"These recipes, most of which are simple, turn out food that's comforting, satisfying, inviting and so often surprising. I love when there's something unexpected in a dish, especially when it's in a dish we think we know well."

— From the Introduction

# EVERYDAY
# DORIE

DORIE GREENSPAN

# EVERYDAY DORIE

## *The Way I Cook*

Photographs by Ellen Silverman

A Rux Martin Book    Houghton Mifflin Harcourt    Boston    New York    2018

For information about permission to reproduce selections from this book, write to trade.permissions@hmco.com or to Permissions, Houghton Mifflin Harcourt Publishing Company,
3 Park Avenue, 19th Floor, New York, New York 10016.

hmhco.com

*Library of Congress Cataloging-in-Publication Data*
Names: Greenspan, Dorie, author. | Silverman, Ellen, photographer.
Title: Everyday Dorie : the way I cook / Dorie Greenspan ;
; photographs by Ellen Silverman.
Description: Boston : Houghton Mifflin Harcourt, 2018. |
"A Rux Martin Book."
Identifiers: LCCN 2017061484 (print) |
LCCN 2018020409 (ebook) |
ISBN 9780544835450 (ebook) |
ISBN 9780544826984 (paper over board) |
ISBN 9781328633521 (special ed)
Subjects: LCSH: Cooking. | LCGFT: Cookbooks.
Classification: LCC TX714 (ebook) | LCC TX714 .G75224 2018
(print) | DDC641.5—dc23
LC record available at https://lccn.loc.gov/2017061484

Book design by Melissa Lotfy
Food styling by Nora Singley
Prop styling by Ayesha Patel

Printed in China
C&C 10 9 8 7 6 5 4 3 2 1

*For Linling and Joshua*
*Love. Always.*

# ACKNOWLEDGMENTS

Writing cookbooks makes me happy. Acknowledging the people who help me do that makes me even happier. And thanking the people who have been at my side book after book makes me happiest of all.

My cookbook family includes Rux Martin, my editor; David Black, my agent; Judith Sutton, my copy editor; and Mary Dodd, my recipe tester. It still seems unfathomable to me that I've been lucky enough to have them in my life for so long. My work shows the marks of their intelligence, talent, energy, creativity and commitment, and I'm richer for having them in my life as friends. I love you.

Once again, as she did for *Dorie's Cookies,* Melissa Lotfy has designed a beautiful cookbook. The extraordinarily lovely pictures are the work of Ellen Silverman, photographer; Nora Singley, food stylist; Ayesha Patel, prop stylist; and their assistants, Gigi de la Torre, Dylan Going and Joan Danahy, who pushed and pushed and never stopped until they had the perfect image. It was inspiring to be in the studio with you.

Making a cookbook is a project with many parts, and I was glad to have Jennifer Herrera of the David Black Agency help sort them out for me. The team at Houghton Mifflin Harcourt is so good at cookbookery that they make it seem easy. Thank you, Sarah Kwak, for your patience and knowledge; Jamie Selzer, for having a sharp eye for errors; and Crystal Paquette, for watching over the printing. Special thanks to Jacinta Monniere, who has the talent of a mind reader when it comes to deciphering a manuscript's hieroglyphics. Extra thanks to Jessica Gilo, Houghton's marketing genie — it's a joy to work with you.

It makes me so happy that, once again, I get to thank Carrie Bachman, the best cookbook publicist in the biz, as well as Breanne Sommer, of HMH's culinary publicity team, for helping to bring this book to cooks across the country. And a toast to my Monday night Riesling pal, Ellen Madere, for advice both generous and good.

Joe Yonan, editor, and Bonnie Benwick, deputy editor, at the *Washington Post* Food section, made a place for me at their table and, for two years, encouraged me to write the Everyday Dorie column. Special thanks to Becky Krystal and Kara Elder, for helping so much during that time.

Thank you, Jake Silverstein, editor, and Jessica Lustig, deputy editor, at the *New York Times Magazine,* for inviting me to write the On Dessert column. And more thanks to Jessica for knowing that Sasha Weiss would be the perfect editor for me.

It is impossible to underestimate what my family means to me and to my work. They are a part of everything I do, my wisest advisers, my best critics and my strongest cheerleaders. I may have written a baker's dozen of cookbooks, but I don't know where to begin to write how much I love you and how much your love means to me. Thank you, Joshua Greenspan, Linling Tao and Michael — the wonderful, wonderful Michael Greenspan.

# CONTENTS

# INTRODUCTION

The recipes in this book are for the food I make all the time. It's the food of weekdays and weekends, of dinners for two and meals for a crowd. It's the food I make in Paris, where I've lived part of the year every year for more than twenty years. It's food from New York City and rural Connecticut, my two hometowns. It's food from supermarkets and from farmers' markets wherever I can find them. But no matter where I am, it's food from the pantry and fridge.

These recipes, most of which are simple, none of which needs skills beyond basic, turn out dishes that are comforting, satisfying and inviting. I've often said that my favorite kind of food is "elbows-on-the-table" — meals that are casual, put people at ease, can sometimes be eaten with your fingers and always encourage guests to linger, sharing stories and passing second helpings. It's the way I like to feed my family and friends.

Whenever I'm cooking, I try to sneak in a little surprise. I love it when there's something unexpected in a dish, especially when it's one we think we know well. The first time I put walnuts and oats in meatballs on a whim and served them to some friends accustomed to their grandmother's Sunday-sauce version, it didn't go unnoticed. People perked up when I put strong mustard in the normally mild, cheesy gougères I always pass before dinner parties. And when I decided to stuff boxy bell peppers with cherry tomatoes and roast them until they were jammy and lightly charred, everyone adored the look of the dish, and no one could guess that what sharpened the flavors were anchovies, cooked until they just about melted into the bread crumbs I'd put in the bottoms of the peppers.

Since I'm an exceedingly practical cook and like to use what I've got on hand, I often change a dish on the spur of the moment because I've found an odd measure of something in the refrigerator, or a leftover from a different dinner. That's how cranberries ended up in the Subtly Spicy, Softly Hot, Slightly Sweet Beef Stew — it turns out their distinctive tang is great with the Korean bottled sauce gochujang, the stew's offbeat seasoner. Mushrooms languishing in the vegetable bin made my regular burger so powerfully flavorful that I call it the Umami Burger.

I've constructed my recipes so that you'll be able to cook this way too. Whenever you see "Choices" or "Playing Around," you'll find ways to riff on a dish so that it will fit into the meal you've got in mind or will let you work with what you might already have in the house. I figure that, like me, when you're ready to cook, you're ready to eat, not shop for a missing ingredient.

If you're a seasoned home cook, you may be comfortable swapping ingredients. You may think, perhaps, that making the Warm Squid Salad with the shrimp you've got in the freezer is a good idea (and it is). Or you may want to substitute pork in the Ponzu Chicken, also a good idea. Or skip the scallops in the Twice-Flavored Scallops and use salmon or swordfish or even eggplant instead — they're all great with my favorite transformer, Lemon "Goop," which you swipe over everything while it's hot.

I also help you work ahead. I feel like a master of the universe when I can pull a dish together quickly because I've done bits of it in advance — or even gotten the whole thing cooked a few days before. Cooking ahead is obvious when stew's on the menu; it's less obvious but just as helpful when you want to set out a bunch of small dishes for a cocktail party, a string of starters that will make an elegant small meal or a tasty and glamorous dish, like the Lower East Side Brunch Tart — I stockpile crusts in the freezer, so whipping it up is a ten-minute construction job.

And just because something is in the starters chapter or found among my favorite vegetable recipes doesn't mean you can't serve it as a main course. If you decide to make the Potato Tourte and call it dinner (I have, many times) or stitch together a meal out of what some would call appetizers, I'll applaud you. I'm a mixer-and-matcher, a play-arounder, a snacker, a nibbler and a picnicker, and you can be too — it's a fun way to cook, a fun way to eat and a fun way to have friends over.

Over the years, cooking food every day in many places for so many different people, I've become more easygoing. You'll see that in my recipes — my food has become simpler, the flavors wider-ranging and my style more spontaneous. If I had a handful of rules when I first started out, most of them have fallen away over time.

These days I have only one rule: There must be dessert! Please follow it.

Cook, bake, share and enjoy.

# NIBBLES, STARTERS & SMALL MEALS

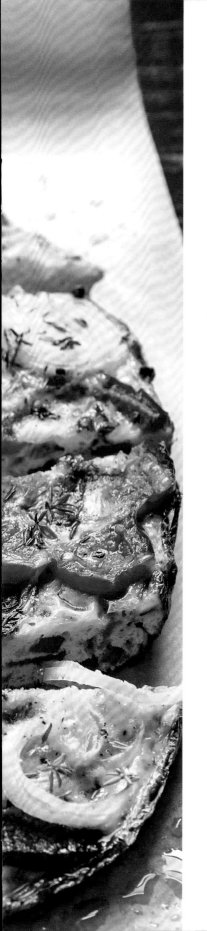

# CANDIED COCKTAIL NUTS

Makes 4 servings

I rarely disagree with Mary Dodd, who tests all my recipes, but we didn't see eye to eye on this one. I thought the recipe served eight, but she said it served only one. So we settled on four, although the recipe can be multiplied infinitely. And it can be varied. In this rendition, I season the nuts salty, sweet, hot and herbaceous, mixing brown sugar, maple syrup and cinnamon, the sweet stuff, with red pepper for heat and thyme for depth.

## a word on multiplication

If you decide to make more than 1 pound of nuts, crisp them on two baking sheets.

## Playing Around

Think about swapping the thyme for rosemary (or even a little lavender), or going more exotic and adding curry powder, smoked paprika, ras el hanout (see page 335) or garam masala (see page 333) to the spice blend.

½ pound (227 grams; about 1½ cups) mixed nuts, such as whole almonds, cashews and walnuts

2 or 3 sprigs fresh thyme

1 tablespoon unsalted butter

1 tablespoon maple syrup

1 teaspoon brown sugar

1 teaspoon fleur de sel (or ½ teaspoon fine sea salt), plus more for sprinkling

¾ teaspoon ground cinnamon

½ teaspoon piment d'Espelette (see page 334) or cayenne pepper

**WORKING AHEAD**
The nuts can be kept for at least 1 week in a tightly sealed container. If they get sticky, pop them back into a 350-degree-F oven for 5 minutes.

Center a rack in the oven and preheat it to 350 degrees F.

Spread the nuts out on a nonstick baking sheet (or use a sheet lined with parchment or a silicone baking mat), scatter over the thyme and roast for 5 minutes.

Meanwhile, put all the other ingredients in a medium saucepan and cook over medium heat, stirring, until the butter melts and the mixture is smooth. You won't have much liquid, but it will be all that you need.

Add the warm nuts to the saucepan and cook, stirring, for 2 to 3 minutes, until they are coated with the mix. Return the nuts to the baking sheet, spreading them out — they won't bake well if they're in clumps.

Bake for 10 minutes, stirring and turning the nuts after 5 minutes. If you want more color, bake for another 5 minutes or so. Transfer the baking sheet to a rack and allow the nuts to cool completely before sprinkling with more fleur de sel (or sea salt).

# MY NEWEST GOUGÈRES

Makes about 55 small gougères or about 35 larger ones

Gougères are French cheese puffs made with a classic dough called *pâte à choux* (the dough used for cream puffs), and it's a testament to their goodness that I'm still crazy about them after all these years and after all the thousands — truly, thousands of them — that I've baked. Twenty or so years ago, I decided that gougères would be the nibble I'd have ready for guests when they visited. Regulars chez moi have come to expect them.

Since then, I've made minor adjustments to the basic technique and more numerous, but equally minor, tweaks to the ingredients. I've flirted with different cheeses, among them Mimolette, smoked Gouda and a French sheep's-milk cheese called Napoleon. I've added pepper — black, red and Turkish. I've snuck in a few different spices, and once, when I had a black truffle, some shavings. The recipe is welcoming.

This version, one of my current favorites, has a structural tweak: Instead of the usual 5 eggs in the dough, I use 4 plus a white — it makes the puffs just a tad sturdier. In addition, I've downsized the puffs, shaping them with a small cookie scoop. And I've added Dijon mustard to the mix for zip, and a surprise — walnuts. These changes are small, but gougère lovers will pick up on them immediately.

½ cup (120 ml) whole milk

½ cup (120 ml) water

1 stick (8 tablespoons; 4 ounces; 113 grams) unsalted butter, cut into 4 pieces

1¼ teaspoons fine sea salt

1 cup (136 grams) all-purpose flour

4 large eggs, at room temperature

1 large egg white, at room temperature

2 teaspoons Dijon mustard (preferably French)

2 cups (about 170 grams) coarsely grated cheese, such as Comté, Gruyère and/or sharp cheddar

⅔ cup (80 grams) walnuts or pecans, lightly toasted and chopped

### WORKING AHEAD

My secret to being able to serve guests gougères on short notice is to keep the scooped puffs in the freezer, ready to bake. Scoop the puffs and freeze them on a parchment-lined baking sheet or cutting board until firm, then pack them airtight. You can bake them straight from the freezer; just give them a couple more minutes of heat.

Position the racks to divide the oven into thirds and preheat it to 425 degrees F. Line two baking sheets with parchment paper or silicone baking mats.

Bring the milk, water, butter and salt to a boil in a medium saucepan over high heat. Add the flour all at once, lower the heat and immediately start stirring energetically with a heavy spoon or whisk. The dough will form a ball and there'll be a light film on the bottom of the pan. Keep stirring for another 2 minutes or so to dry the dough: Dry dough will make puffy puffs.

Turn the dough out into the bowl of a stand mixer fitted with the paddle attachment (or work by hand in a large bowl with a wooden spoon and elbow grease). Let the dough sit for a minute, then add the eggs one by one, followed by the white, beating until each one is incorporated before adding the next. The dough may look as though it's separating or falling apart — just keep going, and by the time the white goes in, the dough will be beautiful. Beat in the mustard, followed by the cheese and walnuts. Give the dough a last mix-through by hand.

Scoop or spoon out the dough, using a small cookie scoop (1½ teaspoons). Or, if you'd like larger puffs, shape them with a medium cookie scoop or a tablespoon and drop the dough onto the lined baking sheets, leaving about 2 inches between the mounds. (*The scooped dough can be frozen on the baking sheets.*)

Slide the baking sheets into the oven and immediately turn the temperature down to 375 degrees F. Bake for 12 minutes, then rotate the pans from front to back and top to bottom. Continue baking until the gougères are puffed, golden and firm enough to pick up, another 15 to 20 minutes. Serve immediately — these are best directly from the oven.

STORING: Although the puffs are best served hot out of the oven, they are still nice (if flatter) at room temperature that same day. If you want to keep baked puffs longer, freeze them and then reheat them in a 350-degree-F oven for a few minutes.

# BLACK BEAN–
# CHIPOTLE DIP

Makes 4 servings

Never underestimate the delicious convenience of having a few cans of beans in the pantry to add to salads or soups or to toss together for this mix, which I'm calling a dip, even if it might just as rightly be dubbed a salsa. It's a thick blend of spiced beans that can be as hot and spicy as you'd like. I usually make it fairly mild, so when I say "season to taste," I mean it.

You can also play around with the texture — if you'd like it chunky, hold back some of the beans to stir into the puree, or add even more beans — and the quantity: The recipe can be doubled or tripled. What I wouldn't change are the accompaniments — tortilla chips, beer and friends.

One 15-ounce (425-gram) can black beans, rinsed and drained

1 tablespoon hot water

½ teaspoon ground cumin

½ teaspoon fine sea salt, or to taste

¼ teaspoon chipotle (or other) chile powder, or more to taste

Grated zest and juice of 1 lime

2 tablespoons finely chopped red onion, rinsed and patted dry, or more to taste

2 tablespoons chopped fresh cilantro, or more to taste

A fat slice of jalapeño, chopped, or more to taste

### WORKING AHEAD
Covered tightly, the dip will keep in the refrigerator for up to 2 days; stir and adjust the seasonings before serving.

Put the beans, hot water, cumin, salt and chile powder in a food processor and whir until smooth. Add the lime zest and as much lime juice as you'd like. Taste and add more salt and/or chile powder if you think it needs it. Drop in the onion, cilantro and jalapeño and pulse just a couple of times to incorporate the ingredients (not to finely chop them).

Spoon the dip into a bowl and serve. Or, cover and refrigerate. (*The dip can be kept in the fridge for up to 2 days.*)

If you serve the dip chilled, taste before serving — spices calm down in the refrigerator and so you might want to boost them a little.

# ROASTED SQUASH HUMMUS

Makes 4 to 6 servings

This hummus, made like traditional chickpea hummus but based on roasted acorn squash instead, owes its existence to a gift of za'atar from a friend, a recommendation for a different brand of tahini (Soom, available online) from a second friend, pomegranate molasses from my pantry and a soupçon of zeitgeist — hummus is everywhere! I like this one for its deep, earthy flavor; its vivacity (not a word usually associated with hummus); and its lightness (again unusual). I also love the way it looks — and tastes — swirled over cool yogurt. Of course you can serve the hummus with pita or in a pocket stuffed with roasted vegetables, but I really like it as a dip, when the dippers are crunchy fresh vegetables.

## a word on quantity

The amounts of tahini and pomegranate molasses are based on getting about 1 cup of puree from the roasted acorn squash. If you end up with more squash, taste and add more tahini and/or pomegranate molasses as needed.

1 small (about 1½ pounds; 680 grams) acorn or butternut squash, scrubbed

1 tablespoon extra-virgin olive oil, plus more for finishing

Fine sea salt and freshly ground pepper

Cayenne pepper

½ cup (120 ml) tahini

2 tablespoons pomegranate molasses (see page 334)

1 to 2 teaspoons za'atar (see page 336), or ½ teaspoon dried oregano plus ½ teaspoon dried thyme, or to taste

1 lemon, halved, for finishing and serving

About ⅓ cup (80 ml) plain Greek yogurt, for finishing

2 to 3 tablespoons pomegranate seeds, for finishing

### For serving (optional)

Toasted pita wedges or sliced flatbread

Carrot spears

Celery sticks

Endive leaves

### WORKING AHEAD

You can roast and char the squash up to 1 day ahead; keep it covered in the refrigerator. The hummus can be made up to 2 days ahead and refrigerated. It's best to add the yogurt, oil and pomegranate seeds just before serving, but in a pinch, you can keep the whole thing overnight.

Center a rack in the oven and preheat it to 400 degrees F. Line a baking sheet with foil.

If you're using acorn squash, cut it in half around its middle. If using butternut, cut it lengthwise. Scoop out and discard the seeds and strings.

Season the tablespoon of oil generously with salt and pepper and sparingly with cayenne. Brush the inside and rim of the squash with the oil, then put the squash skin side up on the baking sheet.

Roast for 35 to 45 minutes, until the squash is easily pierced with a small knife. Remove the baking sheet from the oven and turn the oven to broil.

Cut the squash into wedges or slices and stand them up on their skin sides. Return the sheet to the oven and broil — keeping an eye on the squash — just until it is charred here and there. Figure on about 5 minutes — but keep watching! Remove from the broiler and let cool slightly. (*You can roast and char the squash up to 1 day ahead and keep it covered in the refrigerator.*)

When the squash is cool enough to handle, scrape the flesh from the skin and into a bowl. Use a fork to mash the squash into a puree; you should have about 1 cup. Stir in the tahini, followed by the pomegranate molasses and za'atar (start with 1 teaspoon) or oregano and thyme. Taste for salt, pepper, cayenne and za'atar, keeping in mind that if you chill the hummus, the cold will tamp down the flavors. If desired — and I always desire — squeeze in the juice from one lemon half. Cut the remaining half into wedges to serve alongside the hummus. (*You can cover and refrigerate the hummus for up to 2 days. Taste and season again if needed before serving.*)

When you're ready to serve, put the yogurt in a small serving bowl or on a plate and use the back of a spoon to spread it into a circle. Top with the hummus, leaving a rim of yogurt visible. Run the back of a spoon through the hummus to make a small trough, drizzle some olive oil into it and over the yogurt and scatter over the pomegranate seeds. Serve with the lemon wedges, bread and vegetables, if you'd like.

# RICOTTA SPOONABLE

Makes about 2 cups

Take a peek in my fridge, and you'll find the usual staples — milk, butter, eggs and yogurt, and my favorite plus-one: "ricotta spoonable." I started making it years ago and I've probably never made it the same way twice. It's a mix of ricotta, lots of chopped herbs, freshly grated lemon zest, olive oil and plenty of salt and pepper. It's simple but special.

I prepare this year-round, changing the herbs according to what I have at hand, but I make it most often in summer, when I'm apt to fill the table with small plates of good stuff, things that don't need to be eaten in any order and that lend themselves to mixing and matching. Put the spoonable into the mix, and it will match with beet salad (page 88), frittata (page 27), onion galette (page 54), charred peppers (page 39) and so many other dishes.

## a word on the ricotta

If there's liquid in the container, it's best to drain the cheese. Line a strainer with a double thickness of damp cheesecloth, place it over a bowl, spoon in the ricotta, pull the cheesecloth around the cheese and weight it with a plate or a can of something. Put it in the refrigerator and let it drain for at least 30 minutes, or up to 1 day.

Alternatively, you can make the spoonable, scrape it into a cheesecloth-lined strainer and refrigerate until needed. Do this, and when you turn out the ricotta, the cheesecloth's mesh pattern will be visible — it's pretty.

2 cups (492 grams) whole-milk ricotta, drained if there's liquid (see headnote)

1 large lemon, or more to taste

3 tablespoons minced shallots, rinsed and patted dry

2 scallions, white and light green parts only, thinly sliced

1 tablespoon extra-virgin olive oil, plus more for drizzling

About ½ teaspoon fleur de sel or ¼ teaspoon fine sea salt

Freshly ground pepper

⅓ cup (13 grams) minced mixed fresh herbs, such as dill, parsley, tarragon, thyme, cilantro and/or basil

Put the ricotta in a medium bowl. Finely grate the zest of the lemon over it, then halve and squeeze the lemon and blend in the juice. Stir in the shallots, scallions, olive oil, salt and a healthy pinch of pepper. Taste for salt and pepper, then stir in the herbs. Cover and chill for at least 1 hour before adjusting for salt, pepper and lemon juice and serving.

———————

CHOICES: A dollop of this on a cracker or sliced baguette makes a good appetizer; more of it on dark bread with roasted tomatoes, charred lemons or sliced cucumbers makes a tartine; and a lot of it stirred into pasta makes a dinner.

STORING: The spoonable is best the day it is made, but you can keep it for up to 2 days tightly covered in the refrigerator. Stir well before using.

# PIMENTO CHEESE

Makes about 2 cups

When Mary Dodd, my recipe tester, returned from North Carolina with a mad crush on pimento cheese, along with a can of pimentos, I gave this Southern treasure a try. And I'll admit to a moment of pride when friends from Chapel Hill declared it "spot on."

My version is straight-up and simple, a blend of sharp and extra-sharp cheddar, pimentos, mayo, salt and cayenne. (Don't think that the small amount of cayenne is stingy — its flavor builds as the cheese rests.)

## a word on the cheddar and pimentos

I use Cabot cheddar, and for the sharp cheese, I prefer their wax-wrapped Vintage Choice Extra-Sharp Cheddar. However, now that I'm committed to pimento cheese, I often keep bags of shredded cheese in the fridge. As for the pimentos, Mary told me that Roland-brand whole pimentos are the pepper of choice among pimento-cheese connoisseurs, and so I search them out, often online.

A generous packed ⅓ cup (113 grams) pimentos

8 ounces (227 grams) extra-sharp cheddar (see headnote)

2 ounces (57 grams) sharp cheddar

3 tablespoons mayonnaise

¼ teaspoon fine sea salt

¼ teaspoon cayenne pepper

**WORKING AHEAD**
You can make the pimento cheese up to a week ahead.

Press the pimentos between sheets of paper towels until they are as dry as you can get them and then cut each into a few pieces.

If you're using block cheese, cut it into small chunks; if the cheese is shredded, you're good to go.

Put the pimentos in a food processor and pulse just a couple of times to finely chop them. Add both cheeses and pulse to begin chopping them. Add the mayo, salt and cayenne and pulse and process until the mixture has the texture of tiny-curd cottage cheese. Remove the blade and, using a flexible spatula, give the cheese a last turn — the mix might become smoother and more spread-like, and that's just fine.

Scrape the cheese into a bowl or jar — my favorite is a canning jar or crock; press a piece of plastic wrap against the surface of the cheese if you're using a bowl. Refrigerate for at least 4 hours. If you can wait a day, that's even better: The mixture will pick up punch during that time.

Serve straight from the fridge.

———————————

CHOICES: It's fun to serve the cheese with celery sticks or stuffed into small tomatoes. Not surprisingly, it's good at brunch and nice with a Bloody Mary. I have it on crackers or bread, use it as a sandwich spread (toppped with slices of tomato and cucumber for crunch) and think it's great slathered on corn on the cob and really good on a burger.

# DOUBLE-STUFFED
# DEVILED EGGS
# WITH CRAB

Makes 24 egg halves

Because deviled eggs are so easy to make, I rarely order them when I go out. But in Paris, where there are competitions and prizes for the best *oeuf mayo*, the French version, I'm occasionally tempted. It was at Yves Camdeborde's L'Avant Comptoir de la Mer, his seafood wine bar a few steps from my apartment, that I gave in to that temptation . . . more than once. Chez Yves, the whites are filled with two separate mixtures: One includes crab and the other is the traditional mashed yolks and mayo.

This recipe is my take on his more elaborate rendition. If you want to come closer to Yves', add finely diced pieces of avocado (about half a small one) to the crab mixture. Recipes like this are meant to be played with, so fiddle with the spices, maybe adding a little heat to one or both of the fillings. Have fun, but whatever you do, don't leave out the small bits of apple. Their tartness and crunch are almost as surprising as the crab.

## WORKING AHEAD
Deviled eggs are really best served as soon as they're assembled, but that's not always practical. You can hard-boil the eggs up to 3 days ahead and peel them when needed. You can make the yolk and crab mixtures about 6 hours ahead of time and keep them covered in the refrigerator. And you can stuff the eggs, then cover and refrigerate them for a few hours before serving.

12 hard-boiled large eggs (see page 321 for a how-to), peeled

About ½ cup (120 ml) plus 3 tablespoons mayonnaise

1 to 2 teaspoons Dijon mustard (preferably French)

Piment d'Espelette (see page 334) or cayenne pepper

Fine sea salt and freshly ground pepper

¼ pound (113 grams) lump crabmeat, picked over and patted dry

½ medium Granny Smith apple (don't peel), cored and finely diced

1 slender scallion, white and light green parts only, finely chopped

Freshly squeezed lemon juice

Snipped fresh chives, for finishing

Cut each egg in half the long way and scoop the yolks into a bowl. Using a fork, mash the yolks with ½ cup of the mayonnaise, a teaspoon of the mustard, a little hot pepper and some salt and ground pepper. The mixture will be soft and loose. Taste for mustard, hot pepper and salt and pepper and set aside for the moment.

Put the crabmeat, apple, scallion, the remaining 3 tablespoons mayonnaise and a squirt or two of lemon juice in another bowl. Toss together gently and season with a little hot pepper; add more mayonnaise, lemon juice and/or some salt if needed.

If you're not going to serve the deviled eggs immediately, cover the whites, the yolk-mayo and the crab mixture (separately) and pop them into the refrigerator. (*The filling — and whites — can be refrigerated for up to 6 hours.*)

When you're ready to serve, arrange the whites on a platter. Divide the crab-mayo mixture among them and top with the yolk mayonnaise. I find it easiest — and prettiest — to put the crab into the whites with a spoon, then make an indentation in the crab and use a small cookie scoop to top with the yolk mixture. Scatter over the chives and serve immediately.

# WESTERN FRITTATA

Makes 6 servings

A frittata is a dish that every cook should know how to make, partly because it's so delicious, partly because it's so easy and partly because it's so versatile — it's a happy home for tidbits of all sorts. That it can be made ahead and served at room temperature is a bonus. Essentially an omelet that's cooked for a couple of minutes on the stove and then quickly finished in the oven, a frittata can be made with everything you'd normally put into an omelet, but there's no folding and crossing your fingers that it all holds together. Because I make frittatas so often, and because they're always different, depending on what I've got on hand, it was hard for me to come up with a "real" recipe. This may sound odd to you now, but a couple of frittatas later, you'll be saying the same thing (see the Kale and Onion Frittata on page 28).

This version takes its inspiration from a diner standard: the Western omelet, sometimes called a Denver. It's got onions, bell peppers and some minced jalapeño, as well as chile powder and hot sauce. The original has ham, and you can add that — or bacon or pancetta — if you want to. I like sliced tomato and cheese on this and many other frittatas, but you can leave the top bare or go for scallions or leeks, pepper rings or thin rounds of onion.

## a word on spring onions

Spring onions (sometimes marketed as Texas onions) look like large scallions. They have scallion-like greens, but their base is a bulb, like a regular onion. Spring onions are milder and sweeter than normal onions. You can substitute scallions — you'll need three or four for each spring onion — or an onion.

2 tablespoons olive oil

1 Texas spring onion (see headnote), finely chopped or diced, rinsed and patted dry

1 red or green bell pepper, cored, seeded and finely chopped or diced

½ jalapeño, finely chopped or diced, or more to taste

Pinch of chile powder

Fine sea salt and freshly ground pepper

8 large eggs

Hot sauce

1 tomato, cut into 6 slices, or 12 cherry tomatoes, halved

3 tablespoons shredded cheddar (yellow or white)

2 or 3 sprigs fresh thyme (optional)

Center a rack in the oven and preheat it to 350 degrees F.

Pour the oil into a 9-inch cast-iron or other oven-proof skillet and place the pan over medium heat. Add the onion, bell pepper and jalapeño, season with the chile powder and some salt and pepper and cook, stirring frequently, until the vegetables are moderately soft, about 5 minutes.

Whisk the eggs together with some salt, pepper and chile powder and as much hot sauce as you'd like — keep in mind that you can always season the frittata with more hot sauce after it's baked. Pour the eggs over the vegetables in the skillet and stir just to blend, then let the eggs cook, undisturbed, for 2 minutes. Top with the tomato, sprinkle with the cheese, toss on a sprig or two of the thyme, if you're using it, and slide the pan into the oven.

Bake the frittata for 8 minutes. If you want to serve the frittata in the pan, look at it now. If the sides are puffed and firm, and only the center jiggles a little bit, remove it from the oven (the frittata will continue to cook after it comes from the oven, so as long as you don't want to unmold it, it'll be fine). If you want to turn the frittata out onto a plate, let it bake for another 3 to 4 minutes. If you want a little more color, run the frittata under the broiler for a couple of minutes. Transfer the frittata to a rack and let it rest for 10 minutes.

If you are going to unmold the frittata, have a cutting board and a serving platter at hand. Run a flexible heat-proof spatula around the edges of the frittata, working the spatula under it a bit as you go. Carefully (the pan is heavy . . . and hot!) turn the pan over onto the cutting board; lift off the pan. If anything sticks, see if you can lift it out of the pan and replace it; if not, forget about it. Turn the frittata onto the serving plate (repositioning any tomatoes that have come loose, as they're bound to), sprinkle with additional thyme, if desired, and cut into squares or wedges.

Serve the frittata while it's warm, or allow it to come to room temperature.

———————

STORING: The frittata is best the day it is made, but leftovers can be covered and refrigerated for up to 1 day.

## KALE AND ONION FRITTATA

Instead of the onion, pepper and chile powder, cook ¼ pound kale, trimmed and shredded (or use leaves of baby kale), 3 medium spring onions or other onions, halved and thinly sliced, and 3 garlic cloves, minced, in the oil. Whisk 3 tablespoons Dijon mustard into the eggs, and proceed as directed. You can swap the kale for mustard greens, spinach or chard or add these to the kale. Also think about adding sliced zucchini or mushrooms, chopped bacon or shrimp, or even shreds of leftover chicken or pork — just remember that whatever you put into a frittata has to be cooked first.

# TEMPURA'D VEGETABLES, SEAFOOD OR EVEN FRUIT

Makes 4 servings

I'm not sure how authentic this tempura batter is, but I am sure that it's terrific for everything from fish (think fish and chips) and seafood to vegetables and fruit. It produces a thin, crackle-crisp coating that gives us what we love in fried foods: contrast. This is the batter I use for Shrimp-Mousse Squash Blossoms (see photo, opposite, and recipe, page 33) and Pepper Poppers (page 34), but I use it more often for tempura'd vegetables, such as mushrooms, string beans and slender wedges of winter squash (pumpkin makes excellent tempura) or fruits like sliced apples, pears and bananas.

The batter gets its lightness from flour, cornstarch and a combination of leaveners: baking powder, baking soda and seltzer. It makes enough to coat 1 pound of vegetables, fish, seafood or fruit (18 to 20 small pieces).

As with everything fried, you need to eat the tempura as soon as it's ready, so don't drop in the first bit until you've gathered your group together.

### For the batter

5 tablespoons all-purpose flour

5 tablespoons cornstarch

1 teaspoon baking powder

½ teaspoon baking soda

½ teaspoon fine sea salt

½ cup (120 ml) seltzer, club soda or sparkling water

### For the dipping sauce

½ cup (120 ml) ponzu sauce (see page 334)

1 tablespoon Thai sweet chili sauce (see page 335)

Canola or peanut oil, for deep-frying

### Choose one of the following or mix and match, for a total of about 1 pound

1 pound (454 grams) firm vegetables, such as carrots, potatoes, celery root and/or winter squash, trimmed as necessary and sliced about ⅛ inch thick

1 pound (454 grams) softer vegetables, such as mushrooms, zucchini, onions and/or bell peppers, trimmed as necessary and sliced about ¼ inch thick

1 pound (454 grams) shrimp, shelled and deveined, or scallops, tough muscle removed

1 pound (454 grams) white fish fillets, cut into 2-inch pieces

1 pound (454 grams) fruit, such as pears, apples, pineapple and/or mango, trimmed as necessary and sliced about ½ inch thick

#### WORKING AHEAD

You can prep the fruits, vegetables and/or fish a few hours ahead and keep them covered in the refrigerator. Take the chill off them by leaving them on the counter while you prepare the batter and bring the oil to temperature. It's best to mix the batter at the last minute.

TO MAKE THE BATTER: Whisk together the dry ingredients, then stir in the seltzer. You'll have a smooth batter that's the consistency of heavy cream.

*(Recipe continues)*

TO MAKE THE SAUCE: Mix the ponzu and chili sauce together in a small serving bowl.

TO BATTER AND FRY: Have chopsticks or a fork and a slotted spoon or small strainer at hand. Line a plate with a double thickness of paper towels.

Pour enough oil into a medium saucepan to come 2 inches up the sides. Attach a deep-frying thermometer to the saucepan or have an instant-read one at hand. Heat the oil to 350 degrees F.

Drop a few pieces of whatever you're cooking into the batter, stir them around gently to coat and lift them out (let the excess batter drip back into the bowl), then drop them into the hot oil — don't crowd the pan. Allow the bits to fry, turning them as needed with chopsticks or a fork, until lightly golden on both sides, 1 to 1½ minutes. Lift them out of the oil with the slotted spoon or strainer, letting the excess oil drip back into the pan, and place them on the paper towels. Cover with more paper towels and blot away excess oil. Continue, always making certain that the oil comes back up to temperature before adding more bits.

Serve immediately, with the dipping sauce.

———

# SHRIMP-MOUSSE SQUASH BLOSSOMS

Makes 4 servings

People often complain about a glut of zucchini in their gardens but never about having too many squash blossoms. The blossoms, so beautiful, are a fleeting pleasure. When I can find them in the farmers' market, I grab them to stuff with this shrimp mousse, slip through tempura batter and fry. The mousse can go into mushrooms — choose medium-sized white ones and pipe or spoon it in — or into peppers, hot or sweet, to become poppers (see page 34).

The shrimp mousse itself (though "mousse" seems too fancy a name for it) is made with the flick of a button: It's a food-processor quickie. It's mixed with minced jalapeño, scallions and herbs, and even though you use just a small spoonful of it for each blossom, it never gets lost — it's a mousse with moxie.

See the photo on page 31.

## a word on serving

These have enough flavor to be served with nothing but a sprinkle of flake salt, but if you'd like something more substantial, you can make a ponzu dipping sauce (page 30) or a mayonnaise; the chipotle cream (page 196) is also good with them.

### For the mousse and blossoms

½ pound (227 grams) shrimp (if frozen, thaw and pat dry), peeled and deveined

1 large egg white

1 scallion, white and light green parts only, minced

A slender strip of jalapeño, minced

2 teaspoons minced fresh herbs, such as cilantro, basil and/or parsley

Pinch of cayenne pepper

Pinch of grated lime or lemon zest

Fine sea salt and freshly ground pepper

18 to 20 squash blossoms, the bigger the better

### For the tempura batter

5 tablespoons all-purpose flour

5 tablespoons cornstarch

1 teaspoon baking powder

½ teaspoon baking soda

½ teaspoon fine sea salt

½ cup (120 ml) seltzer, club soda or sparkling water

Canola or peanut oil, for deep-frying

Flake salt, such as Maldon

### WORKING AHEAD

The mousse can be made up to 2 days ahead, covered and refrigerated. You can fill the blossoms a few hours ahead and keep them in the refrigerator, but it's best to make the tempura batter at the last minute.

TO MAKE THE MOUSSE: Put the shrimp and egg white in a food processor and pulse a few times until you have a chunky paste. Add the rest of the ingredients and pulse only a couple of times to incorporate them. (*The mousse can be made ahead and refrigerated, covered, for up to 2 days.*)

TO STUFF THE BLOSSOMS: It's easiest if you scrape the mousse into a piping bag or a zipper-lock plastic bag — push the mousse into a bottom corner of the bag and snip off the tip. Alternatively, you can use a small spoon.

If you'd like, you can reach inside the squash blossoms with tweezers and pull out the tough stamens, but it's fine if you don't. Carefully open the blossoms at the top — if they tear, as they most likely will (they're so fragile), just carry on — and pipe or spoon in a small amount of mousse. Don't be too generous; the mousse will expand when it's cooked. (*You can refrigerate the blossoms for a few hours now, if it's more convenient. Leave them on the counter to warm a bit while you make the batter and heat the oil.*)

TO BATTER AND FRY THE BLOSSOMS: Whisk together the dry ingredients, then blend in the seltzer. You'll have a smooth batter that's the consistency of heavy cream.

Have chopsticks (or a fork) and a slotted spoon or small strainer at hand. Line a plate with a double thickness of paper towels. Pour enough oil into a medium saucepan to come 2 inches up the sides. Attach a deep-frying thermometer to the saucepan or have an instant-read one at hand. Heat the oil to 350 degrees F.

Drop 2 or 3 blossoms into the batter, turn them gently to coat and lift them out (let the excess batter drip back into the bowl), then drop them into the hot oil — don't crowd the pan. Fry, turning as needed with chopsticks or a fork, until lightly golden on both sides, about 2 minutes. Lift them out of the oil with the slotted spoon or strainer, letting the excess oil drip back into the pan, and place them on the paper towels. Cover with more paper towels and blot away excess oil. Continue, always making certain that the oil comes back up to temperature before adding more blossoms.

Serve immediately, with just a light sprinkle of salt.

## PEPPER POPPERS

Choose baby bell peppers of any color or small jalapeños. Cut a slit down one side of each pepper and make a small perpendicular cut at the top — this should give you enough room to pull out the seeds — and then pipe in the mousse. Batter and fry as directed at left.

# CHRISTIANE'S DINNER-PARTY TERRINE

Makes 8 servings

There are some dishes that just stop the show as soon as you bring them to the table, and this is one of them. It's not fancy and it's certainly not hard to make or time-consuming to put together, but it's pretty in a way that says that your host wants to make you happy and feel cared for. That's how I felt when Christiane L'Heritier served this at a dinner in Paris.

While the mention of a terrine often conjures up images of chunky pâtés made with meat, this one is based on a rich egg-and-cream custard studded with vegetables. Christiane's showcased zucchini and toasted pine nuts, and yours can too (see page 36). Mine follows her lead, but it has onions, peppers and lots of herbs, a more year-round mix. Christiane passed around a big pitcher of fresh tomato-basil sauce to pour over each serving. It's a nice but not necessary addition. Like a quiche (my husband calls the terrine a crustless quiche), this dish is good solo or embellished.

### For the terrine

2 tablespoons olive oil

1 large onion, finely chopped, rinsed and patted dry

2 red bell peppers, cored, seeded and finely chopped

Fine sea salt

5 scallions, white and light green parts only, thinly sliced

1 cup (40 grams) chopped fresh basil or a mix of herbs

Freshly ground pepper

9 large eggs

1¾ cups (420 ml) heavy cream

### For the sauce (optional)

4 large or 6 medium tomatoes, peeled, cored and coarsely chopped

A handful of fresh basil leaves, coarsely chopped

1 to 2 tablespoons olive oil, if you'd like

Fine sea salt and freshly ground pepper

**WORKING AHEAD**
The terrine can be made up to 3 days ahead and kept tightly wrapped in the refrigerator.

Center a rack in the oven and preheat it to 350 degrees F. Rub the inside of an 8-by-4-inch loaf pan with a little butter or oil. Line the pan with parchment paper, leaving an overhang on the long sides to use as handles; it's fine if the short ends of the pan are bare. Butter or oil the paper. Have a roasting pan to hold the terrine at hand.

TO MAKE THE TERRINE: Warm the olive oil in a large skillet over medium heat. Toss in the onion and peppers, season with salt and cook, stirring, until the vegetables soften but do not color, about 8 minutes. Scrape the mix into a bowl. Stir in the scallions and basil or other herbs, season with salt and pepper and let cool for about 5 minutes.

In another bowl, whisk the eggs and cream together until well blended. Season with salt and pepper, add the vegetables — leaving behind any liquid that has accumulated in the bowl (it's important that the vegetables not be wet) — and stir to mix well. Turn the mixture out into the prepared loaf pan. Place the pan in the roasting pan and fill the roaster with enough very hot water to come halfway up the sides of the loaf pan. Carefully slide the setup into the oven.

Bake for about 90 minutes, loosely covering the terrine with a foil tent after 45 minutes, until a skewer inserted into the center of the terrine comes out clean. The terrine will rise a little, and it may crack, and that's fine. Carefully remove the loaf pan from the roasting pan and transfer it to a rack. Let rest for about 15 minutes before unmolding the terrine: Run a table knife around the sides, unmold it onto a serving platter and peel away the parchment paper.

The terrine is ready to serve when it is just warm, or let cool to room temperature. You can also refrigerate it and serve it chilled.

TO MAKE THE OPTIONAL SAUCE: Put the tomatoes and basil in a blender or food processor and whir just a few times. Add the olive oil, if you'd like, season with salt and pepper and pour into a pitcher or a bowl. Serve alongside the terrine.

---

STORING: Both the terrine and the tomato sauce can be refrigerated tightly covered for up to 3 days.

CHOICES: The terrine makes a stellar starter, but it could just as rightly be a side dish, or even the main event if you were to add a salad or some well-dressed vegetables. Because it can be served warm, at room temperature or chilled, it's good picnic fare. Since there's nothing I like more than an indoor picnic (some people call it a buffet), I often make this terrine part of the spread.

## ZUCCHINI AND PINE NUT TERRINE

Scrub about 2½ pounds small zucchini, dry them well (don't peel), trim them and cut into small pieces. Sauté the zucchini, along with 2 chopped shallots (or 1 chopped medium onion), in 2 tablespoons olive oil until cooked through, 8 to 10 minutes. Drain the vegetables in a strainer before adding them to the egg mixture. Toss ⅓ cup toasted pine nuts into the mix before baking.

### Playing Around

Any vegetables that you might use to make a quiche can be used in this terrine. Think sautéed leeks, mushrooms or asparagus, for instance. If you'd like, you can use those quiche classics, cubes of ham or bacon. The key is to drain any sautéed ingredients well before adding them to the egg mixture.

# OVEN-CHARRED TOMATO-STUFFED PEPPERS

Makes 6 servings

Every time I make this dish, and I make it lots, I'm surprised by it — surprised by how much I enjoy the process of making it, of stuffing halved peppers with a little bread-crumb mix, some herbs and as many small tomatoes as I can fit into them; surprised by how beautiful the dish is as I'm assembling it and again after it's softened and charred in the oven; and surprised by how all kinds of people love it.

The first layer of bread-crumb stuffing packs bright flavors: anchovies, lemons, herbs and seasonings. The top layer's got the sweetness and acidity of the tomatoes. Be generous with the herbs — before you put the peppers in their baking pan, slick it with olive oil and shower it with a mix of herbs and slices of garlic. I like to have thyme in the bouquet, rosemary too, but parsley, basil and mint are all good players here as well. You may or may not have oil left over for dunking or remoistening the peppers, but that's not the point — this oil-and-herb landscape seasons the bottoms of the peppers and adds another layer of aromatics to the dish.

Since the recipe multiplies easily and endlessly, and because it is good at any temperature, but best, I think, at room temperature, mark it as a party dish.

About 7 tablespoons extra-virgin olive oil

1 garlic clove (or more, if you'd like), germ removed (see page 320) and very thinly sliced

About 8 sprigs fresh thyme, rosemary, mint and/or parsley

6 fresh basil leaves, torn or chopped

Fine sea salt and freshly ground pepper

5 tablespoons unseasoned bread crumbs

8 oil-packed anchovies, minced

1 small lemon

Pinch of piment d'Espelette (see page 334) or cayenne pepper

3 large red and/or yellow boxy bell peppers

1 pint cherry tomatoes (25 to 30), halved

### For serving (optional)

Extra-virgin olive oil

Ricotta or Ricotta Spoonable (page 22)

Snipped fresh chives or finely chopped other fresh herbs

## WORKING AHEAD

You can prep the peppers a few hours ahead and keep them covered in the refrigerator; let them sit at room temperature while you preheat the oven. You can also roast them a few hours ahead and keep them covered at room temperature.

Center a rack in the oven and preheat it to 425 degrees F. Put a deep-dish 9½-inch pie pan (or similar-size baking dish) on a baking sheet lined with parchment or a silicone baking mat. Spread a tablespoon or two of the oil over the bottom and sides of the pan, then scatter over the garlic slices, half of the herb sprigs and half of the basil and season with salt and pepper.

Stir the bread crumbs and anchovies together in a small bowl. Grate the zest of the lemon over and squeeze in the juice from half of the lemon (about 1 tablespoon; precision isn't important here). Cut 6 thin slices from the other half of the lemon, then cut the slices in half; set aside. (If any lemon remains, squeeze the juice from it over the bread crumbs.) Stir in 1 tablespoon oil and season the crumbs with the piment d'Espelette or cayenne. Taste to see if you want some salt (anchovies are salty, so the seasoning might be just fine).

If you'd like (or need room in the pan), trim the peppers' stems. Slice the peppers in half the long way and remove the ribs and seeds. Spoon an equal amount of the bread-crumb mixture into each pepper, scatter the remaining basil over and top each one with 2 lemon slices. Divide the tomatoes among the peppers, placing them as close together as you can, and season with salt and pepper. (I put the tomatoes in the peppers cut side down because I think they look prettier that way, but there is no set rule here.)

Transfer the peppers to the pie pan, crowding them together and cajoling them so that they all fit. One or two might pop up, or their bottoms might not fully touch the base of the pan, but in the end they will be fine. Drizzle over enough of the remaining oil to lightly moisten the tomatoes and then strew over the remaining herb sprigs. (*The peppers can be prepared a few hours ahead to this point and refrigerated, covered; let them stand at room temperature while the oven preheats.*)

Bake the peppers for about 1 hour (check at the 45-minute mark), until they're as soft as you'd like them to be — poke the side of one with the tip of a paring knife to judge. The juices and oil should be bubbling and the peppers charred here and there. Remove and discard the herbs from the top of the peppers.

You can serve the peppers straight from the oven, warm or at room temperature. If you'd like, drizzle them with a bit more oil, top them with a little ricotta (adding a dollop of ricotta is particularly nice if you're serving the dish warm as a starter) and sprinkle with chives or other herbs.

STORING: I think the peppers are best the day they're made, but if you have leftovers, refrigerate them — they'll be soft but still tasty a day later.

# GIVERNY TOMATOES

Makes 4 servings

We went to Giverny, France, to visit the Impressionist painter Claude Monet's house and famous gardens, but we stayed because of these tomatoes. They were the first thing we tasted at Éric Guérin's Le Jardin des Plumes, and they convinced us to make reservations there for dinner that night and lunch the next day.

The tomatoes were listed on the menu as *confites,* a term that can mean either cooked in oil or candied. In this case, they were both, and they were not only surprising but also fabulously delicious. Oh, and they were beautiful too. They arrived whole, red and glistening with olive oil. And there was something else unexpected: The core of each tomato had been removed and the hollow filled with sugar and lime zest, almost invisible, but unforgettable.

This is my go-to summer knockout dish for its taste and beauty and because it takes almost no effort to make. And it can be served warm, room temperature or chilled, making it the ultimate in do-ahead. Because I think these are stunning on their own, I serve them on plates or in shallow bowls with nothing more than some of the oil around them and some salt, pepper and bread on the table. However, a small salad — perhaps dressed with the basting oil and some lemon juice — is a nice accompaniment.

## a word on quantities

Because this is less recipe than guideline, you can easily multiply (or divide) the ingredients. If you add a tomato or even two, you probably won't have to increase the amount of olive oil, since there's enough oil in the recipe to generously baste the tomatoes and to have some left in the baking dish to drizzle over bread (or to dress a small salad to serve alongside the tomatoes).

## and a word on the oil

To add a little more citrus flavor to the dish, I've taken to mixing a few drops of lemon or lime oil (or extract) into the olive oil. If you have a fine-quality lemon-flavored olive oil, you might want to use it in place of half of the recipe's olive oil.

4 large ripe but firm round tomatoes

2 limes (you'll need just the zest)

2 tablespoons sugar

¼ teaspoon lemon or lime oil or pure extract (see headnote and page 334; optional)

½ cup (120 ml) extra-virgin olive oil, or half extra-virgin and half lemon olive oil

Fleur de sel or flake salt, such as Maldon

Freshly ground pepper

**WORKING AHEAD**
You can peel and core the tomatoes a few hours ahead and keep them tightly wrapped in the refrigerator.

Center a rack in the oven and preheat it to 170 degrees F, or as close to that as your oven gets. The lowest temperature on many ovens is 200 degrees F, and that's fine. If yours is at that temperature, your tomatoes will probably be perfect at the 2-hour mark — check them. Have a baking dish that can comfortably hold the tomatoes at hand; a 9-inch deep-dish pie plate works well.

Bring a large saucepan of water to a boil; fill a large bowl with cold water and ice cubes. Cut a shallow X in the bottom of each tomato and, one tomato at a time, drop them into the boiling water; count 15 to 20 seconds and then transfer to the bowl of water. Drain the tomatoes, peel them (save the peels if you want to candy them; see page 42) and remove the cores, creating a V-shaped hollow an inch or so deep in each one. (*At this point, the tomatoes can be tightly wrapped and refrigerated for a few hours.*) Place the tomatoes in the baking dish.

*(Recipe continues)*

Finely grate the lime zest over the sugar and then, using your fingertips, rub the ingredients together until the sugar is moist, fragrant and green. Spoon an equal amount of sugar into the hollow of each tomato. If you're using lemon or lime oil (or extract), mix it into the olive oil, then spoon the olive oil over the tomatoes, allowing just a few drops of oil to go into the hollow of each one.

Bake for 2 to 3 hours, basting the tomatoes three or four times, until they are soft all the way through — poke them with a bamboo skewer or the tip of a thin knife to test. Remove the dish from the oven and season the tomatoes — avoiding the hollows — with sea salt and pepper and decide if you'd like to serve the tomatoes warm, at room temperature or chilled. Spoon some oil from the baking dish over each one just before serving.

STORING: The tomatoes are best the day they're made, but they'll keep for up to a day longer covered in the refrigerator.

## CANDIED TOMATO PEEL

Since you're going to have the oven on low for a long time, you can candy the peels you just pulled from the Giverny Tomatoes.

Line a baking sheet with parchment paper or a silicone baking mat or put a rack over a lined baking sheet. Lay the tomato peels out on the sheet or rack and brush lightly with simple syrup. (To make a simple syrup, stir together ¼ cup sugar and ¼ cup water in a saucepan and bring to a boil, stirring to dissolve the sugar, then cool.) Bake the peels for 1 hour. Turn them over, brush with more syrup and bake for 1 hour more, or until they are dry. Let cool. (*The peels can be kept lightly covered at room temperature for a day or so as long as the room is dry.*) Use the peels to add a flourish to a green salad, a fish dish or, yes, the Giverny Tomatoes.

# POKE TO PLAY AROUND WITH

Makes 4 servings

I'm absolutely positive that this poke (pronounced "poke-*ay,*" meaning literally "to cut or slice" in Hawaiian) is not traditional in Hawaii, the dish's homeland, but I'm not ready to call it inauthentic. Poke, like ceviche, has been riffed on by so many that the only real imperative is that it be extremely tasty.

At its most simple, poke is usually chunks of raw tuna briefly marinated with soy and sesame oil. It's not a fancy dish — more like a snack you'd eat when you're wearing flip-flops — and it's not a dish with rigorous rules. These days, though, the tuna might be replaced by another type of seafood, tofu or vegetables; the marinade might include just about every spice and hot sauce from around the globe; and the add-ins might be salad greens, onions, avocados, mangoes, tomatoes or whatever else is good with fish and bold seasoning.

I'm so crazy about this sweet-salty-hot marinade that I also use it as a dressing for coleslaw, kale and apple salad, beets (I love beet poke) and raw cauliflower. And because it and the fish are versatile, I have fun choosing the add-ins. When summer's the season and the heat and humidity are high, you can't beat poke with very cold watermelon.

I know you're going to have fun with this recipe. Actually, the only "recipe" is for the marinade — the rest is up to you.

### WORKING AHEAD
You can make the marinade up to 3 days ahead and keep it covered in the refrigerator. You can also marinate the tuna or salmon for as long as 3 hours.

### For the marinade

2 tablespoons shoyu (Japanese soy sauce) or other soy sauce

2 teaspoons olive oil

1 teaspoon Asian sesame oil

1 teaspoon minced peeled fresh ginger

¾ to 1½ teaspoons Sriracha (to taste)

½ teaspoon oyster sauce

½ teaspoon unseasoned rice vinegar

1 pound (454 grams) very cold thick-cut sushi-grade tuna or salmon

### Add-ins to pick and choose from

1 teaspoon sesame seeds, white and/or black

Sliced jalapeños or serrano chiles

Diced bell pepper

Sliced scallions

Chopped onions (rinsed in cold water and patted dry)

Slivered garlic

Halved cherry tomatoes

Cubed mango

Cashews, macadamias or peanuts

Broken nori (briefly pan-toasted, or not)

### Go-alongs to pick and choose from

Strong salad greens, like mizuna, kale or arugula

Coleslaw (page 306)

Roasted beet cubes

Cold watermelon cubes

TO MAKE THE MARINADE:  Put all the ingredients in a jar, cover and shake well to blend. (*The marinade can be made ahead and refrigerated for up to 3 days.*)

TO MARINATE THE FISH:  Cut the tuna or salmon into bite-sized cubes and toss them into a bowl. Pour the marinade over, stir to coat the fish, cover and refrigerate for at least 30 minutes, or for up to 3 hours, stirring occasionally.

*(Recipe continues on facing page)*

If you're using the sesame seeds or any of the add-ins, stir them into the poke just before serving. If you're using one of the go-alongs, place on a plate and top with the poke, or mix everything together.

STORING: You can marinate the tuna or salmon for longer than 3 hours, but its texture will soften. Once the poke is on the table, it's best to polish it off, since it won't really keep after that.

# LOWER EAST SIDE BRUNCH TART

Makes 6 servings

After a few weeks of binge quiche-making and a brunch at Russ & Daughters, the Lower East Side Manhattan restaurant that specializes in smoked fish and Jewish tradition, I came up with this recipe. Think bagels and lox, the Sunday-morning meal of millions of New Yorkers, Jewish or not. But to say "bagels and lox" is to shortchange the dish. What you want with your bagel and smoked salmon (lox is one kind) is "the works": cream cheese, red onions, capers, dill and tomato. And that's what you get in this tart.

To capture the spirit and flavor of the weekend special, I did a couple of things I'd never done before for a tart: I used raw red onion, so that it would retain some of its texture (I usually cook the onion before adding it to something to be baked); I speckled the tart with small chunks of cream cheese; and I tossed in capers. As often happens, the oven's heat was the magic ingredient, making all these firsts seem as right as the Lower East Side ritual and just as tasty.

If you'd like your tart to look like the one in the photo, cut the cream cheese into chunks so they won't melt completely, and reserve some of the capers and dill to scatter over the top with the tomatoes

**WORKING AHEAD**
You can prebake the crust up to 2 months ahead and keep it, wrapped airtight, in the freezer.

One 9- to 9½-inch tart shell made with Pâte Brisée (page 329), partially baked and cooled

1½ ounces (43 grams) cream cheese, cut into small bits or chunks

3 ounces (85 grams) smoked salmon, finely chopped (about ⅓ cup)

¼ cup (36 grams) thinly sliced red onion, rinsed and patted dry

3 tablespoons capers, rinsed, patted dry and chopped if large

1 tablespoon chopped fresh dill

¾ cup (180 ml) heavy cream

2 large eggs

½ teaspoon fine sea salt

¼ teaspoon freshly ground pepper

12 to 15 cherry tomatoes, halved

Center a rack in the oven and preheat it to 350 degrees F.

Place the partially baked tart shell on a baking sheet lined with parchment paper or a silicone baking mat. Scatter the cream cheese over the bottom of the crust, followed by the salmon, onion, capers and dill.

Beat the cream and eggs together with the salt and pepper in a bowl until smooth. Pour this into the crust, stopping when you're just below the rim. (It's often hard to judge just how much filling a crust will take, so you might have a few drops left over.) Top with the tomatoes and very carefully slide the baking sheet into the oven.

Bake the tart for 40 to 45 minutes, or until it is puffed and set — a skewer inserted into the center will come out clean. If the center of the tart has risen as much as the sides, you can be certain it's baked through. Transfer the baking sheet to a rack and let rest for at least 15 minutes before serving — it's best just warm or at room temperature.

STORING: The tart is at its prime the day it is made. If you have leftovers, cover and refrigerate for up to 1 day.

# TOMATO TART WITH MUSTARD AND RICOTTA

Makes 6 servings

There is little simpler or more wonderful than this tart, whether you serve it as a starter, for lunch or as part of a pick-what-you-want spread of dishes, indoors or out. While mustard may not be what you think of as a mix-in with tomatoes, it's what makes this tart remarkable. The crust holds sturdy greens, ripe tomatoes, dabs of sweet ricotta and an egg custard, all compatible together and livelier with the mustard. I like grainy French mustard — sometimes called old-fashioned, or *moutarde à l'ancienne* — but you can go with smooth Dijon if you prefer (or if that's what's in the fridge). What's really important is its freshness: The mustard should have good color (it shouldn't have gone brown) and bright flavor. You're depending on it.

## a word on the greens and tomatoes

If you'd like, you can use baby kale or spinach instead of large-leaf greens. And although this tart is best when summer's tomatoes are ripest, I often turn to the recipe when the season is past. The oven's heat sweetens the tomatoes and makes them more satisfying than you'd expect.

One 9- to 9½-inch tart shell made with Pâte Brisée (page 329), partially baked and cooled

2 teaspoons olive oil, plus more for brushing

2 cups (about 100 grams) packed finely shredded greens, such as chard, kale, spinach or arugula

Fine sea salt and freshly ground pepper

About 1 pound (454 grams) tomatoes (3 to 4 medium or a mix of medium and cherry or grape tomatoes)

½ cup (125 grams) ricotta (whole-milk or low-fat)

1 large egg yolk

3 large eggs

6 tablespoons (90 ml) heavy cream

3 tablespoons grainy mustard (preferably French; see headnote)

### WORKING AHEAD

You can prebake the crust up to 2 months ahead and keep it, wrapped airtight, in the freezer. You can prep the ricotta and mustard mixtures ahead and refrigerate for up to 6 hours. You can wilt the greens a couple of hours ahead.

Center a rack in the oven and preheat it to 425 degrees F. Place the partially baked tart shell on a baking sheet lined with parchment paper or a silicone baking mat.

Warm the olive oil in a large skillet, preferably non-stick, over medium heat. Toss in the greens, season with salt and pepper and cook, stirring, until they wilt and soften, 1 minute or less. (*The wilted greens can be kept at room temperature for up to 2 hours.*) Scrape them into the crust, leaving any oil in the skillet.

Remove the little core at the top of each medium tomato and slice the tomatoes. If you've got cherry or grape tomatoes, halve them. Lay the tomatoes out on a double layer of paper towels, cover with more paper towels and pat away the excess moisture.

Mix the ricotta with the egg yolk and season with salt and pepper. (*The ricotta mixture can be covered and refrigerated for up to 6 hours.*)

*(Recipe continues)*

Whisk together the eggs, cream and mustard; season with salt and pepper. (*The mustard mixture can be covered and refrigerated for up to 6 hours.*) Pour into the crust. Add the tomatoes, arranging them so that they're fairly evenly distributed. Finish by spooning dollops of the ricotta mixture over the top.

Bake for about 30 minutes, until the filling is puffed and firm in the center; a skewer inserted into the center should come out clean. Transfer the baking sheet to a rack and let the tart cool for at least 15 minutes before serving, or allow it to come to room temperature — it's good at any temperature.

Just before serving, if you'd like to give the tart a little shine — the tomatoes look good with a gloss — brush a little olive oil over the surface.

STORING: The tart is best served the day it is made, but if you have leftovers, cover and keep them in the fridge — they'll make a good snack the next day.

# MUSHROOM-BACON GALETTE

Makes 6 servings

I often tell beginning cooks to find a few dishes they can perfect and make their own, dishes they can cook with confidence and serve to sighs. Here's one. It's a galette, a free-form tart meant to be ragged and uneven (it's only perfect when it's not perfect), that's filled with a mix of sautéed bacon, leeks and mushrooms tossed with chopped walnuts (both the flavor and crunch are unexpected and fun) and stirred through with herbs and grated Parmesan. You get a lot for only a little effort, and no matter what you do to it, it's beautiful. It also has convenience on its side (see Working Ahead).

The galette has such deep flavors that it doesn't need anything but a glass of wine and maybe a small fluff of salad dressed with something more vinegary than mild.

### For the crust

1 recipe Galette Dough (page 331), ready to roll, or 1 store-bought piecrust

### For the filling

4 slices bacon

1 tablespoon olive oil, plus more for drizzling

½ pound (227 grams) mushrooms—white, cremini, wild or a mix—trimmed and coarsely chopped

2 leeks, white and light green parts only, split, washed and thinly sliced, or 1 large sweet onion, such as Vidalia, thinly sliced, rinsed and patted dry

1 garlic clove, germ removed (see page 320) and finely chopped

Fine sea salt

3 tablespoons dry white wine

2 tablespoons heavy cream

3 tablespoons chopped walnuts

¼ cup (24 grams) finely grated Parmesan

Leaves from 2 sprigs fresh thyme

Freshly ground black pepper

**WORKING AHEAD**
The crust can be rolled out, wrapped airtight and kept in the freezer for up to 2 months. You can make the filling up to 3 days ahead. You can even assemble the galette ahead and keep it in the refrigerator for a few hours; no need to bring it to room temperature before baking.

TO MAKE THE CRUST: If you've made your own dough, place it between two sheets of parchment paper and roll it, occasionally lifting the paper so that it doesn't roll into the dough and turning the packet over so that you roll both sides, until you've got an 11-inch circle. Don't worry about precision and perfect edges; think rustic. Slide the paper-sandwiched dough onto a baking sheet and freeze for at least 1 hour, or refrigerate for at least 2 hours.

*(Recipe continues)*

TO MAKE THE FILLING: Lay the bacon strips out in a heavy skillet and cook over medium heat, turning occasionally, until crispy and golden brown on both sides. Transfer the bacon to a paper towel–lined plate, cover with more towels and pat dry. Pour off all but 1 tablespoon of the fat from the pan and set the pan aside. When the bacon is cool, finely chop it or cut it into slender strips.

Center a rack in the oven and preheat it to 400 degrees F. If the dough has been frozen, leave it on the counter for about 10 minutes while the oven preheats. (You need the dough to be pliable; very cold dough will crack when you work with it.)

Pour the olive oil into the skillet with the bacon fat and return the pan to medium heat. Toss in the mushrooms, leeks or onion and garlic, season lightly with salt and cook, stirring, for about 5 minutes, or until the vegetables are softened — the mushrooms will release liquid and then, as you continue to cook, take it up again. Add the white wine and cook, stirring and scraping the bottom of the pan, until it evaporates, a minute or two. Pour in the cream and cook, stirring, until it's mostly absorbed. Remove the pan from the heat and stir in the bacon, walnuts, 2 tablespoons of the Parmesan, the thyme and pepper. (*You can make the filling ahead; scrape it into a bowl, cover and refrigerate for up to 3 days.*)

TO ASSEMBLE THE GALETTE: If you made the dough, peel the top piece of paper off; leave the dough on the bottom sheet of parchment and keep it on the baking sheet. If you're using store-bought dough, unroll it onto a parchment-lined baking sheet. Scrape the filling onto the crust and use a spatula to spread it into a circle that's about 9 inches in diameter. Lift the bare border of dough and fold it over the filling. As you fold, the dough will pleat on itself, and that's what you want; don't worry about being neat or about getting everything even. (*You can refrigerate the galette for a few hours before baking and bake it straight from the fridge.*)

Bake the galette for 30 to 35 minutes, or until the crust is deeply golden and the filling hot. Transfer the baking sheet to a rack and sprinkle the remaining 2 tablespoons Parmesan over the top of the galette — and, if you'd like, the crust. A drizzle of olive oil is also nice.

The galette is ready to serve after it's cooled for about 10 minutes, or let it cool to room temperature. I usually cut it with a pizza wheel.

---

STORING: The galette is best served within a few hours of baking.

# CARAMELIZED ONION GALETTE WITH PARM CREAM

Makes 6 servings

Although I think of this as being its own very special dish, it's got cousins around the world. A galette is a rustic open-faced tart, and this one, whose chief attraction is a generous layer of slowly caramelized onions, is a bit like a Provençal *pissaladière*, something like an Alsatian *flammkuchen* and sort of like an onion pizza. Without even having met the galette, I'd be disposed to love it based on family ties alone.

The crust is my all-purpose anyone-can-make-it galette dough, which works for fillings both sweet and savory. In fact, the crust is a touch sweeter than it is savory, and that sweetness works beautifully with the onions. (Of course, you can use a store-bought piecrust, if you want.) As for the onions, cooked in butter and lightly bolstered by herbs and garlic, they're almost jammy. The French would call the filling an onion confit. My first thought was to smooth the "jam" over the crust, fold in the edges of the crust and send the galette into the oven. But just as I was about to scrape the onions onto the crust, I had the idea to make a bottom layer of mascarpone and Parmesan. When the galette is fully baked, it's hard to see that the bit of Parm cream is there, but you can taste it. It's a subtle addition, one worthy of the extra attention.

And, yes, just in case you were wondering, you can toss bacon cubes into the pan while you're caramelizing the onions. If you'd like, serve each slice with a handful of bitter greens dressed with lemon juice and a few drops of olive oil.

### For the crust

1 recipe Galette Dough (page 331), ready to roll, or 1 store-bought piecrust

### For the onions

2 pounds (907 grams) sweet onions, such as Vidalia (about 2 large onions)

4 tablespoons (2 ounces; 57 grams) unsalted butter

2 garlic cloves, germ removed (see page 320) and minced, more or less to taste

1 teaspoon sugar

A few sprigs fresh rosemary, thyme and/or oregano

1 teaspoon fine sea salt

Freshly ground pepper

### For the Parmesan cream

⅓ cup (75 grams) mascarpone or full-fat cream cheese

2 tablespoons milk

⅓ cup (33 grams) finely grated Parmesan

Fine sea salt and freshly ground pepper

Fresh herbs, for finishing (optional)

### WORKING AHEAD

The crust can be rolled out, wrapped airtight and kept in the freezer for up to 2 months. The onions can be made ahead, covered and refrigerated for up to 3 days. Ditto the Parm cream. You can even assemble the galette ahead and keep it in the refrigerator for a few hours; no need to bring it to room temperature before baking.

TO MAKE THE CRUST: If you've made your own dough, place it between two sheets of parchment paper and roll it, occasionally lifting the paper so that it doesn't roll into the dough and turning the packet over so that you roll both sides, until you've got an 11-inch circle. Don't worry about precision and perfect edges; think rustic. Slide the paper-sandwiched dough onto a baking sheet and freeze for at least 1 hour, or refrigerate for at least 2 hours.

TO CARAMELIZE THE ONIONS: Cut the onions in half from top to bottom. Place each onion half cut side down on a cutting board, slice it in half the long way and then cut it crosswise into thin slices. Put the onions in a colander or strainer, rinse under cold water and pat dry.

Melt the butter in a large skillet, preferably non-stick, over medium heat. Add the onions and garlic, stir to coat with butter and cook, stirring, for about 5 minutes, until the onions begin to soften. Stir in the sugar, add the herbs and reduce the heat to low. Cook, stirring frequently, until the onions are caramelized; they'll be the color of maple syrup. It will take about 40 minutes (maybe even a bit longer) for the onions to burnish. Be patient and don't rush the process — all the flavor is in the color. When the onions are caramelized, season with salt and pepper and turn out into a bowl; let cool. Pick out the herbs, if you see them, cover the bowl and refrigerate the onions until needed. (*The onions can be made up to 3 days ahead.*)

WHEN YOU'RE READY TO BAKE: Center a rack in the oven and preheat it to 400 degrees F. If the dough has been frozen, leave it on the counter for about 10 minutes while the oven preheats and you make the Parmesan cream. (You need the dough to be pliable; very cold dough will crack when you work with it.)

TO MAKE THE CREAM: Put the mascarpone or cream cheese and milk in a small bowl and stir with a flexible spatula until blended. Watch out for sloshing milk — the milk takes a bit of cajoling to incorporate. Stir in the Parmesan and season with salt (it probably won't need much because of the Parm) and pepper. (*The cream can be made up to 3 days ahead; cover and refrigerate.*)

TO ASSEMBLE THE GALETTE: If you made the dough, peel the top piece of paper off; leave the dough on the bottom sheet of parchment and keep it on the baking sheet. If you're using store-bought dough, unroll it onto a parchment-lined baking sheet. Spread the Parm cream over the dough — make a circle that's about 9 inches in diameter — and then spread the onions over the cream. Lift the bare border of dough and fold it over the onions. As you fold, the dough will pleat on itself, and that's what you want; don't worry about being neat or about getting everything even. (*You can refrigerate the galette for a few hours before baking and bake it straight from the fridge.*)

Bake the galette for 35 to 40 minutes, until the crust and onions are deeply golden; since the onions are already cooked, the long baking time is more for the crust than it is for them. If you'd like, after about 30 minutes in the oven, you can strew some fresh herbs over the onions. When the galette is done, transfer the baking sheet to a rack.

The galette is ready to serve after it's cooled for about 10 minutes, or let it cool to room temperature. I usually cut it with a pizza wheel.

---

STORING: The galette is best served the same day.

# SOUPS & SALADS

# Soups

# Salads

# ROASTED BUTTERNUT SQUASH SOUP

Makes 6 servings

Squash is the Zelig of the vegetable world. Zelig, a character in the Woody Allen film of the same name, is a chameleon who fits into any situation, a guy whose personality turns with every wardrobe change. We don't know if Zelig has his own personality, and I've got similar doubts about squash, doubts that make me love it. What cook doesn't love an ingredient with variable texture and the uncanny ability to welcome disparate flavor combos?

For this soup, I give the squash every opportunity to take on layers of flavor. It's brushed with a mix of oil, soy, maple syrup and spices and roasted, along with carrots, onion and garlic. Then it's simmered in broth with ginger and star anise, pureed and accented with vinegar. You might not be able to pinpoint the flavors in the soup, and it's not likely you'll be able to say that it comes from a particular region or country. Instead you'll just think that, like Zelig, it belongs wherever you are.

Both the vegetables and seasonings are on the sweet side, so I like to finish the soup with a splash of cider vinegar. As vinegars go, apple cider vinegar is not too strong, but it's got enough acidity to tip the soup's balance. I also often drizzle a little cream over the soup. You could think about adding a spoonful of minced fresh herbs. You can also float a few croutons or toasted pumpkin seeds in it — crunch is never a bad idea.

¼ cup (60 ml) olive oil

¼ cup (60 ml) maple syrup

¼ cup (60 ml) soy sauce

Fine sea salt and freshly ground pepper

½ teaspoon ground cinnamon

Pinch of cayenne pepper, or more to taste

1 large (about 2 pounds; 908 grams) butternut squash, scrubbed

1 large (about 1 pound; 454 grams) white onion, peeled and trimmed

1 pound (454 grams) carrots, peeled and trimmed

1 head garlic, cut horizontally in half

6 cups (about 1½ liters) chicken or vegetable broth

5 quarter-sized pieces peeled fresh ginger

1 whole star anise

Cider vinegar, for drizzling

Heavy cream, for drizzling (optional)

## WORKING AHEAD

The soup can be made up to 4 days ahead and refrigerated in a tightly covered container, or frozen for 2 months.

Center a rack in the oven and preheat it to 400 degrees F. Line a baking sheet or roasting pan with foil.

Working in a large bowl, whisk together the oil, maple syrup, soy, 1 teaspoon salt, ½ teaspoon pepper, the cinnamon and cayenne.

Trim the ends of the squash, then cut it in half from top to bottom. Scoop out and discard the seeds and strings (or clean and roast the seeds, if you'd like). Put the squash cut side down on the cutting board and cut each piece into half-moons about 2 inches thick (keep the skin on). Toss the pieces into the bowl with the oil mixture.

Cut the onion into 8 wedges. Cut the carrots in half the long way and then cut each half into 3 chunks. Toss the onion, carrots and garlic into the bowl, turning all the vegetables around until they're coated.

Scoop the vegetables onto the baking sheet and spread them out, putting the halved garlic head cut side down. Pour over any remaining liquid. Roast the vegetables for 30 to 45 minutes (it's hard to give an exact time here), or until they are fragrant, have some color and, most important, can be easily pierced with a small knife. (If any of the vegetables are done earlier than the others, pull them out.)

As soon as the vegetables are cool enough to handle, scrape the squash out of the skin and put it in a Dutch oven or large saucepan. Squeeze the garlic cloves out of their skins and add to the pot. Spoon the onion and carrots into the pot, along with any juices.

Pour the broth into the pot, add the ginger and star anise and bring to a boil. Lower the heat, partially cover and simmer for 30 minutes; add more salt and pepper, if you'd like. Remove the star anise from the soup. Using a blender (stand or handheld) or food processor, puree the soup, in batches if necessary, until it's very smooth. (*You can make the soup ahead and refrigerate it, once cooled, in a tightly covered container for up to 4 days; reheat before serving.*)

Ladle out the soup and drizzle 1 to 2 teaspoons cider vinegar over each portion. If you'd like, drizzle over some heavy cream too.

# BEAN AND TORTILLA SOUP

Makes 4 servings

With its Tex-Mex flavors, this medium-bodied soup has as much (or as little) heat as you'd like and a generous propensity for add-ins. It's based on broth — either store-bought or the liquid you get from cooking a bag of beans (see page 314) — tomatoes (canned diced fire-roasted, if possible), vegetables and chiles: fresh jalapeños, adobo sauce from canned chipotle chiles and chile powder. If you want to toss in a big pinch of Old Bay, do; it's definitely not Tex-Mex, but it's got enough cayenne to fit right in with the other capsicums.

Satisfying on its own sipped out of a mug, the soup is even better when you pile on other ingredients. I like to hold back some of the raw onion and red bell pepper and scatter them over the soup, along with beans, cut-up avocado, a handful of cilantro, shredded cheese, dollops of sour cream or yogurt and scrunched and crumbled tortilla chips (sometimes hot and spicy and sometimes plain). The last touch is a couple of squeezes of fresh lime juice.

The soup is good all through the year and especially good in summer, when it's fun to add some fresh corn.

If you decide to cook beans from scratch, choose either pintos or black-eyed peas and then you'll have the broth and some of the beans for this soup and the rest of them for Cowboy Caviar (page 90).

## For the soup

1 large Spanish or Vidalia onion, chopped, rinsed and patted dry

1 large red bell pepper, cored, seeded and chopped

1½ tablespoons olive oil

2 carrots, peeled, trimmed and thinly sliced

¼ to ½ jalapeño, seeded and chopped

2 garlic cloves, germ removed (see page 320) and chopped

½ teaspoon fine sea salt

Pinch of sugar

¾ teaspoon ground cumin

½ teaspoon chile powder, or to taste

1 teaspoon adobo sauce (from canned chipotles; add half a chipotle, if you'd like)

Pinch of Old Bay seasoning

4 cups (960 ml) vegetable, chicken or bean broth (page 314)

One 15-ounce (425-gram) can diced tomatoes, preferably fire-roasted, with their juice

## For the add-ins

1½ cups (246 grams) cooked (see page 314) or canned beans, such as pinto beans, black-eyed peas or red kidney beans, drained and rinsed if canned

4 to 6 tablespoons sour cream or plain Greek yogurt

1 to 2 avocados, halved, pitted, peeled and cut into bite-sized chunks

Chopped onion and red bell pepper, reserved from soup

Shredded cheese, such as cheddar or Monterey Jack

Chopped fresh cilantro

1 to 2 limes, cut into wedges

Tortilla chips (spiced or plain)

Hot sauce (optional)

## WORKING AHEAD

The soup—minus the add-ins—can be made ahead and kept covered in the refrigerator for up to 4 days or packed airtight and frozen for up to 2 months.

*(Recipe continues)*

TO MAKE THE SOUP:  Measure out ¼ cup each of the onion and red pepper and set aside, covered, until serving time. Pour the oil into a Dutch oven or large saucepan and warm over low heat. Add the remaining onion and pepper, the carrots, jalapeño and garlic, season with the salt and sugar and cook, stirring now and then, for about 20 minutes, until the vegetables are softened but not colored.

Stir in the cumin, chile powder, adobo (and chipotle, if you're using it) and Old Bay and cook, stirring, for 1 minute. Pour in the broth and canned tomatoes with their juice, stir and bring to a boil. Lower the heat so that the soup simmers gently but steadily and cook for 20 minutes. Taste the soup and adjust the seasonings as you'd like. Remove from the heat. (*The soup can be made up to this point and refrigerated for up to 4 days or frozen for up to 2 months.*)

FOR THE ADD-INS:  Put some beans in the bottom of each bowl. Ladle over the soup and top with sour cream or yogurt, avocado, the reserved onion and bell pepper, some cheese and a generous amount of cilantro. Pass the lime wedges and tortilla chips, or squeeze over some lime juice and break some chips into each serving. You might want to have some hot sauce within reach.

# POTATO CHOWDER LOTS OF WAYS

Makes 4 to 6 servings

A chowder so basic you can play it any which way and end up with a satisfying soup. I call it a potato chowder because, well, it's got potatoes, but it might more aptly be called an allium chowder because it's got so many members of that tribe, including garlic, onions, leeks and shallots, which get cooked into the chowder, and scallions and chives, which get added at the end. If you have other family members at hand, maybe garlic scapes or ramps, they'd fit right in. The soup is not very thick or very rich, but it's dense with vegetables and full of flavor. It's also full of possibilities (see Playing Around).

## Playing Around

The chicken broth can be replaced by vegetable broth for a no-meat version. You can easily add other vegetables as they come into season, and spices and herbs are also welcome. Think fresh thyme or rosemary, sage or bay leaf, and consider smoked paprika, harissa powder, Old Bay seasoning or herbes de Provence.

4 slices bacon or 2 tablespoons olive oil

2 leeks, white and light green parts only, split, rinsed, patted dry and thinly sliced

1 large onion, halved, thinly sliced, rinsed and patted dry

1 large shallot, halved, thinly sliced, rinsed and patted dry

2 garlic cloves, germ removed (see page 320) and finely sliced

Fine sea salt

Pinch of sugar

5 cups (about 1¼ liters) chicken or vegetable broth

1 pound (454 grams) potatoes, preferably yellow, peeled and cut into bite-sized cubes

½ cup (120 ml) cream, half-and-half or whole milk (optional)

Freshly ground pepper

### *Toppings to mix and match*

Sour cream or yogurt

Thinly sliced scallions

Snipped fresh chives

Chopped fresh parsley and/or cilantro

**WORKING AHEAD**
You can make the soup a day ahead up to the point where you add the cream; reheat and add the cream just before serving.

If you're using bacon, lay the strips in a Dutch oven or large saucepan and cook over medium-low heat, turning as needed, until cooked and crisp. Transfer the strips to a plate lined with paper towels — leave 2 tablespoons of fat in the pot — and cover with more paper towels; when the bacon is cool, chop into bits and keep until serving. Or, if you're going meatless, warm the olive oil in the pot.

Add the leeks, onion, shallot and garlic to the pot and stir until coated with fat or oil, then season with salt, add the sugar and reduce the heat to low. Allow the

SPRING CHOWDER
(OPPOSITE)

vegetables to cook uncovered, stirring occasionally, until soft but not colored, about 20 minutes.

Pour in the broth, drop in the potatoes and bring the soup to a boil. Reduce the heat to medium-low and cook at a steady simmer, uncovered, until the potatoes are soft enough to break easily when prodded with a fork. You can use a masher or the back of a big spoon to mash some of the potatoes, to add another texture to the soup — an optional step, but one I usually take. (*You can make the soup a day ahead up to this point and refrigerate it, covered.*)

Just before serving, stir in the cream, half-and-half or milk, if you're using it, and heat through, without boiling. Taste for salt and pepper — I think the soup tastes better with a generous amount of black pepper.

Ladle the soup out and, if you'd like, top each serving with a dollop of sour cream or yogurt. Sprinkle with the bacon, if you have it, and, as you like, scallions, chives and/or other herbs.

—————

STORING: The soup can be kept in a covered container in the refrigerator for up to 4 days. If you've added cream or milk, the soup may look a little curdled when you reheat it, but it will still be tasty.

## FALL AND WINTER VEGETABLE CHOWDER

Add cubes of butternut, acorn or Red Kuri squash to the soup either along with the potatoes or in place of them. Or swap the yellow potatoes for sweet potatoes. You could scatter shredded cheese — Gouda or sharp cheddar would be good — on top of the soup or offer cubes of cheese for nibbling alongside.

## SPRING CHOWDER

In addition to the potatoes, drop in pieces of peeled asparagus, sweet peas (frozen or fresh) and/or sugar snap or snow peas. If you'd like, finish with chopped fresh tarragon and dill.

## SUMMER CHOWDER

Keep the potatoes and add zucchini and/or lots of corn cut from the cob. This version would be great with a little pesto drizzled over it and some shards of Parmesan.

# MOROCCAN-SPICED CHICKPEA AND NOODLE SOUP

Makes 8 servings

*Harira* is a traditional Moroccan dish most closely associated with Ramadan — it's often served to break the day's fast — and likely to be found simmering lazily on my stovetop when the weather turns chilly. It's basic, simple to make, thick and satisfying — almost as much stew as soup and, like stew, better the day after it's made. It's the deeply fragrant spices — both very comforting and just a little exotic — that first draw you in and tip you to the fact that the soup's roots are in North Africa. The mix includes ginger, turmeric, cinnamon, cumin and saffron. And then it's the combination of add-ins that keeps you coming back: lentils, chickpeas, tomatoes and broken strands of thin noodles. Some recipes for harira are meatless, some aren't; this one includes small meatballs. Though you can skip them, if you'd like, I usually don't: I like having another texture in the mix, and I love how they pick up and absorb the soup's flavors.

1 tablespoon olive oil (if including the meatballs)

1 pound (454 grams) ground beef, formed into about 20 meatballs, 1 to 2 inches in diameter (optional)

2 tablespoons unsalted butter

2 medium onions, finely chopped, rinsed and patted dry

3 garlic cloves, germ removed (see page 320) and finely chopped

2 celery stalks, including leaves, finely sliced

3½ tablespoons ground ginger

1 tablespoon fine sea salt

1½ teaspoons freshly ground pepper

1½ teaspoons ground turmeric

1½ teaspoons ground cinnamon

¾ teaspoon ground cumin

¼ teaspoon cayenne pepper

Large pinch of saffron threads

One 28-ounce (794-gram) can diced tomatoes in juice or puree

½ cup (20 grams) chopped fresh parsley or cilantro

About 2 quarts (about 2 liters) chicken or vegetable broth or water, or more if needed

¾ cup (180 grams) red (or coral) lentils

One 15-ounce (425-gram) can chickpeas, drained and rinsed

¼ pound (113 grams) angel hair pasta, broken into short pieces

1 to 2 lemons

## WORKING AHEAD

The soup can be made ahead and refrigerated, covered, for up to 3 days. It will thicken considerably, so you'll need to thin it with broth or water and then adjust the seasonings before serving.

If you want to include the meatballs, heat the olive oil in a Dutch oven or large saucepan over medium heat. Add the meatballs and cook, stirring, just until they are colored on all sides, about 5 minutes. (You don't have to cook them all the way through, because they'll be cooked

further in the soup.) Transfer the meatballs to a bowl, pour out the oil and carefully give the pot a swipe with a paper towel.

Melt the butter in the pot over medium-low heat and add the onions, garlic and celery. Cook, stirring, for about 5 minutes, until the vegetables just start to soften. Add the spices, stirring, so they blend with the vegetables and don't burn. Cook the spices for just a couple of minutes, then stir in the tomatoes and half of the parsley or cilantro; return the meatballs, if you've made them, to the pot. Bring to a simmer and cook over low heat for 10 minutes, stirring now and then.

Add the broth or water to the pot, increase the heat and bring to a boil. Adjust the heat so that the liquid simmers, stir in the lentils, partially cover the pot and let everything bubble away gently for 1 hour. Take a peek at what's going on now and then. If it looks as if the liquid is cooking away, add more broth or water, ¼ to ½ cup at a time.

Add the chickpeas and cook, partially covered, for 30 minutes more. Taste and see if you'd like to stir in more of any of the spices.

Just before you're ready to serve, stir in the broken pasta. Cook, uncovered, for 4 minutes, or until the pasta is tender. Stir in the rest of the parsley or cilantro.

Lemon juice is a must, but you have a choice with it: You can add it in the kitchen and then ladle out the soup, or put lemon wedges on the table and make it a do-it-yourself affair.

# CLAM CHOWDER MY WAY

Makes 4 to 6 servings

I started chowdering at home when I realized that I wanted the nourishing soup in winter but was only having it during beach season. While the clam chowder I grew up on was the creamy kind known as New England style, the soup I turn to most is one of my own imagining, a riff on a New England version that nods to Thailand. Instead of cream, I use coconut milk. And instead of the traditional aromatics, I go for ginger and lemongrass, cilantro, basil and, if I can find it, kaffir lime. As for the pancetta, Yukon Golds, Vidalia onions and jalapeño? Not a bit Thai, I know, but so good in the mix.

If you want a more traditional New England chowder, look at page 71.

## a word on the clams and clam juice

I prefer to use chopped raw clams, either fresh or frozen, which I buy from a fishmonger or a supermarket (some markets sell them frozen by the quart; each quart contains about ¾ pound clams and ¼ cup liquid, which I pour into the soup pot). If all you can find are canned minced clams, use them. As for the juice, buy it in bottles or cans, and look for a brand that contains only clam juice or broth and salt. Of course you can make chowder with fresh clams that you cook first in water with aromatics. If you do this, you'll get the clams and the juice, which you'll want to strain (it can be sandy).

3 tablespoons unsalted butter

¼ cup (57 grams) diced pancetta

1 large sweet onion, such as Vidalia, finely chopped, rinsed and patted dry

2 celery stalks, including leaves, thinly sliced

1 tablespoon minced fresh lemongrass (tender inner bulb only) or 1 teaspoon dried or from a tube

1 tablespoon minced peeled fresh ginger

2 garlic cloves, germ removed (see page 320) and minced

About 1 teaspoon minced jalapeño

1 bay leaf

1 kaffir lime leaf (see page 334; optional)

Fine sea salt

2¾ cups (660 ml) clam juice (see headnote)

¾ pound (340 grams) Yukon Gold potatoes, peeled and cut into small cubes

One 13½-ounce (400-ml) can coconut milk (not lite)

¾ pound (340 grams) chopped clams (see headnote)

Freshly ground pepper

¼ cup (10 grams) minced mixed fresh herbs, such as basil, cilantro and dill, for serving

Oyster crackers, for serving (optional)

### WORKING AHEAD

You can make the chowder through the point where the potatoes are cooked and then refrigerate it overnight before finishing.

Working in a Dutch oven or large saucepan over medium heat, melt the butter, then add the pancetta, onion, celery, lemongrass, ginger, garlic, jalapeño, bay leaf and kaffir lime, if you've got it. Stir everything around until it's glossed with butter, season lightly with salt and reduce the heat to low. Cook, stirring, just until the onion is soft and translucent, about 10 minutes. Stay close — you don't want anything to color.

Pour in the clam juice and add the potatoes. Bring to

a boil, lower the heat and let the potatoes simmer until they're cooked through and tender — poke one with the tip of a knife, and it should give easily — about 20 minutes. (*You can make the soup to this point, cover and refrigerate it overnight. Bring to a boil before continuing.*)

Stir the coconut milk into the soup — from this point on, you don't want it to get above a gentle simmer: Coconut milk will curdle if you boil it. Give the milk about a minute to warm, then drop in the clams and simmer until they are cooked through or, if they were cooked to begin with, warm. Taste the soup for salt (it might not need any) and pepper. Remove the bay and lime leaves.

Ladle the chowder into bowls, sprinkle with the herbs and crackers, if you'd like, and serve immediately — this soup is best very hot or chilled; anything in between will be pale and uninteresting.

---

STORING:  The chowder will keep covered in the refrigerator for up to 2 days and can be reheated gently — don't boil.

# NEW ENGLAND CLAM CHOWDER

Omit the lemongrass, ginger, jalapeño and kaffir lime. When you add the bay leaf, add the leaves from a few sprigs of thyme. Before you add the clam juice, sprinkle ¼ cup all-purpose flour over the onions and celery and cook, stirring, for about 2 minutes. Then, if you'd like, pour over ¼ cup white wine, raise the heat and cook until it's almost evaporated. Proceed with the recipe, but instead of adding coconut milk, add 1 cup whole milk and 1 cup heavy cream. Warm — don't boil — and then add the clams. Serve with chopped dill and/or parsley, if you'd like. With this chowder, oyster crackers are not optional — they're a must.

# FRESH-OFF-THE-COB CORN CHOWDER

Makes 4 servings

The season for corn is too short not to make the most of it, and this chowder makes the most of corn down to the cobs. The kernels are cut from the ears and then the cobs are used to flavor the soup, which is built on a base of aromatic vegetables and herbs. When the vegetables are cooked through, the soup is pureed and more fresh vegetables are added, so that you get something smooth and something chunky in each spoonful. I like to add a little half-and-half to the soup at the end, but that's optional, as is a last scattering of herbs. Or, see Playing Around. And if you want to make a meal of the soup, add seafood.

## Playing Around

The soup lends itself to lots of add-ins and swaps. If you don't want bacon, sauté the reserved vegetables in a tablespoon of olive oil. If you opt out of the half-and-half but still want something extra, try a drizzle of chive or even chili oil, a little pesto or some grated Parmesan. As for add-ins, consider small cubes of ham (nice if you're not using the bacon), chunks of cooked shrimp or lobster or even thinly sliced raw scallops—the heat of the soup will cook them perfectly.

4 large ears corn, husked

2 celery stalks, trimmed and finely chopped

1 large sweet onion, such as Vidalia, finely chopped, rinsed and patted dry

1 to 2 garlic cloves, germ removed (see page 320) and minced

1 tablespoon olive oil

Fine sea salt and freshly ground pepper

2 sprigs fresh rosemary

2 sprigs fresh thyme

1 bay leaf

1 slender stalk fennel with fronds (optional)

5 cups (1¼ liters) water

1 tablespoon chicken or vegetable bouillon base (see page 333) or 1 bouillon cube

¾ pound (340 grams) potatoes, peeled, quartered if large, halved if smaller

4 slices bacon

2 tablespoons white wine

½ cup (120 ml) half-and-half (optional)

Minced fresh herbs, such as chives, parsley and/or basil (optional)

### WORKING AHEAD

You can make the soup a day ahead up to the point it's pureed; refrigerate it, reheat and carry on.

Set two large bowls on the counter. Cut the corn kernels off the cobs (see page 217 for a quick how-to) and put half of the corn in each bowl; reserve the cobs. Divide the celery, onion and garlic between the bowls; cover the second bowl and set aside. (Separating the vegetables and then later dividing the potatoes is a bit fussy, but you'll get a soup with great textures.)

Heat the olive oil in a Dutch oven or large saucepan over medium heat. When it's warm, add the vegetables from the first bowl, season with salt and pepper, lower the heat and cook, stirring, just until they soften, about

10 minutes. Toss in the herbs, fennel, if using, and the reserved cobs, pour in the water, add the bouillon base or cube and drop in the potatoes. Turn the heat up, bring the liquid to a boil and season with more salt and pepper, then lower the heat, partially cover the pot and simmer for 20 minutes. Test the potato. If it's tender, the soup is ready. If not, cover the pot completely and cook until a potato can be pierced easily with the tip of knife. Remove from the heat.

Using a slotted spoon, scoop half of the potatoes out of the soup and onto a cutting board, and cut them into small cubes. Set them aside for now. Remove and discard the corn cobs, the bay leaf and any stringy or woody herbs you can see. (*You can make the soup up to this point a day ahead and refrigerate it.*)

Working in batches if necessary, puree the soup in a blender or a food processor, or use a handheld (immersion) blender. Whatever you use, try to get the soup as smooth as possible. I like my chowder super-smooth, but if you like it chunky, don't be as thorough. Rinse out the pot if there's anything stuck to the bottom, then pour in the puree, cover and bring to a simmer over low heat; keep at a gentle simmer while you cook the bacon and the remaining vegetables.

Place the bacon strips in a heavy skillet and cook slowly until crisp, turning as needed. Transfer the bacon to a double thickness of paper towels and cover with more paper towels to remove excess fat (leave the fat in the skillet). Cut the bacon into 1/2-inch pieces.

Put the skillet over medium heat and, when the fat is warm, add the vegetables from the reserved bowl (not the cubed potatoes). Season with salt and pepper and cook, stirring, for about 6 minutes, until barely tender. Pour in the wine, raise the heat and cook until it almost evaporates.

Add the skillet vegetables, bacon and potato cubes to the soup and cook at a simmer for 5 to 10 minutes, until everything is piping hot. Taste for salt and pepper.

Ladle the chowder into bowls and, if you'd like, drizzle with half-and-half and scatter over fresh herbs.

———

STORING: Leftover soup can be kept in the refrigerator for up to 2 days. Bring to a boil and then simmer gently for about 10 minutes before serving. Because of the potatoes, the soup will thicken when chilled; if you'd like it thinner after reheating, add water.

# GINGERED-TURKEY MEATBALL SOUP

Makes 4 to 6 servings

The meatballs in this soup have enough flavor to stand up to just about anything — it's all the ginger, garlic, herbs and onion in them. These are exactly the flavors and scents you want with the soup, a broth that starts out simple and gets more interesting with each addition. First you use it as a poaching liquid for the meatballs, then you drop in lots of vegetables — the choice is yours, but I like to include some strong greens, like mustard, kale and cabbage — and more herbs. Finally there are the noodles, for texture and flavor, of course, but also for fun: Who doesn't love slurping, which seems to be the only way to eat rice noodles? Even with all that goes into the soup, I like to add more — soy sauce, sesame oil, rice vinegar and hot sauce are my druthers. While you can pour as much of these as you'd like into the pot just before serving, I leave the soup as is and put the add-ins on the table, so that each slurper can decide on the best combo and quantity.

## For the meatballs

1 large egg

¼ cup (60 ml) plain yogurt, preferably Greek

½ cup (about 113 grams) finely chopped onion, rinsed and patted dry

½ cup (20 grams) chopped fresh cilantro, basil or a mix

½ cup (30 grams) unseasoned dry bread crumbs

2 garlic cloves, germ removed (see page 320) and finely chopped

1 teaspoon grated peeled fresh ginger

Finely grated zest of 1 lemon

1 teaspoon fine sea salt

½ teaspoon freshly ground pepper

1 pound (454 grams) ground turkey, preferably organic

2½ quarts (2⅓ liters) chicken broth

## For the soup

½ pound (227 grams) rice noodles (sticks or straight-cut)

About 4 cups (about 600 grams) chopped, sliced and/or shredded mixed vegetables, such as peeled carrots, onions, mushrooms, cabbage (Napa or green), mustard greens, kale and/or spinach

Fine sea salt and freshly ground pepper

⅓ cup (13 grams) chopped fresh herbs, such as cilantro, basil, parsley and/or mint

Soy sauce, Asian sesame oil, rice vinegar and Sriracha, for serving

### WORKING AHEAD

You can make the meatballs ahead. Uncooked, they can be kept in the refrigerator for up to 6 hours. Once cooked, you can refrigerate them in some broth for up to 4 days or freeze them in an airtight bag for up to 2 months. The broth can be made up to 4 days ahead and kept in the refrigerator.

TO MAKE THE MEATBALLS: Put the egg in a large bowl and stir with a fork to break it up. Add all the remaining ingredients *except* the turkey and broth and

lightly stir, toss and mix to blend. Add the meat and, using the fork and then your fingers, turn and mix — again, go easy — until blended.

Using a medium cookie scoop (one with a capacity of about 1½ tablespoons) or a tablespoon, scoop out meatballs (you'll get 24 to 30), then roll them between your palms to round them. (*At this point, you can cover the meatballs and refrigerate them for up to 6 hours, or freeze them on a lined baking sheet until they're solid, then pack them in an airtight bag.*)

Bring the broth to a boil in a large pot, then lower the heat so that it simmers.

Drop the meatballs into the broth and, keeping it at a light, steady simmer, poach them, turning them over once, until cooked through, about 8 minutes. You'll probably want to do this in batches. Using a slotted spoon, transfer the meatballs to a large bowl. The broth will be a little murky. If you'd like it to be clearer, line a strainer with dampened cheesecloth (or a triple layer of dampened paper towels) and pour the broth through it into a bowl; rinse out the pot. (*You can put the meatballs in a container and freeze them for up to 2 months. Or cover with broth and refrigerate for up to 4 days; refrigerate the remainder of the broth separately.*)

TO MAKE THE SOUP: Bring a large pot of water to a boil. Drop in the rice noodles and cook for 4 minutes, then drain and transfer the noodles to a large bowl. Cover with cold water, toss in a few ice cubes and set aside until needed.

Bring the broth to a boil in the pot, then lower the heat so that it simmers. If your meatballs have been frozen, drop them into the broth and cook for 10 minutes; if chilled, cook for about 5 minutes; and if just made, simply drop them in. Add the vegetables to the pot and simmer for about 5 minutes. (If you're using carrots, they'll remain slightly firm.) Drain the noodles, add them to the pot and cook until hot — they'll heat very quickly. Taste for salt and pepper.

Ladle the soup, noodles and meatballs into deep bowls, dividing them equally. Sprinkle over the herbs and serve with the soy sauce, sesame oil, vinegar and Sriracha. Encourage everyone to season to taste.

———————

STORING: Once you've loaded the soup with all its add-ins, it is best served that day.

CHOICES: With these meatballs in the freezer, I feel like I'm ready for anything. They're great with pasta, stirred into a stewy bean dish, served as the main event with a side of vegetables or sliced and laid out on a roll (think sub or grinder, depending on where you live) and slathered with Sriracha and mayo — don't forget crisp lettuce. You can also give them the Luang Prabang sandwich treatment (see page 106).

# LETTUCE SOUP

Makes 4 to 6 servings

An elegant soup with a haphazard origin story. Everything that's in this soup — a couple of heads of lettuce, scallions, celery, garlic and a few herbs — was meant to be in a salad to go with some seared scallops. It was going to be lunch on the deck and it was meant to be quick, easy and light. And then two more people showed up and I had to scramble to find a way to stretch what I had. Soup! The ultimate stretcher. A half hour of heat, a good spin in the blender and I was saved. I poured the soup into wide shallow bowls, cut the scallops into quarters (so they'd look more abundant), opened some wine and set out some bread. What was a scramble is now a summer go-to.

**WORKING AHEAD**
The soup can be made ahead and refrigerated for up to 3 days in a tightly covered container. You can reheat it gently (the color will be better if you don't cover the pot) or serve it chilled.

2 tablespoons unsalted butter

3 fat scallions, white and light green parts only, thinly sliced

2 medium shallots, thinly sliced, rinsed and patted dry

1 medium onion, thinly sliced or chopped, rinsed and patted dry

1 celery stalk, trimmed and thinly sliced

1 to 3 garlic cloves (to taste), germ removed (see page 320) and thinly sliced

Fine sea salt and freshly ground pepper, preferably white

2 sprigs fresh parsley

1 sprig fresh thyme

4 cups (960 ml) chicken or vegetable broth or water

1 head romaine lettuce, trimmed and thinly sliced crosswise

1 head Boston (or butter) lettuce, trimmed and sliced

1 tablespoon chopped fresh mint

Freshly squeezed juice of ½ lemon

Optional add-ins (see Choices, opposite)

Working in a Dutch oven or large saucepan over low heat, melt the butter. Add the scallions, shallots, onion, celery and garlic, season with salt and pepper and stir to coat the vegetables with butter. Toss in the parsley and thyme and cook, stirring often, until the vegetables soften, 10 to 15 minutes.

Pour in the broth or water and bring to a boil, then lower the heat to a simmer, partially cover the pot and cook for 10 minutes. Remove the lid, stir in the romaine and Boston lettuce and cook, uncovered, for 3 minutes, or just until the lettuce is wilted. Remove the pot from the heat, pull out the sprigs of parsley and thyme and stir in the mint.

Using a blender, standard or handheld (immersion), or a food processor, and working in batches, whir the soup until you have a very smooth puree. Taste for salt and pepper and add the lemon juice before serving.

*(Recipe continues on facing page)*

Serve the soup while it's steaming hot, or allow it to cool, refrigerate and serve chilled. If you want to add seafood, divide it among the soup plates and pour over the hot soup. If you've chosen to add ravioli, cook them before adding to the soup.

CHOICES: Scallops would make this a meal, but the soup can be served as a starter with just a few croutons, a sprinkling of cheese, a dollop of plain Greek yogurt or a drizzle of pesto or olive oil. It can also be chilled and served in glasses, to be sipped rather than spooned. And it is equally good with shrimp or cooked mini ravioli.

# GREEN-AS-SPRING SOUP

Makes 4 servings

Like crocuses and robins and the first light green leaves on a rosebush, asparagus are a trusty harbinger of spring and a promise of warmth ahead. In this soup, which has enough flavor to be enjoyed hot or cold, they're the star, with a great supporting cast: leeks, shallots and garlic for an aromatic base and zucchini for color and a little more texture. Don't be tempted to peel the squash — the skin is the dish's secret coloring agent. The soup may look rich, ditto the basil-lime cream that makes such a good topper, but neither is: I've kept them both lean so that the flavors of the vegetables can be front and center.

1 tablespoon unsalted butter

1 tablespoon olive oil

2 medium leeks, white and light green parts only, split lengthwise, washed, sliced and patted dry

2 large shallots, sliced, rinsed and patted dry

2 garlic cloves, germ removed (see page 320) and sliced

Fine sea salt

5 cups (1¼ liters) chicken or vegetable broth

1 pound (454 grams) asparagus, trimmed, peeled and cut into 4 pieces each

1 slender zucchini (about ¼ pound; 113 grams), scrubbed, trimmed and sliced

2 sprigs fresh basil

Freshly ground pepper

### For the basil-lime cream (optional)

¼ cup (60 ml) plain Greek yogurt or sour cream

½ lime

Finely chopped fresh basil

## WORKING AHEAD

You can make the soup a day ahead and serve it cold or gently reheated.

Warm the butter and oil in a Dutch oven or large saucepan over low heat. Add the leeks, shallots, garlic and about ½ teaspoon salt and cook, stirring occasionally, for 15 minutes, or until the vegetables are softened, but not colored.

Add the broth and bring to a boil. Toss in the asparagus, zucchini and basil, season lightly with salt and lower the heat. Allow the soup to simmer, uncovered, for 10 minutes, at which point the zucchini and asparagus should be soft. Taste for salt and add pepper. Remove from the heat.

Working in batches if necessary, puree the soup in a blender, standard or handheld (immersion), or a food processor. Run the machine a little longer than you might ordinarily, to be sure that all the ingredients are fully pureed and that the soup is beautifully smooth.

The soup is ready to serve now, or you can pour it into a container, cover and chill.

TO SERVE WITH THE (OPTIONAL) BASIL-LIME CREAM: Place a spoonful of yogurt or sour cream in the center of each bowl of soup, squeeze over a little lime juice and sprinkle on some basil.

———————

STORING: The soup can be kept covered in the refrigerator overnight and served cold or warmed gently. The color will change with time — it is at its most vibrant for a few hours and then it turns a little darker; the taste remains great.

# HOT OR COLD BEET-FENNEL SOUP

Makes 6 servings

I love when you can get a mountain of flavor from a molehill of ingredients — in this case, beets, fennel, onion and garlic. I first made the soup in late spring when, with the enthusiasm that overtakes me as soon as new vegetables come into the markets, I'd bought too many beets. I roasted a bunch, pickled a few and then made this soup, which I continued to make through the summer and into fall. It's good at every temperature, but I think my favorite is cold. The strawberries were a last-minute inspiration and chosen for both their color and their sweet-acidic pick-me-up flavor.

You can serve the soup straight from the fridge or you can double up on the chill, as I do, by pouring it over ice cubes. Sometimes I serve soup-on-ice in highball glasses with a straw, but most of the time I ladle it into bowls and finish it with a scoop of thick Greek yogurt, a few cilantro or parsley leaves, cucumber coins and some strawberries.

### WORKING AHEAD
The soup can be made up to 3 days ahead and kept tightly covered in the refrigerator. If you want to reheat it, do so gently.

1 to 2 tablespoons olive oil

1 medium fennel bulb, trimmed, cored and cut into chunks

1 large red or sweet onion, such as Vidalia, cut into chunks

2 garlic cloves, germ removed (see page 320)

3 sprigs fresh thyme or oregano (optional)

Fine sea salt and freshly ground pepper

6 cups (about 1½ liters) chicken or vegetable broth

5 medium red beets, trimmed, peeled and cut into chunks

### For serving (optional)
Plain Greek yogurt, sour cream or crème fraîche

Strawberries, hulled and cut into small pieces

Cucumber, preferably mini (Persian), peeled (or not) and cut into rounds or small dice

Minced fresh herbs, for sprinkling

Cracked ice cubes

Pour 1 tablespoon of the oil into a Dutch oven or large saucepan and warm over low heat. Add the fennel, onion, garlic and herb, if you're using it, and cook, stirring, until the vegetables soften, about 15 minutes; if you need to, add a little more oil. Season with salt and pepper. Add the broth and beets, turn up the heat and bring to a boil, then lower the heat and simmer, partially covered, for about 45 minutes, depending on your beets. Don't be impatient — the beets must be easily pierced with a knife.

To puree the soup, use a blender, either standard or handheld (immersion), or a food processor. Working in batches and discarding the spent herb sprigs when you come to them, puree the soup, giving it just a minute more than you might normally in order to ensure that you get a silky texture.

You can serve the soup hot or let it cool a bit and then refrigerate until it's thoroughly chilled. If you've refrigerated the soup, stir it before serving. Hot or cold, the soup is good with any of the suggested toppings; the strawberries are especially good when the soup is chilled. For the cold version, I like to put a couple of ice cubes in the bowls (or glasses) before I pour in the soup.

# GREEN GODDESS SIPPER, SOUP OR SHOTS

Makes about 4 cups

The first time I made the Demi-Goddess Dressing (page 304), I just couldn't get enough of its bright flavor. And when I found myself licking my fingers, I realized I had to find a more refined way to get my fill of the stuff. The answer was this soup, which uses some of the dressing and then doubles up on many of the flavors that make it so alluring. There's more buttermilk, more cucumber, more citrus and more herbs. And there are three ways to enjoy this cold treat: traditionally, as a soup; on the rocks, as a sipper; or in shot glasses, as a quick refresher or an accompaniment to a salad that you're serving as a starter.

**WORKING AHEAD**
The soup will keep for up to 3 days in a tightly sealed container.

1 cup (240 ml) buttermilk (well shaken before measuring)

½ cup (120 ml) Demi-Goddess Dressing (page 304)

1 English (seedless) cucumber, peeled, trimmed and cut into small chunks

1 small to medium zucchini, scrubbed, trimmed and cut into small chunks

Juice of ½ lemon or lime

About 1 teaspoon fine sea salt

A small handful of mixed fresh herbs, such as dill, mint, basil, tarragon or fennel fronds, coarsely chopped

Plain Greek yogurt, for serving (optional)

Additional minced fresh herbs, for serving (optional)

Put the buttermilk, Demi-Goddess, cucumber, zucchini, citrus juice and ½ teaspoon of the salt in a blender and whir on medium to high speed until you have a smooth emulsion. Depending on the power of your blender, this might take a little longer than you expect — you want it to be as smooth as possible, so keep going. Taste for salt — you'll probably want more — and then toss in the herbs, whir and taste again. Remember that flavors dull when chilled and this mix is going to be served very cold.

Chill the soup for at least 4 hours and stir well before serving. (If feasible, you can refrigerate the soup in the blender jar and just give it another whir when you're ready to serve it.)

If you're serving this as a sipper, pour it over ice and pop a straw into each glass. If you've got soup in mind, pour it into small bowls. If you'd like, top either with a mini-dollop of yogurt and some herbs. If you're looking for something in between soup and sipper, pour it into shot glasses.

GREEN GODDESS SIPPER AND TOMATO
AND BERRY GAZPACHO (PAGE 86)

# TOMATO AND BERRY GAZPACHO

Makes 4 to 6 small servings

When the weather's hot and you're looking for something fabulously fresh and delicious, quick to make and instantly beloved, pull out your blender and this recipe for a gazpacho based on cherry tomatoes (I like to use Sun Golds for their sweetness, but red ones give you gorgeous color) and strawberries, a combination that should be inscribed in the book of heavenly matches. It's a push-button answer to what to serve on the rocks before dinner, in a bowl to start dinner or late in the afternoon, when you're craving something to tide you over.

Like so many good recipes, this one's easy to play around with. I've given you everything you need to make a first-rate soup, but that doesn't mean there isn't room for improvisation. Of course you can add more mint, basil, ginger, lime, vinegar, harissa or other hottener you want. What you shouldn't do is add less: Gazpacho is meant to be bold and you should catch the vinegar with each sip or spoonful; it's part of what makes the soup so refreshing. Also, remember that spices and salt lose their oomph when chilled and that this soup is meant to be served very cold. You can always add more of anything after the gazpacho has chilled, but you'd do well to make the soup salty and full of flavor from the get-go.

The photo is on page 85.

1 pint (about 300 grams) cherry tomatoes (25 to 30), Sun Golds or red, halved

12 strawberries, hulled (a few more or less won't matter), halved or quartered

3 quarter-sized slices peeled fresh ginger, coarsely chopped

2 scallions, white and light green parts only, sliced

8 fresh mint leaves, torn

8 fresh basil leaves, torn

Juice of 1 lime, or more to taste

2 tablespoons extra-virgin olive oil, or more to taste

2 tablespoons sherry vinegar, or more to taste

1 teaspoon fine sea salt, or more to taste

¼ teaspoon harissa powder (see page 334) or your favorite hot sauce, to taste

Extra-virgin olive oil, for drizzling (optional)

Hot sauce, for serving (optional)

Optional add-ins (see Choices)

## WORKING AHEAD

The gazpacho has to be refrigerated for at least 2 hours, and it benefits from an overnight chill—the texture thickens just a tad and the flavors come together in a more interesting way.

Put all the ingredients in a blender and whir like mad. If you like a chunky gazpacho (I'm a smoothie person), you can whir less madly, but remember that you want to puree the tomato skins and ginger. Taste for seasoning and adjust, going a little heavier on the vinegar and salt, if you'd like, since they'll be tamed in the fridge.

Pour the soup into a storage container, cover and chill for at least 2 hours, or, preferably, overnight before serving. When you're ready to serve, shake or stir the gazpacho well and taste for seasoning.

Serve in glasses, over ice or straight up, or in bowls, with or without optional add-ins. No matter how you serve, there are two constants: cold and sharpness, so check the seasonings and, if you'd like, have some hot sauce on hand for everyone to season as they go.

––––––––––

STORING: Tightly covered, the gazpacho will keep for up to 2 days in the refrigerator.

CHOICES: The soup is luscious with nothing more than a drizzle of olive oil, and even that's optional, but it's also good with a bunch of sprinklers: baby croutons that have been toasted or tossed in a skillet with olive oil; slivers of chile pepper; chopped toasted almonds; small cubes of tomato and/or strawberries (giving a hint of what's to come) or chopped basil, mint or other herbs. For something a little more substantial, try small pieces of highly seasoned cooked shrimp or scallops.

# GINGER-BEET SALAD BOWLS

Makes 4 servings

This is the little recipe that grew and grew. It started life as roasted beets dressed with ginger-harissa vinaigrette, and it was good. Then the beets became the centerpiece of what the French call a composed salad, one in which the elements are laid out or layered rather than tossed, and it was even better. (If you'd like to make a salad like that, use the beets and lettuce and add whatever else you want, or don't — just beets, greens and vinaigrette is fine.) Finally, I added quinoa and it became a delicious meal.

I've outlined my three-step experience with the emphasis on the word "outline." The vinaigrette is a "real" recipe, but after that, while I give you ingredients and amounts, you should feel free to treat these as suggestions and go off on your own.

## a word on the beets

They can be freshly cooked or store-bought cooked — many supermarkets carry good cooked beets in the fresh vegetable section. While I usually roast beets, you can boil them if that's what you prefer; just drain them well and pat them dry, so that they'll absorb the vinaigrette.

### For the vinaigrette

3 tablespoons extra-virgin olive oil

2½ tablespoons white wine vinegar

1½ tablespoons white balsamic vinegar

¾ to 1 teaspoon harissa paste (to taste) or ½ teaspoon harissa powder (see page 334)

½ teaspoon honey

½ teaspoon grated peeled fresh ginger

½ teaspoon fine sea salt

Freshly ground pepper

4 large or 8 small beets, fully cooked, peeled and cut into chunks (about 1 inch)

Fine sea salt and freshly ground pepper

### For the bowls

Lettuce, such as 2 Little Gems, 1 small head romaine, radicchio or endive (red or white)

Fine sea salt and freshly ground pepper

⅔ cup (160 ml) plain Greek yogurt

1½ cups (276 grams) cooked quinoa, warm or at room temperature

2 scallions or 1 spring onion, white and pale green parts, thinly sliced

Quick Pickled Onions (page 320; optional)

2 tablespoons pomegranate seeds

Finely chopped fresh herbs, such as basil, cilantro and/ or mint

**WORKING AHEAD**

The vinaigrette can be made up to 2 days ahead. The beets can be prepared and dressed up to a day ahead; ditto the quinoa. And the pickled onions will keep for a week in the refrigerator.

TO MAKE THE VINAIGRETTE:  Put all of the ingredients in a small jar with a tight-fitting lid and shake vigorously. (*You can make the dressing up to 2 days ahead and keep it in the refrigerator; shake before using.*)

*(Recipe continues on facing page)*

Put the beets in a bowl, season lightly with salt and pepper and toss with just enough vinaigrette to coat them lightly. (*You can cover the beets and refrigerate for up to 1 day.*)

TO MAKE THE BOWLS: Cut off the base of whichever lettuce you've chosen, separate the leaves and wash and dry them. Do the same if you're using endive. If you'd prefer small pieces, tear the larger leaves. Season the leaves with salt and pepper and divide them among four bowls.

Divide the yogurt and beets among the bowls, then spoon in the quinoa. Scatter over the scallions, pickled onions (if you're using them), pomegranate seeds and herbs. Season with salt and pepper, drizzle over the remaining vinaigrette and serve.

The bowls should be eaten as soon as they're made.

# COWBOY CAVIAR SALAD OR SIDE

Makes 4 servings

Helen Corbitt became famous for many of the dishes she created as the culinary director of Neiman Marcus in Dallas. This bean salad, reported to have been served for the first time in 1940, is one that endured. It was originally called Texas Caviar, the name a wink to the shape of expensive caviar mimicked by inexpensive beans. Traditionally made with black-eyed peas, the salad is often served on New Year's Day in the South, when eating beans is said to ensure a year of prosperity.

The salad has cooked (see page 314) or canned black-eyed peas or beans (red, black or pinto) mixed with onions, peppers (hot and sweet), tomatoes, garlic and the (not-from-the-original-recipe) "extras" that make it so good: herbs, spices and lots of lime juice. As with just about anything made with beans, doubling it (or multiplying by almost any number) for a party is easy. The fact that the dish is best made a few hours ahead is another reason to think about it when you're partying, grilling, beaching or buffeting.

## a word on measurements and ingredients

While I've given you measurements, please treat them as a guide. Just as you might want more cumin or paprika, you may want more onion or pepper. Toss, taste and decide. As for the tomatoes, if you'd like, you can use canned fire-roasted tomatoes; drain them well. And if they've got some jalapeños mixed in, that's nice.

¼ cup (60 ml) olive oil

Finely grated zest and juice of 1 lime

1 teaspoon ground cumin, or more to taste

¾ teaspoon fine sea salt

½ teaspoon smoked paprika (sweet or hot)

½ teaspoon honey

About 2 cups (450 grams) cooked or canned beans (see headnote), rinsed, drained and patted dry if canned

3 scallions, white and light green parts only, thinly sliced

1 garlic clove, germ removed (see page 320) and finely chopped

½ red onion, finely chopped or diced, rinsed and patted dry

½ bell pepper, finely chopped or diced

½ jalapeño, seeded and finely chopped or diced

2 to 3 medium tomatoes, finely chopped or diced (or drained canned; see headnote)

½ cup (20 grams) finely chopped fresh cilantro

Hot sauce (optional)

Tortilla chips, for serving (optional)

### WORKING AHEAD

The salad, without the tomatoes and cilantro, which are quick wilters, is best made a few hours, or even a day, ahead and refrigerated. You can make the vinaigrette a day ahead as well.

Put the oil, lime zest and juice, cumin, salt, paprika and honey in a jar with a tight-fitting lid and shake to blend. Set the vinaigrette aside until needed. (*You can make the vinaigrette a day ahead; keep refrigerated.*)

Put the rest of the ingredients *except* the tomatoes, cilantro and optional hot sauce in a large bowl and toss to mix. If you're going to serve the salad now, add the tomatoes and cilantro; if you're going to refrigerate the salad — a good move — hold off and add them just before serving.

*(Recipe continues)*

Toss the salad with about three-quarters of the vinaigrette. Add hot sauce, if you'd like, and, if you've got time, cover and refrigerate for a couple of hours (or up to overnight) before serving.

When you're ready to serve, add the tomatoes and cilantro if you haven't already and taste for salt and spices. Add hot sauce, if you'd like. If the salad has sopped up the vinaigrette, toss it with a little more. (Reserve any leftover vinaigrette — it's good on greens or tomatoes.) Serve chilled or at room temperature, with or without chips.

STORING: It's best to add the tomatoes and cilantro at the last minute, but even with these add-ins, leftover salad will be good a day later.

CHOICES: The salad is terrific alongside anything from burgers to grilled fish, and it also makes a good, heartier-than-it-looks main dish: Add corn, mango and/or avocado, toss in some shrimp and spoon the whole kit and caboodle over kale or spinach.

# CHICKPEA-TAHINI SALAD

Makes 6 servings

The first time I made this dish, it struck me that I should have been making it for years. After all, I'd been crushing chickpeas and mixing them with herbs, spices and tahini almost forever, so why was I so late to the idea of dressing a chickpea salad with tahini, like hummus?

While this salad has many of the same ingredients that hummus does, it only hints at that Mediterranean specialty. Because of the ginger, cayenne and dill, there's more flavor, complexity and general deliciousness than in classic hummus. More texture too, since the chickpeas are left whole and mixed with small chunks of peppers and red onions.

You can make this salad with canned chickpeas — a really good pantry staple — but if you cook your own (see page 314), the flavor and texture will be multiples better. And if you do cook the chickpeas from scratch (see page 314), use the broth instead of water to thin the tahini dressing.

## For the dressing

⅓ cup (80 ml) tahini (stirred well before measuring)

About ¼ cup (60 ml) lukewarm water or warm chickpea broth (see headnote)

2 lemons

1 garlic clove, germ removed (see page 320) and grated or minced, or to taste

1½ teaspoons grated peeled fresh ginger

1½ teaspoons ground cumin

1 teaspoon smoked paprika, or to taste (optional)

1 teaspoon fine sea salt, or to taste

¼ teaspoon cayenne pepper, or to taste

¼ teaspoon honey (optional)

## For the salad

About 5 cups cooked (from 1 pound/454 grams dried) or canned chickpeas, drained

1 red bell pepper, cored, seeded and finely diced

1 small red onion, finely diced, rinsed and patted dry

¼ cup (10 grams) chopped fresh cilantro

¼ cup (10 grams) snipped or minced fresh dill

Freshly ground pepper

### WORKING AHEAD

I like to let the salad chill for a few hours; in fact, it's best after a day in the fridge. The dressing can be made up to 2 days ahead and refrigerated.

TO MAKE THE DRESSING: Put the tahini in a large bowl, pour in the water or cooking broth and whisk until the tahini, which will separate, is smooth. Grate the zest of 1 lemon over the tahini, then squeeze over and whisk in the juice of both lemons. Whisk in the remaining ingredients and taste to see if you'd like to make any adjustments in the seasoning. Remember that chickpeas, as delicious as they are, are bland and they will soak up flavoring, so you don't want a timid dressing. (*The dressing can be refrigerated for a day or two.*)

(*Recipe continues*)

TO MAKE THE SALAD: Add all the salad ingredients *except* the black pepper to the bowl with the dressing and turn with a flexible spatula until all the chunky ingredients are coated, then stir some more — the salad may look a little dry at first, but if you do a good job of enrobing the ingredients in dressing, it will be just right. Season with pepper. (*The salad can be made up to 3 days ahead, covered and refrigerated. Taste for seasoning just before serving.*)

STORING: Kept tightly covered, the salad will hold for up to 3 days in the refrigerator.

CHOICES: You can spoon this out solo, as you would potato salad; add shrimp and make it a main course; or do what I often do: Toss it with kale, arugula or another hearty green. If you add greens, dress them very lightly with a basic vinaigrette (page 305) before mixing them with the chickpeas.

# CAULIFLOWER TABBOULEH

Makes 4 servings

The little grains in this bright, light salad, a culinary trompe l'oeil, are not cracked wheat, tabbouleh's classic ingredient, but slightly crunchy grated raw cauliflower. The florets are cut from their stems (which you can use for soup or cook and add to mashed potatoes), grated and tossed with tabbouleh's traditional flavorings: lemon juice, mint, parsley and just a little olive oil. Made with cauliflower, the time-honored salad moves into the twenty-first century.

I like to add golden raisins (for sweetness and chew) and chopped unblanched almonds (for crunch), but the list of possible toss-ins is endless. Consider celery, carrots, scallions, red onions, beets, apples (rub the cut apples with lemon juice to keep them from browning), cucumbers or even pickles. As long as whatever you add is finely chopped or diced — the salad is nicest when all the ingredients are mini and a similar size — you can go on whatever tangent calls to you. This is less a recipe than a terrific idea and a template for playing around.

## a word on grating

You can grate the florets in a food processor, either by pulsing the machine or fitting it with a grating blade, but I use the large holes on a box grater. It takes about 6 minutes to run through a big head of cauliflower, and the cleanup is quick.

¼ cup (40 grams) moist, plump golden (or dark) raisins

1 large head cauliflower

1 cup (155 grams) cooked (see page 314) or canned chickpeas, drained and patted dry

¼ cup (32 grams) finely chopped unblanched almonds

¼ cup (10 grams) finely chopped fresh mint

¼ cup (10 grams) finely chopped fresh parsley or cilantro

1 to 2 lemons

Fine sea salt and freshly ground pepper

1 tablespoon extra-virgin olive oil, or more to taste

**WORKING AHEAD**
If you have time, it's best to chill the salad for at least 1 hour.

Check your raisins: If they're not plump and soft, put them in a bowl of hot tap water and set them aside to soak. When you're ready for them, drain and pat dry.

Remove the green leaves from the cauliflower. Cut it in half from top to bottom and then crosswise into quarters. There are several ways to grate the cauliflower: You can use the largest holes on a box grater, a Microplane grater with large holes or the grating blade of a food processor. You can also use the regular metal blade of the processor, but make certain that you pulse in super-short spurts and stop the instant you get granules — grate too long, and you'll lose the texture, which is what this dish is all about. If it's not already in a big bowl, put the cauliflower in one now.

Add the chickpeas, almonds, herbs and raisins. Finely grate the zest of 1 lemon over the tabbouleh and then squeeze in the juice, tossing the salad lightly with a fork. Season with salt and pepper, drizzle over the olive oil and toss to incorporate. Taste the salad and see if you'd like more salt, pepper, lemon zest, juice and/or oil. I usually use the zest and juice of 1½ lemons and 2 tablespoons olive oil, but lemons vary in size and tartness.

(Recipe continues)

Serve the salad or, preferably, cover it tightly and refrigerate it for at least an hour.

---

STORING: Packed into a tightly covered container, the salad will keep in the refrigerator for up to 2 days.

CHOICES: I usually serve the salad alongside something grilled — it's great with fish — or as the base of a grain bowl (albeit one that only looks like grain). Or top the tabbouleh with grilled and/or steamed vegetables, salad greens and something pickled; or dress it up and serve it as a dinner-party starter, pairing it with spiced yogurt (page 313) and roasted carrots (page 214), a wedge of roasted squash or sweet potatoes.

# SPRING AVOCADO AND BERRY SALAD

Makes 4 to 6 servings

For just about all of May and June, when I've got local strawberries in the house, those that I don't eat straight from the basket go into desserts (try Eton Mess, page 279); get pickled (page 319), panzanella'd or jumbled on top of ice cream. Or they become part of this surprising salad.

The salad's three star players are avocado, Ruby Red grapefruit and strawberries. The avocados and berries are sliced. The grapefruit is cut into segments, and the membranes that once held them together are squeezed for juice to use in the vinaigrette. Finish the salad with a mix of jalapeño, pink peppercorns, cilantro, basil and a few squeezes of lime juice, and you've got something that's as beautiful as it is tasty.

## WORKING AHEAD

You can make the vinaigrette and cut the grapefruit, strawberries and jalapeño a few hours ahead, but the avocado should be cut and the salad assembled (a matter of minutes) and dressed right before you're ready to serve it.

1 Ruby Red grapefruit

2 or 3 limes (depending on their size)

Tiny pinch of sugar

Fine sea salt and freshly ground pepper

¼ cup (60 ml) extra-virgin olive oil

6 large or 9 medium strawberries, hulled

2 large ripe but firm avocados

½ jalapeño, seeded and finely diced or sliced

About ½ teaspoon pink peppercorns

Fresh cilantro leaves

A few fresh basil leaves, torn

For the grapefruit, you want to remove the fruit in sections and save the juice. You can do this either by cutting away all the peel and slicing the fruit between the membranes, so you get suprêmes (see page 309), then squeezing the juice from the membranes; or by slicing the unpeeled fruit crosswise in half, cutting out the sections (if you have a grapefruit knife or spoon, use it) and squeezing the shells for the juice. Whichever method you use, squeeze the juice into a small bowl and reserve the fruit.

Squeeze 2 tablespoons lime juice (from 1 large lime or 2 smaller ones). Put 1½ tablespoons of the grapefruit juice and the lime juice in a jar with a tight-fitting lid. Add the sugar, a big pinch of salt, some black pepper and the oil and shake vigorously to blend. Taste to see if you want to adjust the seasonings, and set aside.

Slice the strawberries — thin, thick or in half, depending on their size and your preference. (*You can make the salad up to this point a few hours ahead; refrigerate the grapefruit and berries and keep the vinaigrette at room temperature.*)

When you're ready to serve, cut the remaining lime in half. Working with one avocado at a time, slice each one in half from top to bottom, remove the pit and cut each half into long, slender slices — you'll get 6 to 8 slices from each half. Lay the slices out on a platter and immediately sprinkle with lime juice. Season with salt and pepper. Scatter over the grapefruit and strawberries, followed by the jalapeño, pink peppercorns — pinch them between your fingertips to crack them — a few grinds of black pepper and another squeeze or two of lime juice. Shake the vinaigrette to blend again and drizzle it over the salad — you don't want to drown it, so you might not need all of the vinaigrette. Finish with cilantro, basil and a sprinkle of salt.

STORING: If you have leftovers, toss them with spinach leaves — the combo's really good.

# TOMATO AND PEACH PANZANELLA

Makes 6 servings

Like so many good traditional dishes, panzanella was born of thrift, created as a way to use stale bread. It's an Italian salad that has toured the world and picked up ingredients and ingenious additions at every port. The basic dish is chunks of dry bread, sometimes soaked in water and sometimes not, tossed with tomatoes, vinegar (it can take a fair amount of acidity) and oil. The juices from the tomatoes, as well as the oil and vinegar, seep into the bread, saturate it and flavor it deeply. A handful of chopped herbs at the end, and that's all you need.

While that's all you need, it doesn't mean that it's all you might want. I like to add red onion, lemon zest, lemon juice and something unexpected: fruit. I love throwing peaches or nectarines into the mix, as I do here, but the salad can also take watermelon, cherries or pieces of plums. And if the grill is hot, try roasting half of the peaches or nectarines.

You can use any kind of bread you'd like — it's what our founding mothers did. Because my husband is a bread baker, what we've got in the house is usually the remains of a country loaf or baguette. Even if the bread is stale, I find that the salad is better if you put a little extra time into it and oven-toast the bread with olive oil and salt — think croutons.

## a word on measurements

I've measured everything for you, but I think you'll enjoy the salad more if you put it together by look, feel and taste. The amount of bread is really whatever you've got; the oil is as much as you think you need; ditto the onions; and the vinegar is truly to taste. I like the salad sharp — especially when the tomatoes and fruit are summer-ripe — but you might want to tone it down. Taste and add as you go.

1 baguette or other sturdy loaf (about 7 ounces; 198 grams), preferably stale

3 tablespoons extra-virgin olive oil, or more to taste

Fine sea salt or fleur de sel and freshly ground pepper

1 pound (454 grams) ripe tomatoes

2 peaches or nectarines

1 lemon

½ small red onion or more to taste, thinly sliced, rinsed and patted dry

2 tablespoons sherry vinegar or red wine vinegar, or more to taste

Shredded fresh basil leaves or other herb(s)

Center a rack in the oven and preheat it to 350 degrees F. Line a baking sheet with parchment paper or a silicone baking mat.

Tear the bread into pieces just a little bigger than bite-sized, or cut it — often easier when the bread is stale. Spread the pieces out on the baking sheet, drizzle with 1 tablespoon of the oil, season with salt and pepper and toss. Bake for 15 to 20 minutes, turning the bread once or twice, until the cubes are dry and lightly toasted.

Meanwhile, core the tomatoes and cut into chunks. Halve and pit the peaches or nectarines and cut into similar-sized chunks, catching as much of the juice as you can. Toss the tomatoes, fruit and juice into a large serving bowl.

When the bread is toasted, stir it into the bowl. Grate the zest of the lemon over, squeeze over the lemon juice

and stir again. Mix in the onion. Let the salad rest for 5 to 10 minutes (or for up to 1 hour).

Add the remaining 2 tablespoons oil and the vinegar to the salad and season with salt and pepper. Let the salad sit for a couple of minutes again, then taste it for oil, vinegar, salt and pepper. Scatter over the herb(s) and serve.

STORING: Even though this salad is meant to be soft, I think it's best shortly after it's assembled.

CHOICES: You can serve the salad as a starter; as a lunch, in which case you might want to add assertive greens, such as kale or arugula, and perhaps some shrimp; or as a side dish to something light.

# WHITE BEANS AND SMOKED FISH
## (A PANTRY-AND-FRIDGE SALAD)

Makes 6 servings

While my usual forage-in-my-kitchen salad stars chickpeas and tuna, my newest version mixes white beans, preserved lemon and smoked haddock (or other fish). With a double-mustard vinaigrette, some herbs, onions and a splash of fresh lemon juice at the end, it makes a good dinner and will be snackable for a day or two more.

### a word on the haddock

Smoked haddock has a very strong flavor, so you want to cut it into small pieces. If you're using a milder smoked fish, you might want larger pieces, and you might even want a little more fish.

### and a word on the onions

I always have Quick Pickled Onions (page 320) in my fridge. I leave them in their brine; they keep for about a week or so. If you don't have them, use scallions, spring onions or red onion, rinsed in cold water and patted dry.

*For the vinaigrette*

3 to 4 tablespoons extra-virgin olive oil

2 tablespoons white balsamic vinegar

1 tablespoon sherry vinegar

1 tablespoon grainy mustard (preferably French)

1 teaspoon smooth Dijon mustard (preferably French)

Fine sea salt and freshly ground pepper

*For the salad*

4 to 5 cups (about 450 grams) white beans, cooked (from 1 pound dried) or canned, drained and patted dry

2 to 3 celery stalks, trimmed and thinly sliced

1 red bell pepper, cored, seeded and cut into bite-sized pieces (if you'd like, use a hot pepper instead)

½ preserved lemon, peel only, patted dry and finely chopped

Fine sea salt and freshly ground pepper

1 lemon

About 3 tablespoons minced fresh basil, parsley or cilantro, or a mix

3 to 4 tablespoons chopped pickled or plain onions (see headnote)

½ pound (226 grams) smoked haddock (or other smoked fish, or tuna; see Playing Around), skin removed and cut into bite-sized pieces

Salad greens, tossed with a little oil, for serving (optional)

**WORKING AHEAD**

The vinaigrette can be made ahead and refrigerated for up to 5 days.

TO MAKE THE VINAIGRETTE: Put 3 tablespoons oil and the rest of the ingredients *except* the salt and pepper in a jar with a tight-fitting lid and shake vigorously to blend. Taste and decide if you'd like more olive oil (or even more mustard and/or vinegar). Then season with salt and pepper. Beans sop up flavor, so you want the vinaigrette to be sharper than usual. (*You can refrigerate the vinaigrette for up to 5 days. Shake well before using.*)

TO MAKE THE SALAD: Choose a large salad bowl that will give you lots of toss room. Put the beans, celery, bell pepper and preserved lemon in the bowl, moisten with some of the vinaigrette, season lightly with salt (remember that the fish will add salt to the mix) and generously with pepper and toss well. Grate the zest of the lemon over the salad, then add the herbs, onions and a little more vinaigrette and toss again. Mix in the fish and taste to see if it needs more vinaigrette, salt and/or pepper. If you'd like, squeeze the juice of the lemon into the salad — I love this squirt of sharpness and always use it.

Serve as is, or place the salad on a bed of greens.

STORING: Leftover salad will keep covered in the refrigerator for up to 2 days. It may need a little more vinegar, lemon juice and/or salt and pepper — toss and taste before serving.

## Playing Around

Salads like these welcome change-ups — the haddock can be any other sturdy smoked fish, such as salmon, trout or a white fish. If you're a smoked eel lover, go for it — eel and beans are wonderful together. Or, if you want something without smoke, use 2 cans of tuna. The beans can be white, black, red or even firm French lentils. And no one will shake a finger if you decide to add orange or grapefruit segments or sliced tomatoes or avocados.

# CHICKEN

# LUANG PRABANG CHICKEN-CHILI SANDWICHES

Makes 4 sandwiches

Four 8-inch-long soft half-baguettes or sub rolls, split

About ⅓ cup (80 ml) mayonnaise

2 to 3 tablespoons Sriracha (to taste)

2 to 3 Oven-Roasted Chicken Breasts (page 108), depending on size, or other cooked chicken, cut into long strips

About ⅓ cup (80 ml) Thai sweet chili sauce (see page 335)

2 tomatoes, sliced

⅔ English cucumber, peeled or unpeeled and cut into long thin slices

About 2 cups (about 100 grams) shredded crispy lettuce, such as iceberg

When I was in Luang Prabang, Laos, with my son, Joshua, we quickly adopted an evening routine. We'd go to the night market, stroll among the vendors for a while and then turn into the alley where the food merchants set up. The sandwich ladies were at the entrance. Each woman would start putting together a sandwich only when the order came in. The process would start with one of them slicing a bamboo-skewered grilled chicken breast into long strips. Next would come the bread, a soft, almost squishy half-baguette. She'd open the bread wide and place it on the palm of her left hand, then get to work slathering both sides with mayonnaise and hot chile paste, covering the bread with slices of chicken moistened with a little sweet chili sauce, rounds of tomato and long slices of cucumber, tucking in some lettuce and finishing it all off with a prolonged squeeze of sweet chili sauce. Then, the final touch: She'd close the sandwich with a rectangle of paper torn from a magazine and secure the whole bundle with a rubber band.

It's not easy to give a precise recipe for this sandwich, so I've given you the elements and the order in which they can be layered (but don't necessarily have to be). Since grilled chicken is not a year-round staple in our house, I make the sandwiches with sautéed or oven-roasted chicken breasts.

## a word on quantities

This is truly a season-to-taste recipe, so while I've given you measurements, please treat them as guidelines.

Spread both cut sides of the baguettes or rolls with mayonnaise and Sriracha. Arrange the chicken strips over the bottom halves and moisten with some of the chili sauce. Add the tomatoes and cucumber, drizzle with more chili sauce and top with the lettuce. Give everything a last hit of chili sauce and close the sandwiches.

Press the sandwiches down or, if you want the true Luang Prabang experience, secure them with rubber bands and wait for about 15 minutes before snapping the bands and digging in.

———

STORING: The sandwiches are good immediately and best 15 minutes later.

*(Recipe continues)*

# OVEN-ROASTED CHICKEN BREASTS

If you can find small skinless, boneless breasts, use them — they work best with this recipe. If you get big breasts (more usual in supermarkets), cut them horizontally in half. Rub the breasts with a little olive oil and some lemon juice and season with salt and pepper. (*You can marinate the breasts in this mix for a few hours in the refrigerator, or at room temperature just while you preheat the oven.*) Lay the breasts out on a baking sheet lined with parchment paper or foil. Roast them in a 350-degree-F oven for about 20 minutes (longer if they're thick and more than about 5 ounces), until cooked through. Cut into one — it should be opaque at the center or measure 165 degrees F on an instant-read thermometer. Wrapped well, the chicken will keep in the refrigerator for about 5 days.

## Playing Around

Of course you can use a rotisserie chicken here. And you can add other ingredients to the mix, like slices of hot pepper (I sometimes add jalapeños, fresh or pickled), shredded carrots (it's nice but not necessary to toss the carrots and the lettuce with a little seasoned rice vinegar) and/or, my favorite extra, fresh mint and/or cilantro.

# CHICKEN AND SALAD MILANESE STYLE

Makes 4 servings

My friend Tony Fortuna's restaurant, TBar, is the kind of place you could go to every day, and many people do — it's beloved on Manhattan's Upper East Side. I go there often, and many times, despite all the terrific dishes and the seasonal specials, I end up ordering the chicken Milanese. I can't resist the combination of a perfectly breaded, perfectly sautéed chicken breast — in culinary terms, "Milanese" means breaded and sautéed — topped with a bright, citrusy salad and served with a wedge of lemon, just in case you want more tang.

At TBar, the chicken is pounded as thin as an old-school long-playing record; it's as round as one too. I've never been able to come close to TBar's thinness and circularity, but the spirit of the dish is easy to re-create, and the pleasure is the same even if the aesthetics aren't.

### For the salad

1 to 2 celery stalks, with leaves, thinly sliced

½ English (halved lengthwise) or 1 mini (Persian) cucumber, peeled (or not) and thinly sliced

½ bell pepper, finely diced or chopped

1 tablespoon minced mixed fresh herbs, such as parsley, dill and cilantro, or 1 tablespoon minced fresh basil

A handful of baby greens

1½ tablespoons extra-virgin olive oil

1 tablespoon freshly squeezed lemon juice

2 teaspoons white balsamic vinegar

Fine sea salt and freshly ground pepper

### For the chicken

4 boneless, skinless chicken breast halves (trimmed; tenders, if any, removed), each 4 to 5 ounces (113 to 142 grams)

1 to 2 cups (60 to 120 grams) fine dry bread crumbs

3 large eggs

Fine sea salt and freshly ground pepper

2 tablespoons unsalted butter, plus more if needed

¼ cup (60 ml) olive oil, plus more if needed

1 lemon, cut into 4 wedges

### WORKING AHEAD

If you can bread the cutlets and give them a few hours in the fridge before sautéing them, do it. A chill gives the coating time to firm and dry a bit, so you get a crisper cutlet.

TO MAKE THE SALAD: Toss the celery, cucumber, bell pepper, herbs and greens into a bowl. Pour the oil, lemon juice and vinegar into a small jar, season with salt and pepper and shake to blend. Set the salad and vinaigrette aside until needed. (*If you're going to chill the chicken breasts, cover and refrigerate the salad.*)

*(Recipe continues)*

TO MAKE THE CHICKEN: Center a rack in the oven and preheat it to 300 degrees F, to keep the first batch of cutlets warm while you cook the rest. Line a baking sheet with parchment paper or a double layer of paper towels. Have another baking sheet lined with parchment or a rack to hold the breaded cutlets.

Sandwich the cutlets between sheets of parchment or wax paper and pound them with the bottom of a skillet or the flat side of a meat tenderizer.

Set out three shallow bowls (I use soup plates). Put about ½ cup of bread crumbs in each of two bowls and crack the eggs into the third bowl; put the egg bowl between the other two. Season the crumbs and eggs with salt and pepper and lightly beat the eggs to break them up.

One by one, dredge the cutlets in the first bowl of crumbs, run them through the eggs and then coat them in the second bowl of crumbs, placing the breaded cutlets on the lined baking sheet or the rack. Replenish the bread crumbs as you go, if needed. If you have time, chill the cutlets, uncovered. (*The breaded cutlets can be refrigerated for up to 8 hours.*)

Set a large skillet — nonstick is great here — over medium heat. Add 1 tablespoon of the butter and 2 tablespoons of the oil, and when the butter is melted and the bubbling has subsided, slip in 2 cutlets, or as many as fit comfortably in the pan. Cook until the breading is golden on the underside — adjust the heat and tilt the pan as needed so that the chicken, not the butter, browns — then carefully turn the cutlets over to cook and brown the other side. You'll need about 3 minutes on each side, but this will vary according to thickness — it's best to cut into the center of a cutlet to test. When the cutlets are golden and cooked through, transfer them to the second lined baking sheet and pop them into the oven to keep warm.

Wipe out the pan, add the remaining 1 tablespoon butter and 2 tablespoons oil and cook the remaining cutlets.

To serve, season the salad with salt and pepper, vigorously shake the vinaigrette and pour it over the salad. Toss to coat the vegetables.

Place a cutlet on each plate, top with some salad and serve with a lemon wedge.

———————

STORING: Once cooked, the dish should be served immediately.

# PONZU CHICKEN

Makes 4 servings

Ponzu sauce is an ingredient that's easy to love. A mixture of soy and citrus — you buy it ready-made in supermarkets — the sauce can be used right out of the bottle as a marinade or salad dressing. It's sharply citrusy and, because of the soy, packed with magical umami. Here it's the base of a marinade that's bolstered with rice vinegar, Thai red curry paste (sambal oelek or chili with garlic), a bit of sugar and more lemon juice, for more edge. You can marinate the chicken for as little as an hour or give it a day.

I use smallish skinless, boneless chicken breasts without the tenders, but the marinade is also good with chicken thighs, thin pork chops, tofu, tuna or swordfish (particularly when the fish will be grilled). Once the breasts are cooked and the remaining marinade has been boiled so that it can reappear as a sauce, the chicken is ready to serve as is or as the base of a salad, a wrap or a sandwich (see Choices).

### For the marinade

Grated zest and juice of 1 lemon or lime

¼ cup (60 ml) ponzu sauce (see headnote)

2 tablespoons rice vinegar (see page 335)

2 teaspoons olive or vegetable oil

1 teaspoon Thai red curry paste (see page 335), sambal oelek or chili paste with garlic, or more to taste

½ teaspoon sugar

Pinch of fine sea salt

### For the chicken

4 boneless, skinless chicken breast halves (trimmed; tenders, if any, removed), about 5 ounces (142 grams) each

1 tablespoon olive or vegetable oil, or more if needed

**WORKING AHEAD**
The chicken should be marinated for 1 hour at room temperature or up to a day in the fridge.

TO MAKE THE MARINADE: Mix everything together in a zipper-lock bag or a bowl large enough to hold the chicken breasts. Taste and see if you'd like more of any ingredient — you might want a bit more heat. Drop in the breasts, turn them around to coat and seal the bag or cover the bowl. Marinate for 1 hour at room temperature. (*The chicken can be marinated for up to 1 day in the refrigerator.*)

TO MAKE THE CHICKEN: If you've chilled the chicken, take it out of the refrigerator about 30 minutes before you're ready to cook.

Remove the breasts from the marinade — save the marinade — and pat them dry. Pour the tablespoon of oil into a large skillet, preferably nonstick, and warm it over medium heat. When the oil is hot, add the chicken. It's hard to know exactly how long it will take to cook through, but room-temp breasts should be good if cooked, uncovered, for 4 minutes on each side and then, covered, for another 4 to 5 minutes. Add a little more oil during cooking, if needed. Cut into the meat at its thickest part to test for doneness — it should be opaque to the center (and measure 165 degrees F on an instant-read thermometer).

Transfer the chicken to a plate, pour out whatever oil is in the pan and wipe the pan clean with paper towels (and caution). Pour in the reserved marinade and bring to a boil. Boil for 2 minutes, then pour the sauce over the chicken and serve, or into a container if you'll be serving the chicken at room temperature.

---

STORING: The chicken and (boiled) marinade can be refrigerated, together or in separate containers, for up to 3 days. Both are good cold or reheated.

CHOICES: The chicken is delicious just out of the skillet, drizzled with the sauce and served over wilted spinach or with rice, quinoa or another grain. Or turn it into a lettuce wrap, cutting or tearing the chicken into bite-sized pieces; adding a few crunchy ingredients, such as grated jicama, shredded carrots, sprouts, cucumber and/or peanuts; and sprinkling everything with the marinade. Or channel Wolfgang Puck and his famous chicken salad, tossing torn-apart pieces of the chicken with thinly sliced Napa cabbage, carrots and fried wonton chips; I'd add orange or grapefruit segments too. (You might want to blend a little mayonnaise into the ponzu sauce in this case, to help hold the salad components together.) Not surprisingly, the chicken is great in the Luang Prabang Chicken-Chili Sandwiches (page 106).

# SWEET CHILI
# CHICKEN THIGHS

Makes 4 servings

I had my favorite kind of problem with this recipe — I couldn't decide whether to make it with chicken or pork, since it was so good with both. The dish is a simple sauté-then-braise affair and the sauce is a simple chili and soy mixture. Together, they make something so good and so versatile that the only right thing to do is to pull the recipe out regularly.

Whether made with chicken or pork (see page 116 for the tenderloin version), the dish is weeknight-easy, but it's also the kind of recipe that you could happily serve for a party — double it, if you'd like, and make a pile of rice to keep it company. It's not fancy; it's just what everyone wants.

2 tablespoons canola or other neutral oil, or as needed

1 medium onion, finely chopped, rinsed and patted dry

1½ to 3 teaspoons minced peeled fresh ginger

2 garlic cloves, germ removed (see page 320) and minced

Fine sea salt

¼ cup (60 ml) white wine

8 chicken thighs, with or without skin and/or bones, patted dry

Freshly ground pepper

½ cup (120 ml) Thai sweet chili sauce (see page 335)

⅓ cup (80 ml) soy sauce

2 tablespoons Dijon mustard (preferably French)

1 to 1½ teaspoons Sriracha (to taste)

Sliced scallions and crushed red pepper flakes, for serving (optional)

Warm 1 tablespoon of the oil in a Dutch oven over medium heat. Add the onion, ginger and garlic, season lightly with salt and cook, stirring, until they soften a bit and are translucent but not browned, about 5 minutes.

Add the white wine, increase the heat and cook, stirring, until most of the wine evaporates, about 2 minutes. Again, don't color the onions and friends. Transfer the ingredients to a bowl.

Return the pot to medium heat and add the remaining 1 tablespoon oil. Place the thighs in the pot and brown on all sides, adding more oil if necessary. (If the thighs will be crowded, do them in two batches.) Pour off and discard the oil. If you've got burned bits stuck on the bottom of the pot, remove the chicken and scrub the pot, then return the chicken to it. Return the onion mixture to the pot, along with any juices that accumulated, add the chili sauce, soy sauce, mustard and Sriracha and stir to blend. Season lightly with salt and pepper and clap the lid on the pot.

*(Recipe continues)*

Turn the heat down to low and cook the chicken, basting occasionally, for 30 minutes, or until it is opaque in the center; an instant-read thermometer inserted into the thickest part of a thigh should register 165 degrees F.

Transfer the chicken to a serving platter (or don't — serving from the pot is just fine) and spoon over some of the sauce. Sprinkle with scallions and pepper flakes, if you'd like. Pass the rest of the sauce at the table.

STORING: Leftovers can be kept in a tightly covered container in the fridge for up to 3 days.

## SWEET CHILI PORK TENDERLOIN

For 6 servings, use 2 pork tenderloins (each about 1½ pounds/567 grams); pat them dry. Brown them as above and then cook over low heat as above for 35 to 40 minutes, until the meat measures 145 degrees F at its thickest part. With pork, it's always best to test by temperature rather than color — the meat may or may not still be rosy when it reaches the right temperature. When the tenderloins are cooked, transfer them to a cutting board and let them rest for 5 minutes before slicing and serving with the sauce.

# CHICKEN AND WINTER SQUASH TAGINE

Makes 6 servings

Tagines (ta-*jheens*) — stews — are best known and most treasured in North Africa. A little French, a little African, a little Middle Eastern, they are recognized for their slightly sweet spices, their heady aromas, their versatility — they can be based on meat, fish, fowl or vegetables — and the fact that they are traditionally cooked in a pot that carries their name. A tagine is a wide, shallow, round vessel, often made of flameproof pottery, with a cover that looks like a chimney pot or a dunce cap. It's tall and swoops up into a point, and its purpose is to trap every droplet of steam and to send it back down into the stew. But if you don't have a tagine, you can use a Dutch oven.

This particular tagine, combining chicken, slow-cooked onions and chunks of acorn squash, comes more from my imagination and what I have in the pantry than it does from heritage, but the lead seasoning, ras el hanout, originated in Morocco, deep in the heart of tagine country. *Ras el hanout* translates from the Arabic as "head of the shop," suggesting that it is blended from the best spices. As with garam masala, which has the same soft-spice sensibility, and which can be substituted, there are many spices in ras el hanout — and I'd doubt any mixture is the same as any other — but you'll be able to pick out some by scent: cumin and cloves, for sure, and often allspice, cardamom, ginger, chiles and peppers.

About ¼ cup (60 ml) olive oil, or more if needed

2 large onions, halved, thinly sliced, rinsed and patted dry

2 tablespoons water

Fine sea salt

12 chicken pieces, preferably skin-on, bone-in thighs and drumsticks, patted dry

Freshly ground pepper

1 small acorn squash, scrubbed

2 tablespoons ras el hanout (see headnote) or garam masala (see page 335)

1 tablespoon honey

1½ teaspoons ground sumac (see page 335) or finely grated zest of 1 large lemon

2 wide strips lemon zest (if using sumac)

1 teaspoon ground turmeric

¼ teaspoon cayenne pepper

2 cups (480 ml) chicken broth

Juice of 1 large lemon (optional)

Pour 2 tablespoons of the oil into a large tagine or a Dutch oven and warm over medium heat. Add the onions, stirring to coat them with oil, then stir in the water and season with salt. Cover the pot, reduce the heat to low and cook, stirring now and then, until they are very soft but haven't colored, about 30 minutes. This long, gentle cooking brings out their flavor.

Meanwhile, brown the chicken: Working in a large skillet, preferably nonstick, over medium heat, warm the remaining 2 tablespoons oil. Add the chicken pieces — do this in batches if it looks like cooking them all at once will crowd the pan, adding more oil if needed — and cook until golden brown on all sides, about 4 minutes per side. Transfer the chicken to a large plate and season with salt and pepper.

Trim the squash, halve it from top to bottom and scoop out and discard the seeds and strings (or clean the seeds and save to roast). Cut the squash into 8 wedges and then, depending on the length of the wedges, cut

each into 2 or 3 pieces. You want the pieces to be chunks that are easy to eat.

Remove the cover of the tagine or Dutch oven, increase the heat to medium and season the onions with pepper. Stir in the ras el hanout or garam masala, honey, sumac or grated zest, strips of lemon zest (if using sumac), turmeric, 1 teaspoon salt and the cayenne. Stir to blend the spices evenly into the onions and then pour in the broth. Arrange the chicken pieces skin side up in the pot (discard any liquid that accumulated on the plate) and fit the squash among the chicken pieces — don't worry if the liquid doesn't cover the chicken and squash; everything will still cook evenly and be moist.

Bring the liquid to a boil, then lower the heat, cover the pot and simmer gently but steadily for about 45 minutes, until the chicken is fall-off-the-bone soft and the squash is fork-tender. If you can, resist the urge to peek while the tagine is simmering — you want to keep all the aromatic steam in the pot and around the chicken.

Taste for salt and pepper and, if you'd like, add a squeeze of lemon juice. The liquid in the pot will be thin (like jus) but full of flavor. If you cooked this in a tagine, bring the pot to the table; if you used a Dutch oven, transfer the chicken, onions and squash to a large serving platter or bowl, spoon over the jus and serve.

STORING: You can keep the tagine covered overnight in the refrigerator and reheat it the next day, but nothing beats having this dish freshly made.

CHOICES: On weekdays, I serve the tagine with plain couscous. When I've got more time — or when I've got guests — I add chickpeas and sometimes toasted sliced almonds to the couscous and make a sprinkle-over-everything mix of chopped cilantro and parsley, grated lemon zest and a little finely chopped ginger. Think North African gremolata.

# SHEET-PAN SUPPER: BALSAMIC CHICKEN WITH BABY POTATOES AND MUSHROOMS

Makes 4 servings

Here's a recipe that's a quickie — quick to put together and not too long to cook. The "main course" is chicken legs (although you can use breasts; see below) and the "sides" are roasted baby potatoes and mushrooms with shallots and garlic. The flavorings are simple: oil, balsamic vinegar (a brand just a step up from the most basic makes a better dish) and fresh herbs. And what comes out of the oven is seductive. It's the perfect recipe for a during-the-week meal after a crazy-busy day, although it's just as good on the weekends, when you've got more time but might want to spend it away from the kitchen. If you've got a crowd coming, double the recipe and use two pans.

## a word on the chicken

I like to use whole skin-on legs for this dish. If you prefer breasts, I'd suggest you skip cutlets and go for bone-in breasts — buy two split breasts for four people.

1½ pounds (680 grams) small potatoes, scrubbed and halved if large

½ pound (226 grams) white mushrooms, wiped clean, trimmed and cut in half if large

1 large shallot or medium onion, cut into 8 wedges, rinsed and patted dry

4 garlic cloves, unpeeled

8 sprigs fresh rosemary

8 sprigs fresh thyme

Fine sea salt and freshly ground pepper

6 tablespoons (90 ml) extra-virgin olive oil

4 tablespoons balsamic vinegar

4 whole chicken legs (thigh and drumstick), patted dry (see headnote)

Center a rack in the oven and preheat it to 450 degrees F. Rub a baking sheet with a little oil (or line it with foil and oil the foil).

Put the potatoes, mushrooms, shallot or onion and garlic in a large bowl. Toss in 4 sprigs each of the rosemary and thyme, 1 teaspoon salt, a few grindings of pepper, 3 tablespoons of the oil and 3 tablespoons of the balsamic. Mix everything well and spread the ingredients out on the baking sheet.

Put the chicken in the bowl, along with the remaining 3 tablespoons oil and 2 tablespoons balsamic, ½ teaspoon salt and a good amount of pepper, and mix well to coat the chicken. Move the vegetables around to make room for the chicken. Tuck the remaining herbs under each piece.

Roast the chicken for 40 minutes to 1 hour, until a thermometer stuck into the thickest part of a thigh measures 165 degrees F.

Serve everything on the baking sheet or a big platter; pour over the cooking juices.

STORING: The supper is best served straight from the oven, but leftovers are good for a couple of days; cover and refrigerate. If you've got a few potatoes left over, cut them into cubes and toss them into a salad.

# HERB-BUTTER CHICKEN

Makes 4 servings

If you're like me, you'll make this recipe once and then never look at it again — you'll know the template by heart and be able to build variations on it forever after. The basics are simple: herb-speckled butter slipped under the skin of a chicken that's roasted at high heat in a Dutch oven. I've given you a recipe for the butter, which both moistens and flavors the chicken, but nothing about it is sacred. I use a mix of herbs, trying to include some rosemary, tarragon (so good with chicken) and dill, along with the parsley, cilantro and basil that are usually in my fridge, but the next time you make the chicken, you could go Asian, with ginger, garlic and lemongrass, or Mediterranean, with sumac, lemon, za'atar and thyme.

Here are my favorite parts of the recipe: the hands-off roasting (the butter bastes the bird so that you don't have to); the economy of using all the herb and scallion trimmings, as well as the zested-and-squeezed lemon, to flavor the chicken from the inside; the bread that sits under the chicken and soaks up all the drippings (ever since I learned this trick, I've roasted a piece or two of bread under a chicken); the pan juices that come along with the roast; and the fact that you get twice as much flavored butter as you need, so you're ahead on the next chicken or whenever you want to doll up rice or steamed vegetables.

½ lemon

1 stick (8 tablespoons; 4 ounces; 113 grams) unsalted butter, very soft

About 1 cup (40 grams) loosely packed minced mixed fresh herbs (save the stems)

4 scallions, white and light green parts minced, dark green parts reserved

Fine sea salt and freshly ground pepper

2 tablespoons olive oil

1 or 2 slices stale bread

1 chicken, about 4 pounds (1¾ kg), at room temperature, or close to it

1 small onion, sliced

1 bay leaf

⅔ cup (160 ml) white wine or water

1 to 2 teaspoons sherry vinegar, for the pan sauce (optional)

Position a rack in the lower third of the oven and preheat it to 450 degrees F.

Finely grate the zest of the lemon into a small bowl (reserve the lemon). Toss in the butter, minced herbs and minced scallions, season with salt and pepper and mash the ingredients together until well blended. Divide the seasoned butter in half and wrap one piece tightly in plastic wrap; freeze for your next chicken or another use.

Pour the oil into a Dutch oven and swish it around so that it slicks the sides of the pot. Spread a little of the herb butter on one side of the bread, then place it buttered side up in the pot.

Buttering the chicken can be a little tricky — messy too — but there's also something very satisfying about it. Use your fingers to pull the skin away from the meat, loosening it along the breasts and drumsticks. Work from the top and bottom of the chicken, lifting the skin up with your knuckles to help you open up some space without tearing the skin. Using a chunky pat at a time, squish, squiggle and otherwise schmush most of the remaining butter under the skin of the chicken,

spreading it as best you can against the meat. Don't worry about getting an even layer — the butter will melt and baste all the meat in the oven. Pat the skin dry and smear whatever butter remains over it. Season the chicken inside and out with salt and pepper and stuff the cavity with the reserved herb stems and scallion greens. Squeeze the half lemon over the bird and tuck the lemon into the cavity.

Sit the chicken breast side up on the bread. Toss the onion and bay leaf into the pot, pour the wine or water around the chicken and slide the pot into the oven. Roast the chicken, uncovered, for 50 to 60 minutes; if it looks as if the pan juices are running low, add some water. The chicken is done when a thermometer poked into the thickest part of a thigh registers 165 degrees F. Alternatively, you can cut a slit in the chicken between the drumstick and breast and check that the juices run clear.

Transfer the chicken to a cutting board and let rest for about 10 minutes. Meanwhile, skim the fat from the pan juices, discard the bay leaf and stir in some sherry vinegar, if you'd like.

Carve the chicken and serve with the pan juices and the jus-soaked bread (if you haven't already finished it off in the kitchen).

STORING: Cover and refrigerate any leftovers and enjoy them over the course of the next 3 or 4 days.

# CHICKEN-CHILI TAMALE PIE

Makes 6 servings

When I was just married and our cookbook shelf had only a few books on it, I used to make the tamale pie from *Joy of Cooking* just about weekly. The reasons for my devotion were many: The dish was easy enough for me, a novice, to get right (especially since I used a boxed mix for the topping); it could be made in my teeny kitchen; it was inexpensive; the ingredients were readily available; and my husband, Michael, loved it. Although I let it drop from my repertoire decades ago, Michael never stopped loving it and asking for it. So I came up with this version — which has all the attributes of the old pie, plus exciting new flavors and textures.

Tamale pie is two good things in one: chili and corn-bread, one on top of the other. In my dish, the chili is made with cooked chicken (you can use a rotisserie bird or leftover turkey, if that's what you've got); peppers, both hot and sweet; and black beans and diced tomatoes, both from cans. I know it sounds heretical, but I use the canning liquids in the chili — they're too tasty to ditch.

These days, I serve the pie with a crisp green salad — think romaine or a wedge of iceberg. In the old days, I'd top it with sour cream, still a good option.

## WORKING AHEAD
The chili can be refrigerated, covered, for up to 2 days.

### For the chili
1 medium sweet potato

2 tablespoons grapeseed, canola or other neutral oil

1 large onion, finely chopped, rinsed and patted dry

2 garlic cloves, germ removed (see page 320) and finely chopped

Fine sea salt

1 large red bell pepper, cored, seeded and finely chopped

1 medium jalapeño, finely chopped

1 tablespoon ground cumin, or more to taste

¼ teaspoon chipotle (or other) chile powder, or more to taste

One 10-ounce (283-gram) can diced tomatoes with chiles, with their juice

One 15½-ounce (439-gram) can black beans, with their liquid

Freshly ground pepper

1 canned chipotle in adobo sauce, finely chopped, plus 1 teaspoon of the adobo sauce

1 teaspoon honey, or more to taste

1½ to 2 cups (½ pound; 227 grams) shredded or chopped cooked chicken (or turkey)

About ½ cup (120 ml) chicken broth, if needed

About ¼ cup (10 grams) finely chopped fresh cilantro

### For the cornbread
1⅓ cups (200 grams) yellow cornmeal

⅔ cup (91 grams) all-purpose flour

1½ teaspoons baking powder

½ teaspoon baking soda

½ teaspoon fine sea salt

¼ teaspoon chipotle (or other) chile powder, or more to taste

1¼ cups (300 ml) whole milk

2 large eggs

2 tablespoons grapeseed, canola or other neutral oil

1 tablespoon honey

About 3 tablespoons finely chopped fresh cilantro

*(Recipe continues)*

TO MAKE THE CHILI: Bring a medium saucepan of salted water to boil. Meanwhile, peel the sweet potato and cut it into 1-inch cubes. Drop the sweet potato cubes into the saucepan and cook until not quite tender, about 8 minutes, then drain and set aside. The potatoes will be cooked more, so don't let them get too soft now.

Warm the oil in a large skillet over medium heat. Toss in the onion and garlic, season lightly with salt and cook, stirring, for about 3 minutes, until softened. Stir in half of the bell and jalapeño peppers (save the remainder for the cornbread), the cumin and chile powder and cook for another 5 minutes or so, just until the peppers soften. Add the tomatoes and beans, including their juices, 1 teaspoon salt, some black pepper, the chopped chipotle, adobo sauce and honey. Cook for 5 minutes, then add the chicken and cook for about 10 minutes, so the flavors to have a chance to permeate the chili.

Gently stir in the sweet potatoes. If the mixture looks dry — you want to see a little liquid bubbling up around the edges — add some or all of the chicken broth. Taste for salt, pepper, cumin and chipotle powder, adjusting the seasoning as needed. Stir in the cilantro. The chili is ready to be used in the tamale pie — or, if you just can't wait, served as is. (*You can make the chili up to 2 days ahead and keep it covered in the refrigerator. Bring it to a simmer before continuing with the recipe — and check the seasonings again. You'll also probably need to add a little broth.*)

TO MAKE THE CORNBREAD AND BAKE THE PIE: Center a rack in the oven and preheat it to 425 degrees F. Turn the chili out into a 2- to 3-quart rectangular baking dish (I use a Pyrex 11-by-7-inch roaster, but a 9-by-9-inch pan will work).

In a medium bowl, whisk the cornmeal, flour, baking powder, baking soda, salt and chile powder together. In another bowl or a large spouted measuring cup, whisk together the milk, eggs, oil and honey. Pour the liquid ingredients over the dry and, using the whisk, mix — don't beat — until blended. Switch to a flexible spatula and gently stir in the cilantro and the reserved peppers from the chili. Pour and smooth the cornbread batter over the chili. (If you have any batter left over — and you might, as it's hard to judge how the chili will fill the pan — bake it in a small pan or muffin cup alongside the pie.)

Bake the pie for 20 to 25 minutes, until the filling is bubbling and the cornbread is golden brown and firm to the touch all the way to the center; a tester inserted into the center will come out clean. Serve immediately, preferably in bowls — like any chili, this one can be messy.

———

STORING: You can keep leftovers in the fridge for a day or so and reheat them in the oven or a microwave, but the cornbread won't fare as well as the chili.

# ROAST CHICKEN WITH PAN-SAUCE VINAIGRETTE

Makes 4 servings

I taste France in every bite of this dish. The chicken, which roasts undisturbed in a covered pot, is moist and fragrant, having picked up the aromas of its pot-mates: lemon and herbs, carrots, shallots and garlic, which cooks to beyond golden and just about melts in the process. The chicken doesn't get crispy and dark — it's not that kind of dish — but it gets deeply flavorful. And then it gets even more flavor when you pop out some of those garlic cloves and use them and the pan drippings to make a sharp vinaigrette to drizzle over both the meat and a green salad. It's an all-in-one meal, the kind you used to be able to find in classic bistros throughout France and now mostly find only in the homes of cooks with a taste for simple goodness.

The success of the dish doesn't depend on technique — you put a chicken in a pot and don't open the oven until it's done — but on the quality of the bird. The best choice for this is, not surprisingly, an organic, free-range chicken. Be generous with the herbs and don't be disturbed when you lift the lid and discover that some of your vegetables have charred — it's all in the service of making a terrific vinaigrette, since you'll be using the pan drippings to replace the usual oil in a vinaigrette. I like to add a drizzle of walnut oil to the mix — it's a background flavor to be sure, but it adds depth and another touch of Frenchness.

### For the chicken

3 tablespoons olive oil

1 carrot, scrubbed, trimmed and sliced into 1-inch-thick rounds

1 shallot, sliced, rinsed and patted dry

4 sprigs fresh thyme

4 sprigs fresh rosemary

4 sprigs fresh sage

2 bay leaves

Fine sea salt and freshly ground pepper

1 chicken, about 4 pounds (1¾ kg), patted dry

½ lemon

1 head garlic, cut horizontally in half

¾ cup (180 ml) white wine

### For the vinaigrette

About ½ cup (120 ml) water

2 teaspoons Dijon mustard (preferably French)

3 tablespoons sherry vinegar

Fine sea salt and freshly ground pepper

1 teaspoon walnut oil

Mixed salad greens (3 to 4 handfuls), for serving

Fleur de sel or flake salt, such as Maldon, for serving

TO MAKE THE CHICKEN:  Center a rack in the oven and preheat it to 450 degrees F.

Put 2½ tablespoons of the olive oil in a 5-quart Dutch oven. Toss in the carrot, shallot, 2 sprigs each of the thyme, rosemary and sage and 1 of the bay leaves. Season with salt and pepper. Rub the chicken with the remaining ½ tablespoon oil, season inside and out with salt and pepper and stuff with 2 sprigs each of the herbs and the remaining bay leaf.

Put the chicken in the pot. Squeeze over the juice from the half lemon and pop the lemon inside the chicken. Tie the legs together with kitchen twine, if you have it. Put one half of the garlic head, cut side down, on either side of the chicken and pour in the wine. Cover the pot, slide it into the oven and set the timer for 90 minutes.

When the buzzer rings, pull the pot from the oven and very carefully lift off the lid — lift it away from you to avoid the steam. The chicken may not be browned, so if you want some color, you can place it on a foil-lined baking sheet and run it under the broiler. (Reserve the contents of the pot.) Transfer the chicken to a platter, cover it loosely with a foil tent and let it rest while you make the vinaigrette.

TO MAKE THE VINAIGRETTE: Pour off all but 6 tablespoons of the pan drippings from the pot. (If your drippings have mostly cooked away, gotten dark or actually burned, all's not lost — they'll still make a good vinaigrette after you loosen everything with the water.) Discard the vegetables, herb sprigs and bay leaf, but hold on to the garlic. Pour the water into the pot, place over medium heat and cook, scraping, until you've picked up all the good bits (and flavor) that were stuck — add a little more water, if needed. If you the sauce is too chunky, strain.

Squeeze 6 to 8 of the softened garlic cloves into a small bowl and mash them into a paste with a fork or spoon. Whisk in the mustard and vinegar and season with salt and pepper. Whisking gently, slowing pour in the reserved pan drippings and the walnut oil. Taste the vinaigrette and decide if you want more salt and/or pepper, or if you'd like to add more of any of the other ingredients.

Carve the chicken and drizzle over a little of the vinaigrette. Lightly dress the salad greens with some of the vinaigrette. Serve the salad alongside, over or under the chicken, passing the remaining vinaigrette and flake salt for extra seasoning at the table.

———

STORING: Leftover chicken can be kept tightly covered in the refrigerator for up to 4 days; the vinaigrette will keep in a covered jar equally long.

# SPATCHCOCKED CHICKEN

Makes 4 servings

1 chicken, 3 to 4 pounds (1½ to 1¾ kg)

4 tablespoons (2 ounces; 57 grams) unsalted butter, softened

1 teaspoon za'atar (see page 336) or dried oregano (crumble it between your fingertips after measuring)

¾ teaspoon ground cumin

¾ teaspoon ground sumac (see page 335) or finely grated zest of 1 lemon

½ teaspoon ground coriander

Fine sea salt and freshly ground pepper

1 head garlic, cut horizontally in half

1 small onion, sliced, rinsed and patted dry

A few sprigs fresh herbs, such as thyme, oregano, rosemary and/or parsley

¾ cup (180 ml) chicken broth

¼ cup (60 ml) white wine

Country bread, for serving (optional)

Even if the word "spatchcocked" weren't as much fun to say as it is, the dish that it describes would be a favorite: a butterflied chicken, flattened and cooked quickly — a spatchcocked bird cooks in less time than chicken "in the round," and every inch of its skin is crispy, every morsel of its meat juicy. In this recipe, the meat is especially juicy because it's self-basting: You slip seasoned butter under the skin, and it works its way into the bird as it roasts.

The choices for how to season the bird are myriad. I mash the butter with za'atar, cumin, sumac and coriander, but if you fall in love with the technique, you can put it in rotation and fiddle with the flavors each time. (For a slightly French version, see page 132.)

You could just roast the butter-basted bird as is, but I prefer to roast some garlic, onion and herbs along with it — under it, actually — and to pour some wine and broth into the pan too. The aromatics and liquid do two good things: They add more flavor and fragrance to the dish, and they combine to make a delicious pour-over sauce at serving.

Make sure to hold on to the garlic that you tucked under the chicken — the cloves will be soft, sweet, spreadable and luscious swiped across a piece of rough country bread or baguette.

Center a rack in the oven and preheat it to 425 degrees F. Choose a large cast-iron skillet, a 9-by-13-inch roasting pan or a small baking sheet. You want a pan that will hold the chicken snugly and have sides high enough to contain the broth, wine and cooking juices.

Cut down along either side of the chicken's backbone to remove it — you can do this with poultry shears or a knife; discard the backbone. Pull on either side of the bird to open it out and then, using the heel of your hand, press down on the breastbone to flatten the chicken as much as you can. If the breastbone cracks, that's fine. There! You've spatchcocked the bird.

Put the butter in a small bowl and add the za'atar or crumbled oregano, cumin, sumac or zest, coriander, ½ teaspoon salt and ¼ teaspoon pepper. Mash the ingredients together until well blended.

Turn the chicken skin side up and carefully work your fingers under the skin. It's easiest to loosen the skin from the meat if you start at the neck and work your fingers down and along the breast (work on one side and then the other), then work from the bottom of the chicken to wiggle your way along the thighs and legs. Work three-quarters of the butter between the skin and meat in the same way. Don't worry about getting an even layer; once you've got dabs of butter here and there, you can massage the skin to smooth them out. And don't fuss over getting everything just so — when the butter melts, it'll cover the chicken. Pat the chicken dry and rub the remaining butter over the skin.

Put the garlic and onion in the center of whatever pan you've chosen, season with salt and pepper and top with the herbs. Arrange the chicken over these ingredients, then pour the broth and wine around it.

Roast for 45 to 60 minutes — the time depends on your bird — until the chicken is golden brown and the juices run clear when you prick a thigh. (An instant-read thermometer poked into a thigh should read 165 degrees F.) Transfer the chicken to a board and cut it into quarters.

If you've roasted the bird in a skillet, it's nice to return the pieces to the pan and bring the whole thing to the table for a very casual grab, dip and dunk dinner. Otherwise, put the chicken on a platter and pour the cooking juices into a serving pitcher. Either mash the garlic cloves and serve them as a spread instead of butter for the bread, if you're using it, or place the garlic halves alongside the chicken and encourage everyone to squeeze the roasted garlic onto the bread or chicken.

STORING: The chicken is best served soon after it comes out of the oven, but leftovers make great salads or sandwiches — no surprise there.

CHOICES: If you want to, use a roasting pan and add a few cut-up pieces of fennel, celery and carrots and/or some small potatoes to cook along with the chicken.

## TARRAGON SPATCHCOCKED CHICKEN

Mash the butter with 2 tablespoons minced fresh tarragon, the grated zest of 1 lemon, about ½ teaspoon fine sea salt and some pepper. Work this under the chicken's skin. Follow the recipe, using sprigs of tarragon and thyme in the skillet.

# LEMON-FENNEL CHICKEN IN A POT

Makes 4 servings

1 chicken, about 4 pounds (1¾ kg)

1 small fennel bulb, trimmed (reserve a couple of the stalks) and cored

2 lemons

3 large shallots

2 heads garlic, cut horizontally in half

¼ cup (60 ml) plus 1 tablespoon olive oil

1 tablespoon honey

Fine sea salt and freshly ground pepper

4 sprigs fresh thyme

½ cup (120 ml) chicken broth

2 bay leaves

Here's my favorite kind of recipe: It comes together quickly, cooks unattended and arrives at the table ready for its close-up. It can be a hearty supper on Tuesday or a dinner for friends on Saturday. What it's not is a dish for fussbudgets — you want to serve this to people who will be happy to reach across the table, dunk bread into the pot and grab every drop of the tasty, fragrant cooking juices.

The basics of the dish are just that — basic. A head of fennel, a couple of lemons and a lot of garlic and shallots get tossed in a pot with olive oil, honey, thyme and bay leaves and jiggled a bit to make a bed for an oil-massaged chicken. Then you pour over some broth, cover the pot and sit back while the bird turns golden and the vegetables soften and pick up even more flavor.

Serve the dish straight from the oven with a baguette or a country loaf. Done. And done nicely.

Center a rack in the oven and preheat it to 450 degrees F. Take the chicken out of the refrigerator and leave it uncovered on the counter while you prepare the rest of the ingredients — you want to take the chill off it.

Cut the fennel bulb into 6 to 8 wedges and toss into a Dutch oven. Cut one of the lemons in half; set one half aside. Cut the remaining half into 4 wedges and cut the remaining whole lemon into 8 wedges; toss them into the Dutch oven. Trim the shallots, cut each one into 4 to 6 pieces and add to the pot. Toss in the garlic. Add ¼ cup of the olive oil, the honey, 1 teaspoon salt and ½ teaspoon pepper and stir everything together until glossy with oil. (Hands do a good job here.) Make a shallow space in the center of the vegetables so the chicken will have a place to nestle.

Season the inside of the chicken with salt and pepper and stuff it with 1 or 2 reserved fennel stalks. Squeeze the juice from the reserved half lemon over the chicken, rubbing it into the skin, along with the remaining tablespoon oil. Put the squeezed lemon half and 2 sprigs of the thyme inside the bird and place the chicken on top of the vegetables. Pour over the broth, give the vegetables a light stir to incorporate the broth and toss in the remaining 2 thyme sprigs, along with the bay leaves. Cover the pot and slide it into the oven.

*(Recipe continues)*

Roast the chicken for 90 minutes, without peeking into the pot. When the time comes to peek, make sure you the lift the cover away from you — the pot is filled with steam. The chicken should be golden and tender to the point of just about falling off the bone. If you want more color on the chicken, run it under the broiler.

You can serve the chicken directly from the pot — cut it up and return the pieces to the pot (it will keep everything hot and make dunking bread into the "juice" easy). Or you can spoon the vegetables and all their delicious juices into a large serving bowl, cut up the chicken and place it on the vegetables. However you serve the chicken, serve it as soon after it comes out of the oven as possible — when the aromas are most seductive.

STORING: The chicken is best as soon as it's done, but leftovers are delicious reheated a day later. Because the chicken should be soft, you can reheat it and the vegetables in a microwave oven — add a little water if needed. Alternatively, you can warm it in a covered pan over low heat on the stove.

MEAT

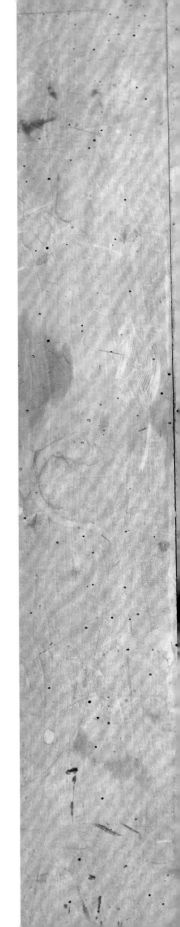

# THREE-PEPPER BURGERS

Makes 4 burgers

If, like me, you're happiest when a burger has as much flavor as the condiments you squeeze, spread or layer on it, this one's for you. The peppers are a mash-up of roasted red bell peppers, Peppadews (sweet, hot or a mix) and jalapeño — and there's also basil, cilantro (or parsley) and sharp cheddar. The cheese is grated, the other ingredients are finely chopped and they're all gently kneaded into the beef. You can form the patties and cook them straight away and get a really good burger. But if you make them ahead, you'll have an even better burger — a few hours or more in the fridge gives the other ingredients time to really flavor the meat.

And just because you've added so many good things to the inside of the burger doesn't mean that you can't add even more outside. Gather your favorites, lay them on the table and let everyone build their burgers as they like. Hint: Mashing avocado onto your toasted bun and then seasoning it with a squirt of lime juice and some salt is a great way to start dressing your patty.

## For the burgers

½ large roasted red bell pepper (store-bought is fine), drained and patted dry

6 Peppadew peppers (sweet, hot or mixed), drained and patted dry

½ jalapeño, seeded

½ cup loosely packed (20 grams) fresh basil leaves

⅓ cup loosely packed (13 grams) fresh cilantro or parsley leaves

½ teaspoon fine sea salt

¼ teaspoon freshly ground pepper

¾ cup (85 grams) grated sharp cheddar

1 pound (454 grams) ground beef

4 soft buns, toasted or not

## For the fixings—any or all

Avocado slices

Tomato slices

Red or Vidalia onion slices

Pickle slices (sweet, hot or both)

Lime wedges

Arugula or lettuce

Mayonnaise

Hot sauce

Ketchup

### WORKING AHEAD
You'll need to get the patties prepped at least 30 minutes ahead. You can keep them wrapped airtight in the refrigerator for up to 1 day or in the freezer for up to 2 months.

Finely chop the roasted bell pepper, Peppadews, jalapeño, basil and cilantro or parsley. Transfer to a large bowl, season with the salt and pepper and add the cheddar and beef. Work everything together with your hands until blended but don't overdo it — you want to lightly mix, not knead, the ingredients. Shape into 4 patties, cover and refrigerate for at least 30 minutes.

*(Recipe continues on facing page)*

(*The burgers can be refrigerated for up to 1 day. If they have been in the refrigerator long enough to chill through, bring them to cool room temperature before cooking.*)

You can cook the burgers on a grill pan or in a heavy skillet; coat either one lightly with cooking spray. Place the pan over high heat, and when it's hot, slip in the burgers. Cook for 4 minutes without moving them — you want to get them nicely charred. Carefully flip them over and cook for another 3 to 4 minutes for medium-rare — make a small cut in one to check the cooking; cook longer if you want the burgers more well done.

Serve the burgers on the buns with the fixings.

———

# UMAMI BURGERS

*Makes 4 burgers*

It all started with the mushrooms. They were languishing in the fridge, having been accidentally left out of a soup I'd made. That they brushed against the unopened jar of Asian oyster sauce as I was pulling them out of the bin was all the inspiration I needed to tinker. One thing led to another, and presto change-o, I had made an umami-packed mushroom mix that ended up in that evening's hamburger and many others since.

The mushrooms are sautéed with onions and then finished with a blend of oyster sauce (or Indonesian kecap manis), soy sauce, gochujang (sometimes referred to as Korean ketchup) and Asian sesame oil. The blend is sweet and hot and spicy and salty and addictively good, which kind of defines umami; worked into ground beef, it's magical. And if you forgo the usual ketchup and slather some bulgogi sauce on your bun, you'll have a wild, wonderful and wholly unusual burger.

1 tablespoon oyster sauce or kecap manis (see page 334)

1 tablespoon soy sauce

½ teaspoon gochujang (see page 334), or more to taste

¼ teaspoon Asian sesame oil

2 teaspoons canola or other neutral oil

10 ounces (300 grams) white mushrooms, wiped clean, trimmed and coarsely chopped

About ¼ cup (36 grams) chopped red or sweet onion, such as Vidalia (rinsed and patted dry)

Fine sea salt and freshly ground pepper

1 tablespoon water

1 pound (454 grams) ground beef

4 buns, preferably lightly toasted

Ketchup or bulgogi sauce (see page 333), for serving

Shredded Napa cabbage, for serving (optional)

Sliced red onion, for serving (optional)

### WORKING AHEAD
You can make the mushroom mix up to 4 days ahead and keep it tightly covered in the refrigerator. The burger patties will have more flavor if you make them ahead and refrigerate them for up to 1 day; you can also freeze them for up to 2 months.

Stir together the oyster sauce, soy sauce, gochujang and sesame oil in a small bowl. Taste and add more gochujang, if you'd like. Set this seasoning sauce aside.

Working in a medium skillet over medium heat, warm the canola oil. When it's hot, add the mushrooms and onion and cook, stirring frequently, for 2 minutes, at which point the mushrooms will have released most of their liquid. Season with a bit of salt and a few grinds of pepper and cook for another 4 minutes or so, until the liquid has evaporated. Add the water and stir to pick up any bits stuck to the bottom of the pan. Remove the pan from the heat, wait 1 minute and then stir in the seasoning sauce. Scrape the mushroom mix into a bowl and let cool. (*You can make this up to 4 days in advance; keep it tightly covered in the refrigerator.*)

Put the beef in a bowl, add the seasoned mushrooms and mix gently to combine evenly. Taste and see if you'd like to add more salt or pepper. Shape into 4 patties. (*If you'd like to give the mushroom flavor time to permeate the patties, wrap them and stow them in the fridge for up to 1 day; bring to cool room temperature before cooking.*)

You can cook the burgers on a grill pan or in a heavy skillet; coat either one lightly with cooking spray. Place the pan over high heat, and when it's hot, slip in the burgers. Cook for 4 minutes without moving them — you want to get them nicely charred. Carefully flip them over and cook for another 3 to 4 minutes for medium-rare — make a small cut in one to check the cooking; cook longer if you want the burgers more well done.

Transfer the burgers to the buns, set out whatever sauce and/or toppings you've chosen and serve immediately.

# MARINATED AND PAN-SEARED HANGER, SKIRT, FLANK OR TAKE-YOUR-PICK STEAK

Makes 2 to 4 servings, depending on the steak

The big flavors in this dish come from the dual-purpose marinade, which is first used to flavor and tenderize the steak and then to sauce it. The marinade itself is Asian-ish with ingredients that hold their own after cooking. The base is soy and oil (the oil helps the marinade stick to the meat), and the aromatics are ginger, garlic, lime, cilantro and Thai red curry paste.

As for the steak, my favorite cut here is hanger steak, often referred to as a butcher's steak. Some people say it got its name because it was an inexpensive, chewy cut that was hard to sell, so the butcher would take it home. Others say that the butcher kept it because it was so delicious. I'm happy with story number two.

There is just one hanger steak on a cow and so the cut is not very common. If you find it, you'll see that the grain runs somewhat the way it does in other sinewy cuts like skirt or flank steak. Any of these would be great with this marinade. And all of them can be cooked on an outdoor grill but, city girl at heart, I reach for a stove-top grill pan or cast-iron skillet.

## a word on the marinade

If you're cooking a large steak or more than one, you may want to double the marinade. Use what you need, and if there's any that you didn't pour over the steak, refrigerate it and use it to marinate chicken cutlets.

### For the marinade

1 teaspoon Thai red curry paste, or a tad more to taste

8 quarter-sized pieces peeled fresh ginger, minced

2 garlic cloves, germ removed (see page 320) and minced, or more to taste

Pinch of sugar

½ cup (120 ml) soy sauce

¼ cup (60 ml) olive oil or neutral oil

Finely grated zest and juice of 2 large or 4 small limes

12 sprigs fresh cilantro, finely chopped (including the stems)

1 hanger steak, 1 flank steak or 2 skirt steaks

Fine sea salt and freshly ground pepper

**WORKING AHEAD**
You can marinate the meat overnight.

TO MAKE THE MARINADE: Put the curry paste in a small bowl, add the ginger, garlic and sugar and mash together. Add the rest of the ingredients and stir to blend. Divide the marinade in half; cover and refrigerate one portion.

Put the meat in a dish that holds it snugly and pour over the remaining marinade. Rub it into both sides of the meat, cover the dish and let it sit at room temperature for at least 1 hour. (*The meat can be marinated at room temperature for about an hour or in the refrigerator for as long as overnight. Remove it from the refrigerator about 30 minutes before cooking.*)

When you're ready to cook, remove the meat from the marinade; discard the marinade. Scrape off and discard whatever solids may be stuck to the meat and pat the meat dry.

If you're going to cook the steak(s) on an outdoor grill, I leave you to it. If your grill or cast-iron pan needs it, spray it with cooking spray, then place it over high heat. When the pan is hot, slip in the meat — if you're cooking 2 steaks, don't crowd them — and cook for 2 to 4 minutes, depending on the thickness. (A flank steak

(*Recipe continues on facing page*)

will cook faster than a skirt or hanger — it may need just 2 minutes on a side.) Flip the steak(s) over and cook until done just as you like. To see how it's doing, cut into the meat and take a peek, remembering that it will continue to cook a bit after it comes off the heat. Transfer the meat to dinner plates or a cutting board, season with salt and pepper and let sit for a few minutes.

Meanwhile, bring the refrigerated marinade almost to a boil in a microwave oven or in a saucepan on the stove.

Cut the steak(s) into portions or slices, spoon the "sauce" over the meat and serve.

STORING: Leftovers, which make great sandwiches and salads, will keep for up to 3 days wrapped in the refrigerator.

# GRILLED DRY-RUBBED RIB-EYE STEAKS

Makes 6 servings

Grab this dry rub when you're looking for instant flavor . . . and color. It gives foods a wonderful burnished hue and, if they're grilled, a delicious crust too. It's a sweet and hot, herby, spicy mixture that you can make in quantity and store for a long time, if you'd like. Because it's nicely balanced, it's good for just about anything. In this recipe, I rub it on rib eyes destined for the grill, but it's just as right for flank or skirt steak, hamburgers (work it into the meat or sprinkle it over the patties), pork chops, chicken (grilled or baked), shrimp or even corn on the cob or wedges of squash.

**WORKING AHEAD**
The rub will keep in a cool dry place away from light for about 6 months. If you want to keep it, make lots.

STORING: Leftovers can be kept covered in the refrigerator for about 3 days.

### For the rub
2 teaspoons brown sugar

1½ teaspoons kosher or other coarse salt

1½ teaspoons chile powder

1 teaspoon paprika

1 teaspoon Old Bay seasoning

½ teaspoon garlic powder

½ teaspoon onion powder or flakes

½ teaspoon Chinese five-spice powder

¼ teaspoon freshly ground pepper

¼ teaspoon ground cinnamon

¼ teaspoon ground cumin

Pinch of crushed red pepper flakes

3 rib-eye steaks, about 1½ inches thick and 1 pound (454 grams) each

Flake salt, for serving (optional)

TO MAKE THE RUB: Put everything in a jar, seal and shake. (*Airtight, the rub will keep for 6 months.*)

About 1 hour (or more) before cooking, pat the steaks dry between layers of paper towels. Rub each steak generously on both sides with the spice mixture. If you'll be grilling within an hour, keep the steaks, covered, at room temperature; if you'll be waiting for a few hours, cover the steaks and refrigerate; pull them out about 30 minutes ahead to come to a cool room temperature.

Heat an outdoor grill to medium-high (or heat an oiled or sprayed grill pan on the stove over high heat). Cook the steaks to your preferred degree of doneness. If you like rare steaks, take a look after 4 minutes on each side; for medium-rare, 5 to 6 minutes. If your steaks are less than 1 inch thick, reduce the cooking time. It's hard to give a rock-solid time, because grills vary. (A rare steak should reach 120 to 125 degrees F on an instant-read thermometer.) Remember that the steaks will continue to cook a bit once they come off the grill, so err on the side of less done. Transfer the steaks to a platter, tent with foil and let rest for 5 minutes before cutting each steak in half and serving with flake salt, if you like.

# BEEF AND BEER STEW

Makes 6 servings

This is my take on the Flemish dish beef carbonnade, a slowly braised stew characterized by an abundance of onions, a little bacon and a base of dark beer (Belgian ale, if you can find it). As with anything that's cooked for a long time, the magic is the way the ingredients meld over time. Here you start with slowly caramelized onions that only become sweeter in the oven. A look at the ingredients and the knowledge that the onions are caramelized can't but lead you to think that the dish will be sweet, but the sweetness is offset by the beer, the herbs and spices (the allspice is a wonder) and the mix of vinegar and grainy mustard. It's a terrific cold-weather dish. Traditionally it would be served over broad noodles; I suggest you follow tradition.

4 allspice berries or ½ teaspoon ground allspice

2 cloves or a pinch of ground cloves

¼ cup (34 grams) all-purpose flour

Fine sea salt and freshly ground pepper

2½ pounds (about 1 kg) chuck or other stew beef, cut into 2-inch cubes and patted dry

About 3 tablespoons canola or other neutral oil

6 slices thick-cut bacon, cut crosswise into 1-inch pieces

2 tablespoons unsalted butter

4 medium onions, thinly sliced, rinsed and patted dry

4 garlic cloves, germ removed (see page 320) and finely chopped

One 12-ounce (360-ml) bottle Belgian ale, such as Chimay, or other dark ale or beer

1½ cups (360 ml) beef broth

2½ tablespoons brown sugar

2 tablespoons cider vinegar

1 tablespoon grainy mustard (preferably French)

1 tablespoon tomato paste

4 sprigs fresh thyme

3 bay leaves

Wide noodles, for serving

¼ cup (about 10 grams) chopped fresh parsley, dill, chives, tarragon or mixed herbs, for serving

**WORKING AHEAD**
You can make the stew up to 3 days in advance and refrigerate it.

Put the whole allspice and cloves, if using, in a tea ball (or a paper tea bag) or tie them in a bundle using cheesecloth; set aside.

Put the flour in a large bowl, season with salt and pepper and drop in the beef; toss it around to coat.

Warm 2 tablespoons of the oil in a Dutch oven over medium-high heat. Add as many beef cubes as you can (shaking off the excess flour as you do) without crowding the pot — the beef will steam, not brown, if the pot is too full. Cook, seasoning the meat once more with salt and pepper and turning to brown on all sides. As the meat is browned, transfer the pieces to another bowl. Add more oil as needed to finish browning the meat. Hold on to any leftover flour.

If the oil has burned, wipe out the pot, leaving whatever solids have stuck to the bottom. Toss the bacon into the pot and cook, stirring, until it's browned. Spoon out the pieces and put them in the bowl with the beef.

Add the butter, onions and garlic to the pot and cook over medium to medium-low heat, stirring occasionally, until the onions are caramel-colored; adjust the heat as needed. Be patient — this will take at least 20 minutes, perhaps longer. Season with salt and pepper.

While the onions are caramelizing, center a rack in the oven and preheat it to 300 degrees F.

If you had leftover flour, stir it into the onions, along with the ground spices, if you're using them, and cook for a minute or two, until the flour is browned. Add ½ cup of the ale and cook, stirring and picking up whatever solids remain on the bottom of the pot. The mixture will thicken and the ale will almost evaporate.

Return the meat and bacon to the pot, along with whatever juices accumulated in the bowl. Pour in the remaining ale and add the broth, brown sugar, vinegar, mustard, tomato paste, thyme, bay leaves and the whole allspice and cloves, if you're using them. Give everything a good stir and bring to a boil over medium-high heat. Taste for salt and pepper, then cover the pot with foil and its lid. Slide it into the oven.

Cook the stew for 2½ to 3 hours, until the meat is tender enough to cut with a spoon. Remove the packet of whole spices, if you used it, and the bay leaves and thyme sprigs. (*Once cooled, the stew can be wrapped well and refrigerated for up to 3 days or frozen for up to 2 months.*)

You can serve this on plates, of course, but I think it's easiest and most enjoyable to eat if you put it into bowls or shallow soup plates. Spoon the stew over the noodles, sprinkle with the herbs and serve.

---

STORING: Leftover stew can be frozen, covered airtight, for up to 2 months.

# BEEF CARBONNADE CHOCKFUL OF VEGETABLES

Root vegetables will add color and more textures and flavors to the stew. Because it cooks for such a long time, it's best to either steam the vegetables and add them to the stew 30 minutes before it's done or to drop the raw vegetables into the stew when it's half-cooked. (Or, if you'd like, you can steam the vegetables at the last minute and stir them into the finished stew — they won't have the flavor of the carbonnade, but they'll have good color.) Carrots, parsnips, turnips, celery root and winter squash are nice here. Peel the vegetables and cut into 2- to 3-inch pieces no matter how you plan to cook them.

# SUBTLY SPICY, SOFTLY HOT, SLIGHTLY SWEET BEEF STEW

Makes 6 to 8 servings

My bottle of gochujang sauce says it's good for every-thing, so I shrugged and put some in the beef stew I was working on. Perhaps "everything" is an exaggeration, but it certainly was good in this dish. Great, in fact. The sauce is chile-based but not all that hot. (The balance of hot to sweet can differ according to brand, so find one you like and then, if necessary, adjust the amount you use.) It's mostly umami-packed and not easily describ-able, and the same could be said about this stew. The mix of spices is Asian, but the aromatics are standards in French cooking; ditto the technique of marinating the beef in wine and then cooking it slowly. The gremolata is similar to the herb mix you might sprinkle over osso buco, the classic Italian dish. And the cranberries? I noticed them in the fridge when I went to grab the carrots, and it made me think that their sweet-tart flavor might just be terrific with this cross-cultural mash-up. Bingo!

## a word on beef cuts

You can make the stew with boneless stew meat or you can mix it up with a few chunky bone-in cuts, like oxtails and short ribs, which will add more flavor and texture. Play around and see what you like, remembering that bony cuts usually have less meat and more fat, so you might have to increase the amount you need for the stew.

### For the beef and marinade

1 bottle (750 ml) red wine, preferably fruity but dry

¼ cup (60 ml) soy sauce

3 tablespoons gochujang (see page 334), or more or less to taste

5 quarter-sized slices peeled fresh ginger

3 garlic cloves, smashed and peeled

Scallion greens, reserved from the gremolata, below (optional)

Cilantro stems, reserved from the gremolata, below (optional)

3 pounds (about 1½ kg) beef stew meat (see headnote)

### For the stew

3 tablespoons canola or other neutral oil

Fine sea salt and freshly ground pepper

1 large onion, trimmed, cut into 8 pieces, rinsed and patted dry

6 carrots, trimmed, peeled and cut into 4 pieces each

3 garlic cloves, germ removed (see page 320) and slivered

One 1-inch piece fresh ginger, peeled and slivered

½ cup (50 grams) fresh cranberries

⅓ cup (80 ml) water

2 cups (480 ml) beef broth

1 tablespoon honey

2 points star anise

Pinch of black peppercorns

A small sliver of cinnamon stick

1 bay leaf

A strip of orange peel (save the orange for the gremolata)

### For the gremolata

3 scallions, white and light green parts only, thinly sliced

2 tablespoons minced fresh cilantro

1 teaspoon finely grated peeled fresh ginger, or more to taste

1 teaspoon finely grated or minced garlic, or more to taste

Finely grated zest of 1 orange (orange reserved from the stew)

Fleur de sel or fine sea salt

Cooked rice, quinoa or egg noodles, for serving (optional)

*(Recipe continues)*

## WORKING AHEAD

The stew is tastier if you marinate the beef overnight, or even up to 3 days in advance, and it's easier to skim off whatever fat accumulates during cooking if you chill the broth for a couple of hours before serving time. You can also make the stew itself up to 3 days ahead. The gremolata can be made a few hours ahead and refrigerated.

TO MARINATE THE BEEF: You can marinate the beef in a Dutch oven or a jumbo zipper-lock plastic bag. (I prefer a bag because it takes up less room in the refrigerator.) Mix the wine, soy sauce and gochujang together until blended, then add the remaining marinade ingredients and stir. Add the meat and turn it around so that it's submerged; cover or seal and refrigerate overnight. (*The meat can marinate in the refrigerator for up to 3 days.*)

When you're ready to cook, transfer the beef to a plate lined with a triple thickness of paper towels. Cover it with three more towels and pat dry. Strain the marinade into a bowl; discard the solids. If some of the solids have stuck to the meat, remove and discard them (without being too fussy).

TO MAKE THE STEW: Warm 2 tablespoons of the oil in a Dutch oven over medium heat. Add the beef in batches — don't crowd the pot — and cook, turning to brown all sides for about 8 minutes. Let each side of the beef get dark before turning it and browning another side. As the pieces brown, transfer them to a bowl and season with salt and pepper.

Pour off the fat from the pot and add the remaining 1 tablespoon oil. When it's hot, add the onion and carrots, season with salt and pepper and cook over high heat, turning as needed to color the vegetables — don't be afraid of getting a little char here and there. Add the vegetables to the beef. Lower the heat and toss in the garlic, ginger and cranberries. Cook, stirring frequently and taking care not to blacken the garlic and ginger, until the mixture is fragrant and the cranberries have popped. Scrape over the beef and vegetables and stir.

Return the pot to high heat, pour in the water and cook, scraping the bottom, until you've picked up all the browned bits and most of the liquid has evaporated. Return the beef and vegetables to the Dutch oven and stir in the broth and all the remaining ingredients, including the reserved marinade. Bring to a boil, reduce the heat to low, cover the pot and simmer for 2½ to 3 hours, until the beef is fork-tender.

Transfer the beef to a bowl — be gentle; you want to keep the pieces intact. Strain the broth and discard the vegetables, herbs and spices (they've done their job and they're too tired to be good now).

If you've got time, put the broth in a shallow pan and freeze it until the fat rises to the top so you can skim it off and then reheat the broth when needed. If you want to serve the stew now, skim off as much of the fat as you can. Taste the broth for salt and pepper, return the meat to the pot and reheat. (*The stew can be made up to 3 days ahead and refrigerated.*)

MEANWHILE, MAKE THE GREMOLATA: Stir all the ingredients together. (*You can make the gremolata a few hours ahead and keep it covered in the refrigerator.*)

I like to serve this in wide shallow soup plates, although bowls are fine. If you're serving rice, quinoa or noodles with the stew, spoon it into the plates or bowls and top with the beef. Ladle over the broth and sprinkle with gremolata, or pass the gremolata at the table.

———

STORING: Stored in an airtight container, leftover stew can be frozen for up to 2 months.

# SLOW-COOKER BRISKET WITH CARROTS AND SWEET POTATOES

Makes 6 servings

Brisket's a tough cut of meat that needs long, slow cooking to make it tender and flavorful. You can get that gentle heat by cooking it in a Dutch oven on the stovetop, in a low oven or in a slow cooker, a tool that's perfect for the job. No matter how I'm going to braise the brisket, I like to give it a preliminary sear over high heat to color and lightly crust it; ditto the carrots and sweet potatoes that make this a one-pot dinner. The quick high-heat treatment gives everything a roasted flavor, which is nice in a long-cooking dish. (If you're in a hurry, you can skip this step and just stir everything together in the pot.)

## a word on cooking methods

If you want to make the brisket on the stovetop, use a large Dutch oven and cook, covered, over low heat. If you choose the oven, put the brisket and other ingredients in a roasting pan, cover with foil and cook in a 350-degree-F oven. In either case, add the bigger cuts of carrots and the sweet potatoes after about 1½ hours of cooking. Start checking the meat at the 3-hour mark and, if necessary, continue to cook until fork-tender.

1 pound (454 grams) carrots, peeled and trimmed

About 3 tablespoons canola or peanut oil

1 large or 2 medium onions, halved, thinly sliced, rinsed and patted dry

4 garlic cloves, germ removed (see page 320)

2 celery stalks, trimmed and sliced into 1-inch pieces

Fine sea salt and freshly ground pepper

One 3-pound (about 1½-kg) beef brisket, trimmed, but with a thin layer of fat on one side

2 cups (480 ml) fruity red wine, such as Syrah

One 14-ounce (397-gram) can diced tomatoes, with their juice

12 pitted prunes

1 bay leaf

1 whole star anise

½ teaspoon Urfa pepper (see page 335) or a pinch of smoked paprika

2 medium sweet potatoes, peeled and cut into 2-inch pieces

Chopped fresh parsley, for serving (optional)

Flake salt, such as Maldon (optional)

**WORKING AHEAD**

The brisket is easiest to cut when it's chilled, so if you have time, refrigerate the meat and the sauce separately — it will be easier for you to spoon off and discard the fat if the sauce is in its own container. You can make the brisket up to 5 days ahead. Reheat over gentle heat.

Cut 3 of the carrots into 2-inch-thick pieces — these will go into the pan at the start. Cut the remaining carrots into thirds and set them aside.

Warm 1 tablespoon of the oil in a large skillet over medium heat. Toss in the onions and garlic and cook, stirring, until softened, about 4 minutes. Add the smaller pieces of carrot and the celery, season with salt and pepper and cook, stirring, for 4 minutes. If the pan seems dry, add a little more oil. Turn up the heat and stir the vegetables around for a minute or so to get a little char on them. Scrape the vegetables into a slow cooker and discard whatever oil is left in the skillet.

Put the skillet over medium-high heat, add another tablespoon of oil to the pan and add the brisket fat side down. Cook until browned, about 3 minutes, then turn and brown the other side. Season with salt and pepper, then transfer the beef to the cooker and discard whatever oil remains in the skillet.

Put the skillet over high heat, add the wine and bring to a boil, scraping the bottom of the pan to pick up whatever bits have stuck to it. Lower the heat and add the tomatoes with their juice, the prunes, bay leaf, star anise and Urfa pepper or paprika. Stir well, then pour the mixture into the slow cooker.

Give everything a good stir, cover, set the slow cooker to low and cook for 4 hours.

Drop in the remaining carrots and the sweet potatoes and cook for 4 more hours, or until the beef and the second-round vegetables are fork-tender. (*The brisket and vegetables can be covered and refrigerated now for up to 5 days, or wrapped airtight and frozen for up to 2 months. While the dish is cold, skim off any surface fat and slice the brisket — it's much easier to cut when it's cold, and you'll get neater slices.*) Taste for salt and pepper, adjust the seasonings as needed and, if you can find them, remove the star anise and bay leaf before serving (if not, warn your tablemates).

Cut the meat into long slices, always cutting against the grain, and reheat in the sauce over low heat.

Arrange the sliced meat, vegetables and sauce on a large platter and sprinkle with parsley and flake salt, if you'd like.

STORING: You can freeze the brisket for up to 2 months.

CHOICES: Because the braise has carrots and sweet potatoes, you can serve it on its own, but I think it's especially good over mashed potatoes, small pasta, chewy barley or toasty kasha. Also, if you'd like, about an hour before the brisket is done, you can stir in some shredded greens, such as kale, chard or spinach.

# STUFFED CABBAGE

Makes 6 to 8 servings

If you've never made stuffed cabbage, I urge you to stop everything and do it now. Earthy and rustic, stuffed cabbage is beloved in many cultures, revered in Europe and known to cause arguments among cooks who are convinced that their recipe is superior to all others. My version, which mixes beef, pork, rice and my mother-in-law's long-secret addition, ketchup, is idiosyncratic but one I'd argue for. Passionately. I make my stuffed cabbage in bundles, the way I had it when I was growing up. It's a nod to childhood memories, but I do it this way partly because I enjoy the arts-and-crafts nature of the project. That it makes the dish easier to serve and more attractive is a bonus. For me, the sauce, both pungent and a little sweet, is the prize: It's built on tomatoes, sweetened with apple juice and spiked with vinegar. The cabbage packets are layered between the sauce and a cushion of grated apples, shredded onions and cabbage and braised for 3 hours — the aromas draw everyone into the kitchen.

### For the cabbage bundles

1 large head green cabbage—regular or Savoy

1½ pounds (680 grams) ground chuck

½ pound (227 grams) sausage meat—sweet, hot or a combination (or an equal amount of ground chuck)

1 medium onion, finely chopped, rinsed and patted dry

2 shallots, finely chopped, rinsed and patted dry

2 garlic cloves, germ removed (see page 320) and finely chopped

1½ teaspoons fine sea salt

½ teaspoon freshly ground pepper

¼ teaspoon cayenne pepper

½ cup (100 grams) basmati or other long-grain rice

Grated zest of 1 lemon

¼ cup (60 ml) ketchup

1½ tablespoons soy sauce

### For the sauce and add-ins

Two 28-ounce (794-gram) cans whole tomatoes, with their juice

⅓ cup (80 ml) unsweetened apple juice

3 tablespoons brown sugar

2 tablespoons cider vinegar

1 teaspoon fine sea salt

Pinch of cayenne pepper

1 onion, sliced, rinsed and patted dry

1 apple, grated

## WORKING AHEAD

I like to make this a day ahead if I can. An overnight in the fridge gives you the chance to easily spoon off and discard any fat, and it gives all the flavors a chance to deepen.

TO MAKE THE CABBAGE ROLLS: Bring a large pot of water to a boil.

Meanwhile, pull off and discard any tough outer leaves from the cabbage. Turn the cabbage upside down and, working carefully with a heavy knife, cut out the

core. I usually have to do this in increments — cutting out a divot and then going back in to cut away more. Pull off the outer 18 or so leaves (the largest on the head). Drop a couple of leaves at a time into the boiling water and leave them there for a minute or two, just until they're softened. Shake off the excess water as you remove the leaves from the pot and then pat them dry.

Working with one leaf at a time, spread it out on a cutting board, with the outer part — the side where the thick center rib sticks up — facing up. Using a paring knife or a strong vegetable peeler, cut or shave down the thick rib so that it's (kind of) even with the leaf and, most important, flexible — don't worry about being precise. Set the trimmed leaves aside; they're the ones you'll stuff. Thinly slice the remaining cabbage — think thick-cut coleslaw — and set aside for the sauce.

Put the ground chuck and sausage in a bowl, add all the remaining ingredients and mix together as though you were making meatballs — be thorough, but try not to knead or work the stuffing too much.

To construct the bundles, lay a cabbage leaf inner (cup) side up on a work surface. Shape about ¼ cup of the stuffing into a little log. Place the log horizontally across the cabbage, keeping it within the bottom third of the leaf, and lift the bottom of the leaf up and against the meat — or over it, if you have enough leaf. Fold the two sides over the log and then start rolling the log up in the leaf until you get to the top. (Imagine that you're making a burrito and the cabbage leaf is the tortilla.) Make the roll as compact as you can and secure the seam with a toothpick. Repeat with the remaining leaves and stuffing.

TO MAKE THE SAUCE AND COOK THE BUNDLES: Center a rack in the oven and preheat it to 350 degrees F.

Open the cans of tomatoes and, using kitchen scissors and working in the cans, snip the tomatoes into small pieces (alternatively, you can break them up with your hands). Pour the tomatoes and juice into a large bowl and stir in the apple juice, brown sugar, vinegar, salt and cayenne. In another bowl, toss together the sliced onion, grated apple and reserved sliced cabbage.

Pour one third of the sauce into a large Dutch oven or a large ovenproof sauté pan with a lid. Cover with half of the apple mixture and top with half of the cabbage bundles. Repeat with half of the remaining apple mixture and the rest of the cabbage bundles. Finish with a layer of the remaining sauce and apple mixture. Cover with a piece of parchment paper cut to fit snugly inside the pot and against the ingredients (or seal the top of the pot with aluminum foil). Cover with the lid and slide the pot into the oven.

Let the stuffed cabbage cook undisturbed for 3 hours. Taste the sauce, which will be thin, and add more sugar, vinegar, salt or cayenne if you think it needs it. Then test a cabbage bundle to make certain that the rice is tender. If it isn't — unlikely, but . . . return the pot to the oven until it is.

The stuffed cabbage can be served now or cooled, refrigerated and reheated when you're ready — I think the flavors get even better after an overnight rest.

STORING: You can keep leftover cabbage bundles and sauce in a covered container in the refrigerator for up to 4 days. The stuffed cabbage can be frozen for up to 2 months packed in an airtight container. If frozen, gently thaw before reheating in a covered pot.

# MEATBALLS AND SPAGHETTI

Makes 4 to 6 servings

My husband used to reminisce about his mother's meatballs — until, at last, I made these. They do exactly what the best meatballs do: They drink up the sauce and have great texture and so much flavor on their own that you'd be happy to put them on a sub or over a crisp romaine salad.

I make the meatballs with ground beef and sausage meat. Then I add two unusual ingredients: oats and walnuts, the former for texture, the latter for surprise, flavor and texture too. As for the sauce, the secret little extra is balsamic.

## a word on quantity

If you'd like, you can double the recipe — use a Dutch oven or large saucepan to simmer the sauce and meatballs.

### For the sauce

One 14½-ounce (411-gram) can whole tomatoes, preferably San Marzano (diced tomatoes are fine), with their juice

One 14½-ounce (411-gram) can crushed tomatoes, preferably San Marzano

2 garlic cloves, germ removed (see page 320), pressed or minced

1 tablespoon sugar

1 teaspoon balsamic vinegar

1 teaspoon fine sea salt

½ teaspoon freshly ground pepper

### For the meatballs

1 pound (454 grams) ground beef, not too lean

½ pound (227 grams) hot Italian sausage meat

½ cup (71 grams) finely chopped red or Spanish onion, rinsed and patted dry

¼ cup (20 grams) rolled oats (not instant)

¼ cup (30 grams) chopped walnuts

1 tablespoon chopped fresh herbs, such as thyme, oregano, rosemary and/or basil, or more to taste

1 teaspoon fine sea salt

½ teaspoon freshly ground pepper

1 large egg, lightly beaten

2 tablespoons olive oil, or more if needed

¾ pound (340 grams) spaghetti or linguine

Grated Parmesan or Grana Padano, for serving (optional)

Finely chopped fresh herbs, for serving (optional)

**WORKING AHEAD**
You can make the meatballs and sauce up to 3 days ahead and keep them covered in the refrigerator. When you're ready to serve, simmer for about 30 minutes in a covered pot over low heat.

*(Recipe continues)*

TO MAKE THE SAUCE: If you're using whole tomatoes, plunge a pair of kitchen scissors into the can and snip until the tomatoes are bite-sized (or break them up with your hands). Turn the tomatoes out into a large deep skillet or saucepan. Add the remaining ingredients and stir to combine. Place the pan over very low heat, cover and let cook while you make the meatballs.

TO MAKE THE MEATBALLS: Put all the ingredients *except* the egg in a large bowl. Gently mix — I use my fingers — until evenly blended. Add the egg and mix just to combine. Form the mixture into 24 to 28 small meatballs, being careful not to work the meat too much. I use a medium-sized cookie scoop (1½-tablespoon capacity) for this job — a cinchy way to get all the balls the same size.

Have a large plate with a double thickness of paper towels close to the stove.

Warm the oil in a large skillet, preferably nonstick, over medium heat. Add as many meatballs as you can without crowding the pan and cook, turning them as needed, until they're browned on all sides. You just want to sear the outside of the meatballs; you're not looking to cook them through.

Transfer the meatballs to the plate and pat them lightly to remove as much oil as you can, then drop them into the sauce. Repeat with the remaining meatballs, adding more oil to the pan if needed.

Push the meatballs around to make sure that they're submerged — it might be a tight fit — then cover the pan and cook at the lowest possible simmer for 1 to 1½ hours. This long, gentle simmer will flavor the sauce without overcooking the meat and producing the dreaded tight, bouncy meatballs of my childhood — and maybe yours. (*You can cool the meatballs and sauce, pack them into a container and refrigerate for up to 3 days.*)

When the meatballs are almost ready, cook the pasta in a large pot of boiling salted water following the package directions; drain well. If the pan with the sauce is large enough, you can turn the pasta out into it and give everything a good stir. If not, put the pasta in a large bowl and pour over the meatballs and sauce. Finish with cheese and herbs, if using, and get this to the table — it's a dish that should reach the table looking like it's sending out smoke signals.

———————

STORING: The cooled meatballs and sauce can be stored airtight in the refrigerator for up to 3 days. You can reheat leftover sauce and meatballs in the microwave, but be careful: You really don't want to overcook the meat.

# MEDITERRANEAN SHEPHERD'S PIE

Makes 4 to 6 servings

There's a lot of fancy food in this world, and then there's shepherd's pie, a rustic hodgepodge often made with leftovers, seldom made the same way twice and always satisfying. For this version, one that's been on my favorite shepherd's pie list for a while now, I start from scratch with sausage and ground meat. I often use turkey, but chicken, lamb and beef are all good. It's the herbs and spices that make this one Mediterranean. The potatoes could just as nicely be sweet potatoes, and I like to cook butternut squash into the filling (so easy — you can buy it already peeled and cubed, fresh or frozen) because I like its sweetness with the spices.

A shepherd's pie is a one-dish meal and not a light one, so I serve a leafy salad alongside, or even on top of it. Add a little extra mustard or vinegar to your favorite dressing — it's nice to have a bit of bite and tang to go with the pie's slight sweetness.

## For the potatoes

About 2½ pounds (about 1 kg) Yukon Gold potatoes, peeled and cut into 2-inch chunks

2 tablespoons unsalted butter

4 to 6 tablespoons whole milk or heavy cream

Fine sea salt and freshly ground pepper

## For the filling

2 to 3 tablespoons olive oil

1 pound (454 grams) ground lamb, beef, turkey or chicken

½ pound (227 grams) hot or mild sausage meat (pork, chicken or turkey)

1 medium onion, coarsely chopped, rinsed and patted dry

2 garlic cloves, germ removed (see page 320) and minced

1½ teaspoons fine sea salt

Freshly ground pepper

½ cup (120 ml) chicken broth

1 tablespoon ground cumin

1½ teaspoons ground sumac (see page 335) or grated zest of 1 lemon

1½ teaspoons za'atar (see page 336) or 1 teaspoon dried oregano

½ teaspoon harissa paste or 1½ teaspoons harissa powder (see page 334)

1 cup (200 grams) canned crushed tomatoes

½ pound (227 grams) peeled butternut squash, cut into 1-inch cubes

2 handfuls baby kale or spinach

1 tablespoon unsalted butter, cut into bits, or olive oil (optional)

### WORKING AHEAD

You can make the filling up to 2 days ahead and keep it refrigerated, covered. Alternatively, you can assemble the pie, freeze it for up to 2 months and bake it straight from the freezer. To do this, preheat the oven to 350 degrees F and count on it taking about 1 hour to heat through. If the potatoes brown too much before the liquid starts to bubble, tent the pie loosely with foil.

*(Recipe continues)*

I like to get the potatoes going while I'm working on the filling. If you'd prefer, make the filling first. Either way, keep in mind that the potatoes will be easier to spread over the filling if they're warm.

TO MAKE THE POTATOES:  Drop the potato chunks into a large pot of cold salted water. Bring to a boil over high heat and cook until the potatoes mash easily when pressed against the side of the pot, 15 to 20 minutes.

Drain the potatoes, put the empty pot back over medium heat, return the potatoes to the pot and cook, stirring and turning them, for about 1 minute, until they are dry. Spoon the potatoes into a food mill or ricer set over a bowl and run them through it. (Of course, you can mash the potatoes with a fork, but a mill or ricer will make them fluffier.) Stir the butter and ¼ cup of the milk or cream into the potatoes, along with ample salt and pepper, and taste them — add more of whatever you think they need. Set aside.

Center a rack in the oven and preheat it to 375 degrees F. Put a deep-dish pie plate (or an ovenproof casserole with a capacity of about 2 quarts) on a baking sheet lined with parchment paper or foil.

TO MAKE THE FILLING:  Put a large skillet over medium heat, add 1 tablespoon of the oil and when it's hot, add the ground meat and sausage. Cook, stirring and pressing the meat with a wooden spoon to break it up, for about 2 minutes; as you're cooking, drizzle in up to 1 more tablespoon of oil if you think you need it. Then add another tablespoon of oil, along with the onion and garlic, season with the salt and a few grinds of pepper and cook over low heat until the onions soften, about 10 minutes.

Add the chicken broth, turn the heat up a little and use the spoon to scrape up any browned bits stuck to the bottom of the skillet. Stir in the spices and cook for a minute, then add the crushed tomatoes and bring to a gentle simmer. Scatter over the pieces of squash, cover the pan (with its lid or a baking sheet) and cook over low heat until the squash is fork-tender, about 20 minutes. Stir in the kale or spinach and taste for salt and pepper. (*You can make the filling up to 2 days ahead and keep it tightly covered in the refrigerator.*)

Spoon the filling into the pie plate, adding enough of the liquid in the pan to come up and around the edges of the mix. (There's usually just the right amount left in the skillet. My own preference is to go for juicier rather than drier.) Top with the potatoes, smoothing them over the filling or making swoops and swirls out to the edges of the pie plate. (*At this point, the pie can be refrigerated until cool, wrapped airtight and frozen for up to 2 months.*) If you'd like, dot the top of the potatoes with the butter or brush them with a little olive oil.

Bake the pie for 30 to 40 minutes, until the filling is bubbling and the potatoes are browned here and there. If you'd like to get them crusty brown, run them under the broiler. Serve immediately, preferably in shallow soup plates.

---

STORING:  You can keep leftover pie covered in the refrigerator for up to 2 days. Reheat, covered, in a conventional or microwave oven.

CHOICES:  You can use turnips or green peas instead of the squash, or just skip the extra vegetable. You can also forgo the potatoes and the pie part of the dish entirely — the filling is so fragrant, tasty and chunky that you might want it just the way it is. Pull out a bun and make a sloppy Joe, or grab a wedge of cornbread and smother it with the juicy meat. If you plan ahead, you can make some rice or a pot of beans and use the filling as a spoon-over.

# BRAISED LAMB SHANKS WITH TOMATOES AND OLIVES

Makes 4 servings

I fell in love with lamb shanks, braised until tender enough to eat with a spoon, at New York bistros during the time when every chef with good classic training was going rustic. I knew the dish was actually simple, yet there was something about the way the slow-cooked meat seemed almost glazed, and the sauce, chunky and natural, seemed to tack between sweet and acidic, herbaceous and fruity, that made me think it was beyond the reach of mortal home cooks. Good thing I got over that! In truth, shanks are as easy to make as stews — they just look more impressive. The secret is patience. Spend a little time browning the meat and then just a few minutes more building the layers of flavor in the sauce — a mix of tomatoes, olives, herbs and strips of citrus zest that looks meek but, over time in the oven, turns bold and gives character to the dish.

## a word on leftovers

The sauce is great over pasta — I like it with a short pasta, like fusilli. If you've got leftover meat, shred it over the pasta.

### WORKING AHEAD

Like all classic braises, this is even better the day after it's made. Keep it well covered in the refrigerator—you can hold it for up to 3 days—and reheat it gently on the stovetop or in a 325-degree-F oven.

4 lamb shanks

2 tablespoons grapeseed, peanut or other neutral oil

Fine sea salt and freshly ground pepper

2 tablespoons olive oil

1 garlic head, loose skin removed

2 carrots, peeled, trimmed and thinly sliced

1 large or 2 medium onions, finely chopped, rinsed and patted dry

Leaves from 2 sprigs fresh rosemary

One 28-ounce (794-gram) can whole tomatoes, preferably San Marzano, with their juice

1 tablespoon anchovy paste or 4 oil-packed anchovies

1½ cups (360 ml) white wine

1 cup (240 ml) chicken broth

1 cup (about 150 grams) oil-cured black olives, pitted

2 wide strips tangerine, orange or lemon peel, white pith removed

¼ teaspoon Urfa pepper (see page 335) or a pinch of cayenne pepper or crushed red pepper flakes

Center a rack in the oven and preheat it to 350 degrees F. Line a baking sheet with parchment paper or a silicone baking mat — your insurance against drips on the oven floor.

Choose a stockpot, Dutch oven or a large deep skillet with a cover — although the shanks will shrink as they cook, you need to be able to arrange them in a pot with all the other saucy ingredients and give everything room to bubble.

Pat the shanks dry with paper towels. Heat the vegetable oil in the pot over medium heat and brown the shanks on all sides, about 10 minutes. You'll probably need to work in batches. When the shanks are browned, transfer them to a bowl and season with salt and pepper. Pour out the oil in the pot and pour in the olive oil. Cut off just enough from the top of the head of garlic to reveal the cloves, and toss the garlic, carrots, onions and rosemary into the pot. Season with salt and cook over low heat, stirring, until the vegetables are softened but not colored, 10 to 15 minutes.

Meanwhile, plunge kitchen scissors into the can of tomatoes and snip until they are bite-sized (or break them up with your hands).

Stir the anchovy paste or anchovies into the pot and cook, stirring, until dissolved into the mixture, a minute or two. Add 1 cup of the wine, turn up the heat and boil until it is just about evaporated. Add the remaining ½ cup wine, the broth, tomatoes with their liquid, the olives, citrus peel and pepper and stir everything around. Return the shanks to the pot, doing your best to almost submerge them. Seal the pot with a piece of foil and then the lid. Place the lined baking sheet in the oven and put the pot on it.

Braise for 2 hours and then check the shanks — if the meat is falling off the bone, they're done; if it's not, give them another 30 minutes or so. Pick out the garlic if you can — it may have fallen apart — and serve the shanks with the sauce.

———

STORING: Wrapped airtight, leftover shanks and sauce can be frozen for up to 2 months.

## LAMB OR VEAL OSSO BUCO

The shank is the cut that gives us osso buco, thick rounds of meat with the marrow bone in the center. If you'd like, ask the butcher to cut the shank into rounds, and cook the pieces as you would the full shanks, but for about half the time — check the pot after 1 hour. You can also do this with veal, the more traditional meat for osso buco.

# ROLLED, STUDDED AND HERBED BONELESS LEG OF LAMB

Makes 4 to 6 servings

A boneless leg of lamb, rolled, studded with slivers of garlic and rubbed with herbs, oil and lemon zest, is a feast worthy of a very special occasion yet doable on any weeknight. One part of what makes this roast so delectable is the rub; the other is the way it's cooked — it's oven-braised. A quick run in a hot oven, followed by less than an hour of unattended slow cooking, turns out a succulent, potently aromatic roast. If it's spring, serve the lamb with something green; if the weather's cold, something rich, like the Potato Tourte (page 220), would be splendid.

Depending on your market, you may find a leg of lamb that's already rolled up (some are wrapped in oven-proof netting and ready to roast). Otherwise, buy a boneless leg of lamb and roll it yourself, rolling it so that the layer of fat is on the outside, and tying it into a chubby bundle with kitchen twine.

1 head garlic

1 boneless leg of lamb, 2½ to 3 pounds (1 to 1½ kg), rolled (see headnote), at room temperature and patted dry

¼ cup (60 ml) olive oil

2 tablespoons minced fresh herbs, such as thyme, rosemary and/or oregano (reserve the stems)

1 lemon

Fine sea salt and freshly ground pepper

1 medium onion, sliced, rinsed and patted dry

3 to 6 sprigs fresh herbs, such as thyme, rosemary and/or oregano

¼ cup (60 ml) white wine

1¼ cups (300 ml) chicken broth

**WORKING AHEAD**

If you prefer lamb that isn't rare, you can make the roast up to 3 days ahead and reheat it very gently in a covered Dutch oven, adding a little more wine, broth or water if needed.

Center a rack in the oven and preheat to 450 degrees F.

Remove 1 or 2 garlic cloves from the head, peel them and slice them into slivers with a knife or do this with a small (Benriner-type) mandoline. Using the tip of a paring knife, pierce the lamb all over and then stud it with the garlic, using the knife to help you push the slivers into the meat. Separate the remaining cloves (no need to peel) and toss them into a Dutch oven.

Mix 2 tablespoons of the olive oil and the minced herbs together in a small bowl — toss the stems into the Dutch oven — and grate the lemon zest over the oil. Season generously with salt and pepper and rub the seasoned oil over the lamb.

Thickly slice the lemon and add the slices to the Dutch oven, along with the onion and herb sprigs. Pour over the remaining 2 tablespoons oil and the white wine, season with salt and pepper and stir to mix well. Center the lamb in the pot.

*(Recipe continues)*

Roast the lamb for 15 minutes, then cover the pot and lower the oven temperature to 350 degrees F. Continue to cook until a thermometer inserted into the center of the roast reads between 120 degrees F (rare) and 135 degrees F (medium-rare), about 30 minutes. The total cooking time will be about 45 minutes. If you'd like the top of the roast to be a little darker, run it under the broiler very briefly. Remove the roast and tent with foil; let it rest while you make the pan sauce.

Put the Dutch oven over high heat and bring the liquid in the pot to a boil, crushing the garlic cloves as you do. Cook for about 2 minutes, then add the broth, lower the heat and simmer for 5 minutes. Taste for salt and pepper and strain the sauce.

Slice the roast and serve, either moistening the meat with the pan sauce or passing it at the table.

STORING: If you like your lamb rare, your only chance to have it the way you want it is to eat it as soon as it's ready or at room temperature for a few days after that. Leftovers make great sandwiches, and they're also good in Mediterranean Shepherd's Pie (page 161) — cut the lamb into small cubes and use it instead of the ground meat.

# LIGHTNING-FAST TAHINI PORK

Makes 4 servings

Pork tenderloin should be called "the cook's best friend." It can be braised or roasted, sliced into cutlets and pan-seared or cut into cubes, as it is here, and quickly skillet-cooked in a sauce that's got more complexity and flavor than you'd expect from anything this easy. The sauce, which lightly coats the meat, gets its creaminess from a small amount of tahini and its sophisticated flavor from spices most closely associated with North Africa. Because of the tahini, a paste made of ground sesame seeds, I like to finish the dish with a sprinkling of the same seeds.

If you don't have tahini in your cupboard, you can use an equal amount of creamy peanut butter and, if you'd like, finish the dish with chopped peanuts instead of sesame seeds.

Sautéed spinach is delicious with this.

STORING:  While you can keep any leftovers in the refrigerator overnight and reheat them gently the next day, the dish is really best just-made.

½ teaspoon harissa powder (see page 334) or chile powder

½ teaspoon ground ginger

½ teaspoon ground cumin

¼ teaspoon ground turmeric

¼ teaspoon fine sea salt, or more to taste

1 pound (454 grams) pork tenderloin, cut into 1½-inch cubes

2 tablespoons tahini (stirred well before measuring) or creamy peanut butter

Juice of 1½ lemons

2 tablespoons olive oil

2 tablespoons honey

2 tablespoons cider vinegar

2 tablespoons water

Freshly ground pepper

Chopped fresh cilantro, for finishing

Sesame seeds, for finishing

Stir together the harissa or chile powder, ginger, cumin, turmeric and salt to blend. Toss the pork with the spices, coating all sides.

Mix the tahini with 2 tablespoons of the lemon juice. The tahini will thicken, and that's fine.

Warm the olive oil in a large skillet — I like nonstick for this — over medium heat. Add the pork cubes and cook for a minute or so, just to brown them on all sides. Pour in the honey, stir to coat the meat and cook for 1 minute. Add the vinegar, quickly followed by the water, and stir to deglaze the pan, picking up whatever bits have stuck to the pan. Lower the heat, stir in the tahini mix and cook for a few minutes until the sauce is smooth and the pork is cooked through. Remove from the heat, stir in the remaining lemon juice, taste for salt and season with pepper.

Turn the pork out onto a serving platter and sprinkle with the cilantro and sesame seeds.

# BOURBON-ROASTED PORK LOIN

Makes 6 servings

One 3-pound (1½-kg) boneless pork loin roast (not tender-loin), at close to room temperature

¼ cup (60 ml) bourbon

¼ cup (60 ml) grainy mustard (preferably French)

2 tablespoons honey

2 tablespoons brown sugar

1 teaspoon Sriracha

Fine sea salt and freshly ground pepper

2 tablespoons olive oil

2 medium onions, thinly sliced, rinsed and patted dry

2 apples, such as Gala or Fuji, unpeeled, cored and cut into 6 pieces each

The day after I returned from a weekend of good eating in Louisville, I made this pork roast. Four days surrounded by some of the best bourbon, the lifeblood of the city, made me want to cook with it. Turns out that bourbon and pork are as good together as pitmasters say they are.

The foundation of this dish is onions and apples, classic pork go-withs in both France and America, while the flavorful wet rub — grainy mustard (French), honey, brown sugar, Sriracha and bourbon (from Kentucky) — is a mélange. Roasted in the oven for under an hour, everything comes together in a mix of sweet and hot that calls for some dunkables — biscuits or baguette.

I'm sure you know this, but just in case: Save the good stuff to drink before, during or after the roast. The pot is no place for splurge bourbon.

**WORKING AHEAD**
If you've got the time, you'll get even more flavor if you give the pork up to 8 hours in the refrigerator after you coat it with the bourbon rub.

STORING: The leftover roast will keep tightly wrapped in the refrigerator for about 4 days. You can heat it gently if some pan juices remain. Or slice it and make great sandwiches.

Using a sharp paring knife, cut a shallow crosshatch pattern in the roast's top layer of fat, taking care not to cut into the meat.

Mix the bourbon, mustard, honey, brown sugar, Sriracha, 1 teaspoon salt and a few grinds of black pepper together. Rub this over the pork, covering all sides. If you're cooking the roast now, just set it aside while the oven preheats. Or put it in a covered container and refrigerate until needed. (*The rubbed pork can be refrigerated for up to 8 hours — pull it out of the refrigerator about 30 minutes before cooking.*)

Center a rack in the oven and preheat it to 400 degrees F.

Warm the oil in a Dutch oven or other heavy-high-sided ovenproof casserole over medium heat. Toss in the onions and apples, season with salt and pepper and cook, stirring regularly, for about 10 minutes, until the onions are translucent and the apples are starting to soften.

Center the roast on top of the apples and onions, pour in whatever liquids from the rub have accumulated and slide the pot into the oven. Roast the pork, uncovered, for 45 to 55 minutes, basting it a couple of times, until a thermometer inserted into the center of the roast registers 135 to 140 degrees F.

Allow the roast to sit for a few minutes before slicing and serving it with the onions, apples and delicious pan juices.

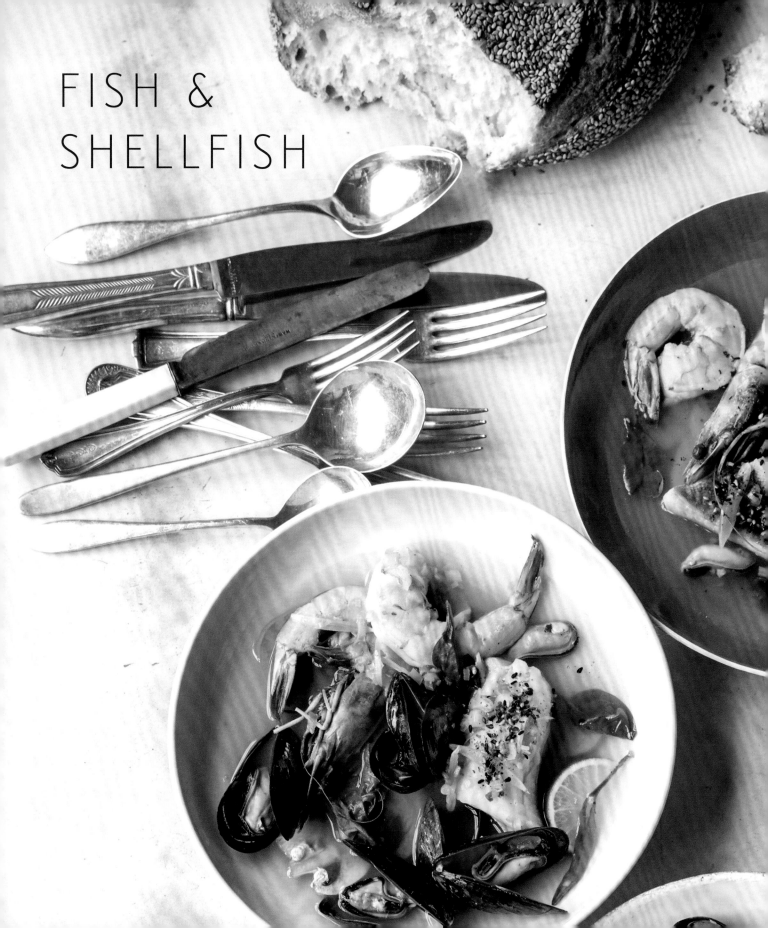

# FISH & SHELLFISH

# SALMON BURGERS

Makes 6 burgers

When we were shooting the photos for my last book, *Dorie's Cookies*, lunch was a highlight of the day, as each of us took turns cooking. One morning, Claudia Ficca, the food stylist, announced that she'd bought some salmon and had an idea for lunch: salmon burgers. Like everything Claudia does, these are special. They get a supersized helping of zip from lemons, capers, two kinds of mustard, scallions, lots of dill and Greek yogurt, which adds tang and, most important, moisture.

You can serve these juicy burgers on buns — I usually put them between Martin's Potato Rolls, topping them with slices of tomato and avocado, relish or even Quick Pickled Onions (page 320) — and offer them up with coleslaw (page 306), cucumber salad or my favorite go-along, Basta Pasta Potato Salad (page 225). You can also switch up the herbs — parsley or cilantro can stand in for the dill or be mixed with it — and you can swap the capers for chopped pickles.

The blend for the burgers is so packed with flavor that you could even skip the pan-grilling and serve it raw, as tartare. It makes a great starter or, with a green salad and slices of toasted baguette, a main course.

## a word on the salmon

My favorite for these burgers is wild Alaskan salmon; sockeye and Chinook are good choices. Because wild salmon is seasonal, I often use frozen fillets.

1½ pounds (680 grams) skinless salmon fillets (see headnote), cut into chunks and patted dry

½ cup (120 ml) plain Greek yogurt

½ cup (42 grams) finely chopped scallions (white and light green parts only)

½ cup (20 grams) chopped fresh dill

2 tablespoons smooth Dijon mustard (preferably French)

1 tablespoon grainy mustard (preferably French)

1 tablespoon capers, rinsed, patted dry and coarsely chopped if large

1 lemon

¾ teaspoon fine sea salt, or to taste

Canola or olive oil, for cooking

6 buns (see headnote)

Toppings (see headnote)

### WORKING AHEAD

You can keep the burger mix in the refrigerator for up to 8 hours before cooking.

Put the salmon in a food processor and pulse about 6 times, just until it is finely chopped. Stop before you have a paste!

Put the yogurt, scallions, dill, both mustards and the capers in a large bowl and stir to blend. Finely grate the zest of the lemon into the bowl. Stir in the salmon — use a flexible spatula and a light touch — and season with the salt. Taste and decide if you'd like more salt or want to squeeze some lemon juice into the mix. Cover the bowl, pressing a piece of plastic wrap against the surface of the mix, and refrigerate for at least 2 hours. (*The burger mix can be refrigerated for up to 8 hours.*)

When you're ready to make the burgers, divide the salmon into 6 portions and shape each one into a patty. Lightly coat a grill pan or skillet, preferably nonstick, with a small amount of oil or spray and place it over medium-high heat. Cook the burgers in two batches

(*Recipe continues on facing page*)

(don't crowd the pan) for about 2 minutes on each side — you want to crisp the exterior and just warm the insides.

Serve immediately, sandwiching the burgers between the buns and topping them with whatever you choose.

STORING: If you have leftover burgers, wrap and refrigerate them for up to 1 day; serve cold on top of a salad or reheat in a microwave.

# WARM SQUID SALAD

Makes 4 servings

This is a "minute" dish — and a stellar one. You cut all the ingredients for the salad — celery, pepper, red onion that's given a quick dunk in vinegar, capers, tomatoes, avocado and lemon zest — then whisk together a lemon-lime dressing and, when you're ready to serve, poach the squid for just 60 seconds. One minute is all it takes for the squid to become tender, ready to absorb the dressing's sharp flavors and add its own to the salad's mix of vegetables, both crunchy and soft. A light supper that can be enjoyed year-round, this is one of my favorite kinds of recipes: It seems restaurant-fancy but it's really a cinch.

You can serve the salad on a bed of greens — it's good with both dark greens, like kale and spinach, and crisp ones, like romaine or shredded iceberg.

## a word on the squid

If you're buying squid from a fish market, ask to have the skin removed, if it hasn't already been, and the squid bodies cut into ringlets. If you're buying it frozen — a good option — the skin will have been removed, so all you have to do is defrost it just until it's easy to slice and cut the bodies with a chef's knife into rings about 1/4 inch wide. If the squid's got tentacles, cut them into bite-sized pieces.

2 tablespoons white wine vinegar

1 tablespoon water

1/2 medium red onion, thinly sliced and rinsed

Juice of 1 lime

Juice of 1/2 lemon, plus 2 wide strips of the zest

1 tablespoon capers, rinsed, patted dry and chopped if large, plus 1 teaspoon of the brine

1/4 cup (60 ml) extra-virgin olive oil

Fine sea salt

About 8 baby potatoes, cooked, cooled and quartered or halved, depending on size (optional)

2 celery stalks with leaves, bottoms trimmed and thinly sliced

1 red bell pepper, cored, seeded and cut into small pieces

1 pint (about 300 grams) grape tomatoes, halved or quartered

Freshly ground pepper

1 pound (454 grams) squid, cut into rings (see headnote)

Crushed red pepper flakes (optional)

1 avocado, halved, pitted and cut into chunks (optional)

**WORKING AHEAD**

You can make the salad up to 1 hour in advance and refrigerate it, and the onions can be pickled up to 1 day ahead.

Whisk the vinegar and water together in a small bowl and drop in the onion slices. Let the onions pickle — stir now and again — while you prepare the rest of the salad. (*You can pickle the onion in the fridge for up to 1 day.*)

Make the dressing in another bowl by whisking together the lime and lemon juice and the caper brine. Whisk in the olive oil and 1/2 teaspoon salt; set aside.

Bring a medium pot of generously salted water to a boil.

Meanwhile, finely chop the lemon zest and toss it into a large serving bowl. Add the potatoes, if you're

using them, the celery, bell pepper, tomatoes and capers. Drain the onion and add it to the bowl. Season lightly with salt and pepper and toss with a little bit of the dressing.

Drop the squid into the boiling water, stir and cook for 1 minute. (Don't worry if the water doesn't return to a boil.) Taste, and if you like the texture, drain well; if you'd like the squid firmer, cook for 30 seconds more.

Add the squid to the salad, toss with the remaining dressing, taste for salt and pepper and add a pinch of red pepper flakes, if you'd like. (*The salad can be chilled for an hour.*) If you're using the avocado, gently stir it in, and head for the table.

STORING: You can refrigerate leftovers overnight — the squid will be great, but the salad stuff, particularly the tomatoes and the avocado, if you used it, will soften.

# MISO-GLAZED SALMON

Makes 4 servings

3 tablespoons miso paste (white or red)

1 tablespoon honey

1 tablespoon freshly squeezed lemon juice

1 tablespoon soy sauce

4 salmon fillets, preferably center-cut, 5 to 7 ounces (142 to 198 grams) each

Before I'd ever heard the term "umami," I knew that every time I had something with miso, I'd wanted seconds. I just didn't know why. Turns out that miso, a paste made of fermented soybeans, is the poster child for umami, the fifth flavor in the family that includes sweet, salty, bitter and sour. The word is sometimes translated from the Japanese as "delicious;" I think of umami as the taste that makes you keep coming back for more.

I don't know where the idea of marinating and glazing fish with miso started, but my first memory of it was a dish of miso-marinated black cod that the chef Nobu made famous around the world. My version uses salmon, although if you can find black cod, you can use it, and it's made rather quickly: an hour of marinating (more, if you'd like; I think Nobu marinated his fish for 3 days) and about 10 minutes of cooking. I bolster the miso with another umami ingredient, soy, and add honey and lemon juice. Together, they don't just hit each of the five flavors, they glaze the fish beautifully.

## a word on size

The dish is best with individual fillets. I've made it with large pieces of salmon (roasting a center cut of about 1¼ pounds for 25 minutes or so) but, although it's still very tasty, it's awkward and the servings don't look as attractive.

**WORKING AHEAD**
You can marinate the fish overnight.

Mix the miso, honey, lemon juice and soy together in a baking dish that will hold the fish in a single layer. Miso is not an easy mixer, so mash and press it a bit to get the mixture as smooth as possible.

Brush the marinade over the fish, covering all sides (except the bottom if the fillets have skin), arrange the salmon in the dish and cover with plastic wrap. Let marinate at room temperature for 1 hour. (*The salmon can be refrigerated for as long as overnight; remove it from the refrigerator at least 20 minutes before cooking.*)

Center a rack in the oven and preheat it to 425 degrees F. Line a baking sheet with parchment paper. If the fillets have a thick coating of marinade on them, you might want to brush off whatever seems like excess, but in all likelihood the marinade will just be skimming the surface, and that's fine for roasting. Place the fillets skin side down on the lined sheet and slide them into the oven.

Roast for 8 to 10 minutes, until the salmon feels firm to the touch. You can wiggle a fork into the center to get a peek at the color: It should be pinker at the center. The best way to check for doneness is to use an instant-read thermometer: Wild salmon should be cooked to 120 degrees F; farmed to 125 degrees F. If the marinade hasn't fully dried and glazed the fish, turn on the broiler and give the fillets a minute or so under it.

The fish is good served as soon as it comes from the oven or at room temperature. It's even good the next day, flaked into or over a salad.

STORING: Leftover cooked fillets can be wrapped tightly and kept in the refrigerator for up to 1 day.

# CITRUS-MARINATED HALIBUT WITH MANGO SALSA

Makes 4 servings

I use this marinade year-round on whatever fish is best in the market, but I especially like to pair it with halibut in the winter. The marinade's bright combination of fresh lemon and orange juice, made still more piquant with a little hot pepper, is exactly right when skies are heavy and dull. The marinade is a twofer: First it's used to flavor and lightly moisten the fish, and then it's heated and drizzled over the pan-roasted fillets.

You might think of the colorful mango salsa with tomatoes, bell pepper and mango as optional, but I hope you won't. I always top the fish with it so that I can pack more flavor, texture and color into the dish.

I sometimes add a salad, placing it under the fillets or between the fish and the salsa. Use mixed greens or arugula (you need just a handful), season with salt and pepper and dress with equal measures of extra-virgin olive oil and lemon juice. And, if you make this with a "steak-fish" like tuna or swordfish, think about cooking the fish on the grill and warming the reserved marinade in a pan.

### For the marinade and fish

Grated zest of 2 lemons

5 tablespoons freshly squeezed lemon juice

Grated zest of 2 tangerines or 1 large orange

¼ cup (60 ml) freshly squeezed tangerine or orange juice

¼ cup (60 ml) extra-virgin olive oil

4 scallions, white and light green parts only, thinly sliced

1 to 2 tablespoons chopped fresh cilantro stems (reserve the leaves for the salsa)

A sliver of jalapeño, finely chopped

1 teaspoon fine sea salt

Pinch of sugar

Pinch of cayenne pepper

4 halibut fillets, about 5 ounces (142 grams) each and about 1 inch thick

### For the salsa

About 12 grape or cherry tomatoes, halved

1 large ripe but firm mango, peeled, pitted and cut into small cubes

½ red bell pepper, finely chopped

½ cup (about 20 grams) chopped fresh cilantro

¼ cup (38 grams) chopped red onion, rinsed and patted dry

2 tablespoons shredded fresh mint or basil leaves (optional)

¼ teaspoon fine sea salt

Freshly ground pepper

Pinch of cayenne pepper

1 tablespoon extra-virgin olive oil

1 tablespoon freshly squeezed lemon juice

1 tablespoon canola oil (more if you're cooking in batches)

### WORKING AHEAD

The salsa, except for the lemon juice, can be made up to 2 hours ahead and refrigerated.

*(Recipe continues)*

TO MARINATE THE FISH: Put all the marinade ingredients in a jumbo zipper-lock bag and stir together. Add the fillets, seal the bag and turn until they're covered. Let the fish marinate, turning it from time to time, for 1 hour at room temperature. (*The fish can be marinated for up to 4 hours in the refrigerator. Remove it from the refrigerator about 20 minutes before cooking.*)

TO MAKE THE SALSA: Mix everything *except* the lemon juice together. (*You can do this a couple of hours ahead and keep the salsa covered in the refrigerator. Remove the salsa from the fridge about 20 minutes before you start cooking the fish.*)

TO COOK THE FISH: Remove the fish from the marinade and scrape any ingredients that have stuck to it back into the marinade; reserve the marinade. Using paper towels, pat the fish dry.

Working in a large skillet (preferably nonstick) over medium-high heat, warm the canola oil. When it's hot, add the fish, domed side down. If your skillet isn't large enough to hold all the pieces, cook the fish in two batches, adding more oil to the pan as needed, or use two skillets. Cook for 3 minutes, then carefully turn the fish over and cook for 3 to 5 minutes more, until the fish separates easily when prodded with a small knife; it should be opaque all the way to the middle — these tests are more important than the exact time you cook the fish. Transfer the fillets to a large platter.

Wipe out the pan, pour in the reserved marinade and bring it to a boil (or do this in the microwave or a small saucepan on the stove). Spoon some sauce over each fillet. If there's extra, pour it into a small pitcher and pass it at the table.

Stir the lemon juice into the salsa, spoon some over each fillet (bring any extra to the table as well) and serve.

———

STORING: The dish is best eaten as soon as it's made or when the fish reaches room temperature. If you have leftover fish, pack it in a container with whatever sauce you have and refrigerate for up to 1 day. Sadly, the salsa doesn't keep well.

# SALMON BRANDADE

Makes 6 to 8 servings

I created this dish out of a longing for traditional brandade but a reluctance to make it. A blend of very creamy mashed potatoes and salt cod, brandade is rich, filling and deeply satisfying — but not the kind of dish I'd do at home. Salt cod needs to be soaked in several changes of water over several hours or even days before you can start cooking it — and I rarely plan that far in advance.

My version keeps everything that I love about brandade but swaps smoked salmon for the salt cod. The milk and smoked salmon are boiled together, left to steep and then used to make the mashed potatoes. I've also channeled the goodness of shepherd's pie and added a surprise underlayer, a mix of quickly cooked fresh salmon, onions, herbs and more smoked salmon. This brandade celebrates everything that's warm and comforting about the original while adding a touch of luxe — it's brandade for dinner parties. Serve with a salad and white wine. Maybe even Champagne.

## a word on the smoked salmon

This is not the time to buy the most expensive smoked salmon you can find; this is the time for scraps and ends. Since you'll be chopping the salmon to bits and then cooking it, it needn't come from the coveted center of the salmon or be hand-sliced by a master.

1½ cups (360 ml) whole milk

½ pound (227 grams) smoked salmon (see headnote), finely chopped

2 to 2¼ pounds (1 to 1¼ kg) Yukon Gold potatoes, peeled and cut into medium chunks

Kosher salt

3 tablespoons unsalted butter, cut into 6 pieces, plus ½ tablespoon cold butter

Fine sea salt and freshly ground pepper

1½ tablespoons olive oil

1 large onion, finely chopped, rinsed and patted dry

2 garlic cloves, germ removed (see page 320) and minced

6 to 8 ounces (170 to 227 grams) skinless salmon fillet, cut into small cubes

¼ cup (60 ml) white wine or dry vermouth

2 to 3 tablespoons minced mixed fresh herbs, such as dill, chives, parsley and/or tarragon

Plain dry bread crumbs, for finishing

### WORKING AHEAD

You can make the salmon mashed potatoes up to 1 day ahead and keep them covered in the refrigerator. You can even assemble the brandade and hold it covered in the fridge for a day.

Bring the milk just to a boil in a medium saucepan. Stir in half of the smoked salmon, turn off the heat and let steep while you make the potatoes.

Put the potatoes in a tall pot (I use a pasta cooker for this — it makes draining easy), cover generously with cold water, salt the water copiously with kosher salt and bring to a boil. Cook the potatoes until they're so tender that you can easily crush them against the side of the pot with a fork, 15 to 20 minutes. Drain well.

The potatoes must be mashed, a job best (and most elegantly) done with a food mill or ricer, which produces fluffier potatoes than you get with a fork or masher. Mash them in a large bowl and then, using a spatula or

wooden spoon, stir in the salmon-milk mixture, followed by the 6 pieces of butter. The potatoes will be softer and looser than you might be used to. Season with sea salt and pepper. Press a piece of plastic wrap against the surface of the potatoes and set aside while you make the onion-salmon base. (*You can cover the potatoes and refrigerate them overnight.*)

Center a rack in the oven and preheat it to 350 degrees F. Butter a 9-inch pie plate or gratin pan (preferably one that's not metal) and place it on a baking sheet lined with parchment paper.

Warm the olive oil in a large skillet over medium-low heat. Toss in the onion and garlic and cook, stirring, until the onion is soft and translucent, about 10 minutes. Season with sea salt and pepper — go light on the salt — and stir in the cubed fresh salmon. Increase the heat to medium-high and cook, stirring, for 1 to 2 minutes. Add the wine or vermouth and cook, stirring, until the wine almost evaporates, then remove the pan from the heat and stir in the herbs and the remaining smoked salmon. Taste for salt and pepper and scrape the mixture into the buttered pan. Top with the mashed potatoes, spreading them all the way to the edges of the pan. Dot with bits of the cold butter and sprinkle over the bread crumbs. (*At this point, you can cover the dish and refrigerate it for as long as 1 day.*)

Bake for about 30 minutes, or until the potatoes are hot all the way through (poke a knife into them and then touch the knife to test for heat), the juices from the onion and salmon are bubbling and the top is golden brown. If you want more color, you can run the brandade under the broiler.

Serve immediately — brandade is meant to be so hot that you've got to blow on every forkful.

————————

STORING: The brandade is best as soon as it's made, but if you've got leftovers, they'll be good reheated the next day.

# PORTUGUESE-STYLE COD AND BEANS EN PAPILLOTE

Makes 1 serving, but multiplies easily

*En papillote,* French for "in a pouch," is a way of cooking that's fascinated me ever since I first tried it. It's essentially oven-steaming, which doesn't sound very glam, but it's one of the simplest and most efficient ways to mix and bring out flavors. Sealing the ingredients in a bundle — I use parchment, but foil works too — means the flavors and aromas have no place to go but deeper into each other. The technique works for fish and shellfish, small pieces of poultry, vegetables and fruits. Here I'm making what could be a big-pot braise in miniature. Enclosing the cod with white beans, herbs and tomatoes in a white wine sauce (I use the word "sauce" very, very loosely) flavored with smoked paprika and garlic creates a dish that bends toward Portugal.

I've given you directions for making a single packet, so that you can multiply this construction project as many times as you want — the number will depend on the space you've got in your oven. You can make and refrigerate the packages ahead of time, but once baked, the papillotes should not be kept waiting. I like to serve this in shallow soup plates or bowls. The best way is to bring the packs to the table and let each person open his or her own — that first burst of aroma is fabulous.

⅓ cup (87 grams) cooked or canned cannellini beans, rinsed, drained and patted dry

1 garlic clove, germ removed (see page 320) and slivered

½ teaspoon balsamic vinegar, or more to taste

1½ tablespoons extra-virgin olive oil

About ½ teaspoon smoked paprika (sweet or hot)

Fine sea salt and freshly ground pepper

2 lemon slices

3 slices from a small to medium tomato

2 sprigs fresh thyme

1 scallion, white and light green parts only, cut into 1-inch lengths, or 3 tablespoons chopped spring or white onion, rinsed and patted dry

One 5-ounce (142-gram) cod fillet, with or without skin, at or close to room temperature

1 tablespoon white wine

### WORKING AHEAD
You can make the packets and refrigerate them for up to 8 hours ahead. Remove before you preheat the oven.

Center a rack in the oven and preheat it to 450 degrees F. Line a baking sheet with parchment paper, foil or a silicone baking mat. Cut a 15-inch (or close) square piece of parchment or foil, and have kitchen twine at hand.

Mix the beans, half of the garlic, the balsamic and ½ tablespoon of the olive oil together in a small bowl. Stir in a generous pinch of paprika and season with salt and pepper. Taste and add more balsamic, paprika, salt and/or pepper, if you'd like.

Place the sheet of parchment or foil on the counter. Start building the dish in the center of the packet: Lay down a slice of lemon, top with 2 slices of tomato and a sprig of thyme and season with salt and pepper. Spoon on the bean mixture and scatter over half of the scallion or onion. Rub the cod with some paprika, salt and pepper and nestle it into the beans. Scatter over the remaining garlic slivers and scallion (or onion). Top with the remaining tomato, lemon and thyme and, once again, season with salt and pepper. Pour over the remaining 1 tablespoon oil and the wine. Lift up the edges of the paper or foil to make a kind of hobo's sack and tie it tightly at the "neck," leaving a couple of inches between the ingredients and where you're securing the bundle. Put the packet on the baking sheet. (*The packet can be prepared up to 8 hours ahead and kept in the refrigerator; let it sit on the counter while you preheat the oven.*)

Bake for 15 minutes, or until the fish is opaque at the center; poke it with a paring knife and peek in. If your fillet was under 5 ounces, check at 12 minutes; if it was heavier or cold, check at 15 — you might need a minute or two longer. Because you're steaming the fish, the risk of overcooking is minimal.

Serve the packet immediately, paying attention when you open it — the initial puff of steam is very hot. Wonderfully fragrant too.

STORING: There is no keeping this dish once it is cooked.

# FLOUNDER MEUNIÈRE WITH ONION-WALNUT RELISH

Makes 4 servings

Anything *meunière* is always simpler and more rustic than you'd think from its French name. *La meunière* is "the miller's wife," and so you can be certain that what's being cooked will be dredged in flour. You can also be sure it will be cooked in butter. The technique for meunière is easily mastered, as long as you stay close to the pan for the 5 or so minutes that the fish cooks — you need to let the butter brown and then toss in little pieces of cold butter to keep it all from getting too dark.

The fish for meunière is most classically sole, often cooked on the bone, but filleted flounder can be easier to find and is perfect for the dish. Just as classically, the fish is finished with lemon juice, and brought to the table dusted with parsley. My version is almost classic: It keeps the flour, butter and lemon juice and it even has the parsley, but the herb is mixed into a lively relish (if you dice rather than chop the onions, you'll get a more interesting texture), whose cast of ingredients also includes anchovies, lemon zest and juice, chopped walnuts and small toasted-in-olive-oil croutons.

## For the relish

⅓ cup (40 grams) chopped walnuts

About 2½ tablespoons extra-virgin olive oil

⅓ cup (80 ml) very small cubes stale bread, preferably baguette or country loaf, crust on or off

5 oil-packed anchovies, drained and finely chopped

Finely grated zest of ½ lemon

1 tablespoon freshly squeezed lemon juice, or more to taste

Fine sea salt

½ medium onion, finely diced or chopped, rinsed and patted dry

Freshly ground pepper

## For the fish

⅓ cup (45 grams) all-purpose flour

Fine sea salt and freshly ground pepper

4 flounder fillets, about 5 ounces (142 grams) each, with or without skin, patted dry

3 to 6 tablespoons (1½ to 3 ounces; 42 to 85 grams) cold unsalted butter

½ lemon

Chopped fresh parsley

TO MAKE THE RELISH: Toss the walnuts into a dry skillet set over medium heat and cook, stirring and shaking the pan, until they are lightly toasted — catch a whiff of them and you're done or near to done — about 2 minutes. Set the nuts aside.

Return the skillet to the heat and pour in a teaspoon or two of the oil. When it's hot, add the croutons and cook, stirring, until golden brown. Set these aside with the walnuts.

Working in a medium bowl, stir the anchovies, 1 tablespoon of the oil, the zest, lemon juice and a large pinch of salt together. Add the onion, nuts, croutons and a few grinds of pepper; taste for salt and add more lemon juice, if you'd like. If the relish looks a little dry to you — it's nicest when there's some oil in the bowl that hasn't been absorbed by the bread — add more olive oil. Stir in as much parsley as you'd like just before serving.

TO MAKE THE FISH: If you think you're going to have to cook the fish in batches, preheat the oven to 200 degrees F so that you can keep the first batch warm while you're working on the second.

Spread the flour on a large plate and season it generously with salt and pepper. Run the fillets through the flour, making sure that both sides are covered, then tap off the excess.

Set a large skillet, preferably nonstick, over medium heat and drop in about 1½ tablespoons of the butter — measurements are not key here, you just want enough butter for the fish to brown easily. When the butter has melted and the bubbles have calmed down, slip in as many fillets as you can fit without crowding. Cook for about 3 minutes, until the flour is golden and the fish is cooked halfway through — you'll see it turn opaque around the edges; the butter will be a nutty brown. Carefully flip the fish over — I like a fish or offset spatula for this job — and cook for 2 minutes or so, adding another ½ to 1 tablespoon butter in small pieces and spooning the brown butter over the fillets as they cook. Transfer the fish to a serving platter. If you've got more fillets, keep the first batch warm in the oven while you repeat the process.

Spoon the butter from the pan over the fillets, or don't — the fish is fine flavored with only the butter it absorbed during cooking. Squeeze over some lemon juice. Stir the parsley into the relish, and then top the fish with the relish or pass the relish at the table.

———————————

STORING: The fillets are a make-them-and-eat-them treat. At least they are for most people — but my husband likes a chilled leftover fillet in a sandwich with lettuce, tomato and either mayo or ketchup (sometimes both).

# ROSA JACKSON'S BOURRIDE

Makes 4 servings

Even before Rosa Jackson was my friend, she was an authority I turned to when I wanted to know more about the foods of Paris and Nice, the food-lover's Eden on the French Riviera. Rosa arrived in France from Canada in 1995 and did what so many people dreamed of doing: stayed! She is well known for her tours of the Nice market and recently opened a cooking school, Les Petits Farcis, in a sun-filled studio in the Old City, so that you can shop at the market with her and head right to the kitchen. Which is what I did and how I learned to make this *bourride Sétois*, a fisherman's stew from the seaside town of Sète.

The word *bourride* tells you that it's a fish stew with aioli (garlic mayonnaise), sometimes referred to as the butter of Provence. In the traditional version, the fish is poached in broth; Rosa braises it with vegetables, making a stew — well, not really a stew, since it's not at all soupy — that's more colorful, more flavorful and surprisingly quick (as in weekday-quick) to pull together. At Rosa's, we had the bourride with steamed baby potatoes, and that's how I do it at home too.

## a word on the bread and potato

The aioli is thickened with a base of bread or cooked potatoes. If you want to use potato, cut up a baby spud and boil it for 10 minutes or so, then drain and mash it. If you prefer to use bread, soak a slice of sandwich or country bread in a small amount of milk only until it's thoroughly moistened, then remove it from the soaking bowl and squeeze out the excess liquid.

### For the aioli

1 garlic clove, preferably young, germ removed (see page 320)

Coarse sea or kosher salt

2 large egg yolks, preferably organic (the yolks are barely cooked), at room temperature

1 slice (¾ ounce; 22 grams) stale bread, soaked in milk, or 1 small (1 to 1½ ounces; 28 to 43 grams) boiled potato (see headnote)

½ cup (120 ml) mild-tasting olive oil

½ lemon

Freshly ground pepper

### For the bourride

1 medium carrot, peeled and trimmed

10 celery leaves (optional)

4 Swiss chard, spinach or Tuscan kale leaves, center ribs removed

2 young leeks, white and light green parts only, rinsed and patted dry

2 tablespoons olive oil

Fine sea salt

4 cod, halibut or skinned monkfish fillets, 5 ounces (142 grams) each

Freshly ground pepper

About ½ cup (120 ml) water or vegetable or fish broth

Celery leaves or fennel or dill fronds, for serving (optional)

**WORKING AHEAD**
You can make the aioli up to 1 day ahead and keep it tightly covered in the refrigerator.

TO MAKE THE AIOLI: The aioli can be made using a mortar and pestle or a handheld (immersion) blender. To use a mortar and pestle, crush the garlic with a pinch of coarse salt. Add the yolks. Squeeze out the milk from the bread, if you're using it, then add it or the potato to the mortar and crush to mix coarsely. Drop by drop, add the olive oil — here Rosa cautions to always turn the

pestle in the same direction. The mixture will thicken into a mayonnaise. (To use a handheld blender, first crush the garlic to a puree on a cutting board with the pinch of salt or push it through a garlic press; put it in a medium bowl. Mash in the yolks and the bread or potato, then blend in the oil by droplets. No matter which tool you used, squeeze in some lemon juice, then taste to see if you'd like more juice and/or salt. Season with pepper. (*You can make the aioli up to 1 day ahead and hold it in the refrigerator. Bring it to room temperature before using.*)

TO MAKE THE BOURRIDE: Cut the carrot into small pieces — think cubettes. Slice the celery leaves, if using, and the chard, spinach or kale into thin shreds. Cut each leek lengthwise into quarters and thinly slice.

Heat the oil in a large saucepan or Dutch oven over medium-low heat. Add all the vegetables and a good pinch of salt and cook, stirring, until they soften but don't color, about 5 minutes. Season the fish with salt and pepper and add it to the pan. Cover and cook over low heat for 4 to 6 minutes on each side (cod and halibut cook faster than monkfish). Test it early by piercing it at the center with a small knife — cod or halibut will flake and be opaque; monkfish will cut easily and be opaque. (The cooked fish should measure about 145 degrees F on an instant-read thermometer, though you can go a little lower, because the fish will rest a bit and the residual heat will cook it a tad more.) Transfer the fish to a plate; cover loosely and put in a warm place.

Stir the aioli into the vegetables and cooking juices. Add as much water or broth as needed to create a sauce that just coats a spoon; better to err on the side of a little thick than a little too thin. Taste for salt and pepper.

Serve the fish and vegetables in shallow soup plates with a sprinkling of celery leaves or fennel or dill fronds, if you'd like.

STORING: The bourride is a make-and-enjoy dish.

CHOICES: The aioli is stellar as a go-along with crudités, steamed vegetables, hot or cold hard-boiled eggs or potatoes and as a spread for sandwiches.

# TWICE-FLAVORED SCALLOPS

Makes 4 to 6 servings

Two flavoring combos make this stunningly simple dish exceptional: a bold marinade that becomes a sauce and a lemon-confit jam (page 308) — call it "goop"— that becomes a glaze. If you haven't already stocked some of this in your refrigerator, I urge you to do it now and to never be without it — it's culinary magic.

The marinade mixes ginger, soy, lemon and yuzu kosho, a Japanese seasoning paste made with chiles and citrus (you can swap it for an equal amount of Thai curry or chile paste and a scrape of lemon zest — not the same, but still delicious). The jam is a slow-cooked mash of lemon zest and segments, sugar and salt.

After they're briefly marinated, the scallops are skillet-seared (they can be grilled, if you'd like) and then, as soon as they're cooked, they get a swipe of the jam — that's the one-two flavor punch. Boil the leftover marinade in the pan or in a microwave, and presto! You've got a sauce.

Juice of 1 lemon (about 2 tablespoons)

4 teaspoons soy sauce

1 teaspoon minced peeled fresh ginger

1 teaspoon yuzu kosho (red or green; see page 336, or see headnote)

½ to 1 teaspoon honey

24 sea scallops, tough muscle removed, patted dry

About 1 tablespoon olive oil

Lemon Goop (page 308), to taste

## WORKING AHEAD
You can marinate the scallops up to 6 hours ahead.

Choose a container — a glass loaf pan is good here — that will hold the scallops snugly and whisk together the lemon juice, soy, ginger, yuzu kosho and ½ teaspoon honey in it. Taste, and if you think it needs to be a bit sweeter, add more honey. You don't want a sweet marinade, but you do want to cut the bite of the chile and citrus just a smidge. Add the scallops, turning them around in the marinade, cover and set aside at room temperature for 30 minutes, turning them once. (*You can marinate the scallops in the refrigerator for up to 6 hours, turning them a few times. Remove them from the refrigerator about 20 minutes before cooking.*)

Remove the scallops from the marinade, but hold on to the marinade. Do a cursory job of scraping off the bits of ginger — you won't get them all, so don't fuss — and pat the scallops dry between paper towels.

Pour just enough oil to slick the bottom of the pan into a large skillet and heat over medium-high heat. When it's hot, add the scallops. Cook, without turning, for 2 minutes, then flip them over and cook for another minute, or until they are just opalescent in the center (cut into one to check). Transfer the scallops to a serving platter and swipe the tops with the goop.

Heat the marinade in the skillet or in a microwave — bring it just to a boil. Pour the marinade around the scallops or pass it at the table.

*(Recipe continues)*

STORING: If you have any leftover scallops, refrigerate them and use them in a salad the next day.

CHOICES: While there's nothing wrong with serving the scallops on their own, it's nice to give them a bed to rest on. In the summer, they're lovely over a pouf of salad or slices of ripe tomatoes — just salt and pepper the tomatoes and brush or drizzle them with olive oil. When tomato season is over, try them on Slow-Roasted Tomatoes for Everything (page 315). They're also excellent over quickly wilted greens such as spinach, chard or kale.

## Playing Around

Turn to this recipe when you want to do something quick and good with shrimp, swordfish, tuna, salmon, pork chops or cutlets, chicken cutlets or thighs or grilled eggplant or zucchini.

If you use chicken or pork, you'll need to boil the marinade for 2 minutes.

# SHRIMP TACOS

Makes 4 servings

Anytime you can encourage people to play with their food, mix and match things and eat with their fingers, I think you should. And there's no way around using your fingers with these tacos. The mix-and-matchers are: tortillas (corn or flour); avocado mash, made with as much jalapeño as you'd like; quick-cooked chile-dusted shrimp; shreds of crunchy lettuce; peach-pineapple salsa; and a light chipotle cream made with mayo and Greek yogurt. You can even ditch the taco part and use all the ingredients to make a colorful salad or lettuce wraps, in which case, reach for a soft lettuce.

## a word on heating the tortillas

Heat tortillas directly over a gas flame or in a dry skillet to toast them before serving. You can keep the tortillas warm, wrapped in foil, in a 250-degree-F oven.

## Playing Around

When the season changes, you can replace the peaches with grapefruit segments or use only pineapple. You can swap white fish for the shrimp; cook it in a little oil in a skillet. You can forgo the avocado mash altogether or just toss some avocado cubes over the shrimp or into the salsa.

### For the chipotle cream

¼ cup (60 ml) mayonnaise

¼ cup (60 ml) plain Greek yogurt

1 to 2 canned chipotles in adobo sauce, minced

Fine sea salt

Freshly squeezed lime juice

### For the salsa

¼ pound (113 grams) ripe tomatoes (plum, round or grape)

¼ medium red onion, finely chopped or diced, rinsed and patted dry

¼ large red or yellow bell pepper, finely chopped or diced

1 to 2 peaches, peeled or not, pitted and finely chopped or diced

⅛ pineapple, cored and finely chopped or diced

1 wide strip jalapeño, or to taste, finely chopped

½ teaspoon fine sea salt

Freshly squeezed lime juice

Hot sauce

¼ cup (10 grams) finely chopped fresh cilantro

### For the avocado mash

Finely grated zest and juice of 1 lime, or more juice if desired

Fine sea salt

2 wide strips jalapeño, or more to taste, finely chopped

2 ripe avocados

### For the shrimp

1½ pounds (680 grams) medium or large shrimp, peeled, deveined and patted dry

1½ to 2 tablespoons olive oil

½ to ¾ teaspoon Old Bay seasoning or chile powder

Pinch of fine sea salt, or more to taste

Squirt of fresh lime juice

*(Ingredients continue)*

### For serving

8 tortillas, toasted (see headnote), or lettuce leaves if you want to make wraps

Shredded romaine or iceberg lettuce (if making tacos)

Hot sauce

Sprigs fresh cilantro

**WORKING AHEAD**

The cream, without the lime juice, holds up really well even if made about 2 days ahead. Although you can make the salsa and avocado mash a few hours ahead, it's better to wait until shortly before you cook the shrimp.

**TO MAKE THE CREAM:** Whisk the mayonnaise, yogurt and chipotles together in a bowl. Season with salt and add as much lime juice as you'd like. (*You can make this without the lime juice up to 2 days ahead and keep it covered in the refrigerator; add the juice and whisk before serving.*)

**TO MAKE THE SALSA:** Toss the tomatoes, onion, bell pepper, fruit and jalapeño in a large bowl and stir gently. Squeeze in some lime juice and taste for the juice as well as for salt and jalapeño, adding more if you'd like. Just before you're ready to serve, add hot sauce to taste and the cilantro. (*You can make this a couple of hours ahead and keep it in the refrigerator, but it's better made as close to serving time as possible, and best if you add the lime juice at the last minute.*)

**TO MAKE THE MASH:** Stir the lime zest, juice, some salt and jalapeño together in a medium bowl. Halve the avocados, pit them, scoop out the flesh and add it to the bowl, then mash it with a fork until chunky. Taste for salt, juice and jalapeño. Press a piece of plastic wrap against the surface and set aside at room temperature. (*The mash can be refrigerated for up to 2 hours.*)

**TO MAKE THE SHRIMP:** Mix the shrimp and 1½ tablespoons of the oil with ½ teaspoon of the Old Bay or chile powder. Place a large skillet — nonstick is great here — over medium-high heat and, when it's hot, toss in the shrimp. Cook, turning only once, until they are pink and cooked through; if needed, add more oil to keep them from sticking. Depending on the size and how cold the shrimp were when you started, count on anywhere from 3 to 6 minutes. Turn the shrimp out into a serving bowl, squeeze over a little lime juice and season with more salt and/or Old Bay or chile powder, if you'd like.

**TO ASSEMBLE:** Lay out the cream, salsa, avocado, shrimp, tortillas, shredded lettuce (or lettuce leaves for wraps), hot sauce and cilantro on the table and encourage everyone to construct their own perfect taco.

# HOLIDAY FISH SOUP

Makes 6 servings

This substantial fish soup turns toward Asia for its inspiration, fragrance and flavor. The broth gets its vivacity from a usual aromatic trio of scallions, shallot and garlic, and a less usual one of lemongrass, ginger and yuzu kosho. It gets its depth from the mix of fish that's poached in it. I like to use mussels — nothing gives you a more flavorful base for fish; cod (or another firm-fleshed white fish, such as halibut or monkfish); and shrimp. The soup becomes even more beautiful once you add mushrooms, scallions, sweet potatoes and a scattering of cilantro leaves or seaweed flakes.

The dish takes its name from the fact that I often make it for our lots-of-people-around-the-table holiday dinners in Paris. It's perfect for a celebration — it's elegant, good-looking, delicious and very easy to make, even for a crowd (the recipe multiplies easily). Make the broth in advance and have the fish and vegetables ready to go, and when it's time, you'll have just a few minutes of kitchen work ahead of you.

### WORKING AHEAD
You can make the broth ahead and keep it covered in the refrigerator for up to 3 days or freeze it for up to 1 month.

## For the broth

1 tablespoon olive oil

6 scallions, white and light green parts only, sliced paper-thin

3 garlic cloves, germ removed (see page 320)

1 large shallot, thinly sliced, rinsed and patted dry

1 stalk lemongrass, tender inner bulb only, very thinly sliced

One 1-inch piece fresh ginger, peeled and very thinly sliced

1 sliver of chile pepper

A thin strip of lime zest

Fine sea salt

1 teaspoon red yuzu kosho (see page 336)

¼ cup (60 ml) white wine or dry vermouth

5 cups (1¼ liters) chicken, fish or vegetable broth

Pinch of sugar

## For the fish and vegetables

24 mussels, scrubbed and debearded if necessary

1½ pounds (680 grams) skinless cod fillet or other firm-fleshed white fish fillet (see headnote), cut into 6 portions

24 medium shrimp, peeled and deveined

6 large head-on shrimp, unpeeled (optional)

6 scallions, white and light green parts only, cut into 3 pieces each

2 large white or brown mushrooms, such as cremini, wiped clean, trimmed and thinly sliced (preferably with a mandoline)

1 shallot, very thinly sliced, rinsed and patted dry

½ sweet potato (cut crosswise), peeled, cut lengthwise in half and thinly sliced (preferably with a mandoline)

A handful of baby spinach

Fine sea salt, to taste

## For serving

1 lime, halved

Chopped fresh cilantro and/or dried seaweed flakes or furikake (see page 333)

*(Recipe continues)*

TO MAKE THE BROTH: Warm the oil in a Dutch oven or heavy soup pot over medium-low heat. Add the scallions, garlic, shallot, lemongrass, ginger, chile and lime zest, stirring to coat the ingredients with oil. Season with a pinch of salt and cook, stirring, for about 5 minutes, until the mixture is softened and fragrant. Add the yuzu kosho and cook, stirring and mashing, until the paste is evenly mixed into the aromatics. Pour in the wine, raise the heat and cook, stirring, until it just about evaporates, a minute or two. Add the broth and bring to a boil, then lower the heat to a simmer, cover the pot and cook for 20 minutes.

Taste the broth for salt and add the sugar. Strain into a bowl or pitcher and discard the solids; return the broth to the pot. (*You can make the broth up to 3 days ahead and keep it covered in the refrigerator or freeze it for up to 1 month.*)

TO MAKE THE FISH AND VEGETABLES: Bring the broth to a light boil, lower the heat so that it simmers and drop in the mussels. Cover the pot and cook for 2 minutes. Add the remaining ingredients and cook, uncovered, for 3 minutes or so more, until the shrimp are pink, the fish is cooked through and the mussels have opened (discard any that don't). Remove the pot from the burner.

Divide the fish and vegetables among six shallow soup plates and ladle over the broth — there will be more fish than broth in each bowl. Give each portion a squeeze of lime juice and a sprinkling of cilantro and/or seaweed or furikake. Serve immediately.

# PASTA WITH SARDINES, FENNEL AND PINE NUTS

Makes 4 to 6 servings

There are probably as many recipes for pasta and sardines as there are cooks who want to turn out tasty food in a flash. As with so many great pasta dishes, if you do the prep while the water's coming to a boil, you can pull the sauce together in the time it takes for the pasta to cook to al dente. But I'd make this dish even if it took hours — the mix of sweet and salty, savory and mild, familiar and surprising is too good to pass up.

The recipe is based on what I remember from my first taste of this popular Sicilian dish. The fennel and pine nuts are traditional. I'm not so sure about the raisins and capers, and the tomatoes are outliers, but I toss them in when I have them. You can use whatever sardines you have, but if you get best-quality sardines packed in olive oil, the dish will shine more brightly. I prefer to bone the sardines myself rather than buying them boneless, and I leave the skin on — by the time the sardines mix with everything else, the skin has almost melted into the sauce. (I have friends who also leave in the bones, which are slender, crunchy and calcium-packed.)

¼ cup (40 grams) raisins

1 pound (454 grams) pasta, such as penne, fusilli or fettuccine

⅓ cup (50 grams) pine nuts or, less traditionally, chopped walnuts

½ to ¾ cup (120 to 180 ml) extra-virgin olive oil

1 medium onion, finely chopped, rinsed and patted dry

1 small fennel bulb or ½ large bulb, trimmed (reserve the fronds), quartered, cored, and thinly sliced

2 garlic cloves, germ removed (see page 320) and finely chopped

Fine sea salt

1 to 2 medium tomatoes, cut into bite-sized cubes (optional)

2 tablespoons capers, or more to taste, rinsed, patted dry and chopped if large

2 cans (about 4 ounces; 115 grams each) sardines (see headnote), drained (reserve the oil if it's tasty), cut into bite-sized pieces

1 lemon

Freshly ground pepper

1 to 2 tablespoons finely shredded fresh basil leaves (optional)

Put the raisins in a small bowl and cover with very hot tap water; drain when you're ready for them.

Bring a large pot of generously salted water to a boil. When it's boiling, stir in the pasta and cook until barely al dente — you're going to be cooking it for a few minutes in the sauce, so you want to stop the cooking early.

Meanwhile, set a large skillet, preferably one with high sides, over medium heat, toss in the pine nuts or walnuts and cook, stirring and shaking the pan, until they're toasted, a minute or two. Transfer the nuts to a bowl and return the skillet to the stove.

Pour 3 tablespoons of the oil into the skillet, add the onion, fennel and garlic, season lightly with salt and cook over medium-low heat, stirring often, until softened, about 4 minutes. If the vegetables color a bit, it's fine. Stir in the tomatoes, if you're using them, the

raisins, capers and the oil from the sardines — or, if you don't want to use the sardine oil, ¼ cup olive oil. At this point, the pasta should be done; if it's not, keep the skillet over very low heat until it is.

When the pasta is cooked, scoop out about ½ cup of the cooking water and set it aside. Drain the pasta, shaking off most of the water, and turn it into the skillet (or return it to the pasta pot and scrape in the sauce), stirring to coat it with sauce. Add more olive oil a little at time, if you'd like — you want the pasta to shine. Grate in the zest of the lemon and squeeze its juice over the pasta. Top with the sardines and gently fold everything together. Taste for salt and pepper and drizzle in pasta water or more oil if you think the sauce needs it. Stir in the nuts, reserved fennel fronds and basil, if you're using it, and serve.

STORING: There are people who enjoy leftover pasta, and I happen to be one of them. If you've got some left over, cover and refrigerate it. You can eat it cold from the fridge or reheat it gently and quickly in a microwave, adding more oil, if you'd like.

# PASTA WITH SHRIMP, SQUASH, LEMON AND LOTS OF HERBS

Makes 4 servings

3 large lemons

1 pound (454 grams) green and/or yellow zucchini, scrubbed and trimmed

1 pound (454 grams) small pasta (see headnote)

½ cup (120 ml) extra-virgin olive oil

1 pound (454 grams) large shrimp, peeled and deveined

Fine sea salt and freshly ground pepper

Cayenne pepper

2 tablespoons unsalted butter

2 tomatoes, cored and cut into ½-inch pieces (save the juice if possible)

½ cup (20 grams) chopped fresh dill

½ cup (20 grams) snipped fresh chives

Like so many "everyday" dishes, I first made this as a quick toss-together, and then, because it was so good and easy — it's dinner in under 30 minutes — I shopped for the ingredients so I could make it again and again. The pasta is simple, clean and flavorful. The secret is the lemons — you use every bit of them: The juice flavors the sauce (I use the word "sauce" loosely); the squeezed halves add zip to the pasta cooking water; and the zest goes in at the end for freshness. And the herbs: Dill and chives are my choice for this, but you can mix it up with mint, oregano, basil and/or cilantro. Finally, I like to use large shrimp and small pasta, like fusilli, penne or mini-rigatoni, so the pasta and the shrimp are similar in size.

Finely grate the zest of the lemons and toss it into a large serving bowl. Squeeze the juice into a cup (you want a scant ½ cup) and hold on to the lemon halves. Cut the squash into quarters the long way, then cut each piece crosswise into ¼-inch slices (they'll be wedge-shaped). Fill a large pot with generously salted water, toss in the lemon halves and bring to a boil. Add the pasta and cook according to the package directions until al dente.

As the pasta bubbles away, pour ¼ cup of the oil into a large skillet set over medium-high heat. Add the shrimp (do this in batches if you think the pan will be crowded), season with salt, pepper and a pinch of cayenne and cook for about 3 minutes, turning once, until the shrimp are pink; you want them to stay tender, so taste them as soon as they turn color. Using a slotted spoon, transfer the shrimp to a bowl.

Add another 2 tablespoons oil to the skillet and, when it's hot, toss in the squash (again, working in batches if necessary). Season with salt and pepper and cook over high heat, turning as needed, until the squash is lightly golden, 3 to 5 minutes. With a slotted spoon, transfer to the bowl with the shrimp.

When the pasta is cooked, scoop out ½ cup of the cooking liquid and set it aside, then drain the pasta.

*(Recipe continues)*

## Playing Around

When zucchini and tomatoes are not in season, think about spinach, kale or eggplant and sun-dried tomatoes.

Return the skillet to medium-high heat, add the remaining 2 tablespoons oil and the pasta and toss the pasta around in the oil until it's coated. Add the shrimp and squash, the reserved pasta water, the lemon juice and butter, stir to blend, taste for salt, pepper and cayenne and cook for just a minute or two — the sauce will thicken slightly and the pasta will have a nice shine.

Stir in the tomatoes and whatever juices there are. Turn everything out into the serving bowl with the zest, top with the herbs and stir to mix. Serve immediately.

STORING: While this dish is primo as soon as it's made, it can be satisfying as a salad the next day; store, covered, overnight in the refrigerator. If you're having the leftover pasta cold, taste for salt and pepper — it will probably need more. It might need a splash more oil too.

# SEAFOOD PASTA

Makes 4 to 6 servings

It was only after I'd committed to enough seafood to feed ten that I thought to ask the fishmonger's wife what to do with it. I'd gone to my usual fish stand in my Paris neighborhood and said that I had pasta for a crowd in mind. I was thinking about something based on butter, white wine and herbs, but Madame suggested I start with slow-cooked squid in tomato sauce and that I shouldn't forget a little hot pepper at the end. "It's what we do in Portugal," she said. And it's what I did and continue to do, although the fish changes according to what I can get. These days I'm likely to cook squid rings (most often bought frozen and sliced when they're still a little icy) and then add chunks of a firm fish, like monkfish, swordfish or tuna, and shrimp.

It'll take an hour or so to simmer the sauce — you'll want to go slow for the sake of the squid — but it bubbles away merrily without your having to do much. You can also do this part ahead, making it a dish that's good for parties, which is how it all started.

For the clam juice, look for a brand that includes only clam juice and salt. Finally, choose your crushed tomatoes carefully — I like San Marzano tomatoes here.

I like long pasta for this dish. I usually use spaghetti, linguine or fettucine, but I'm always happy when I can get something fanciful, like mafaldine — it's the pasta that's in the photo on page 208.

You can multiply this recipe as much as you'd like — I've more than halved it from my original. And feel free to stray as far as you'd like from my suggestions for the seafood and fish, but try to get squid. It's a big-bang choice: You get a lot of flavor and texture for not much money and very little effort.

2 tablespoons olive oil

1 large onion, finely chopped, rinsed and patted dry

2 garlic cloves, germ removed (see page 320) and finely chopped

Fine sea salt

¼ cup (60 ml) white wine or dry vermouth

1 pound (454 grams) cleaned squid, cut into ¼- to ½-inch-thick rings and patted dry

One 14½-ounce (411-gram) can crushed tomatoes (see headnote)

1 sprig fresh rosemary

1 sprig fresh thyme

1 cup (240 ml) clam juice (see headnote)

¾ pound (340 grams) long pasta (see headnote)

¾ pound (340 grams) firm fish fillets (see headnote), cut into bite-sized pieces

12 to 16 large shrimp (more if they're small), peeled and deveined

Crushed red pepper flakes

2 tablespoons tomato paste

1 to 2 tablespoons cold unsalted butter

Grated zest and juice of 1 lemon (optional)

Chopped fresh herbs, such as parsley, chives and/or tarragon, for serving (optional)

## WORKING AHEAD

You can get the squid and sauce done a couple of hours or up to a day ahead; refrigerate it if you're keeping for more than 2 hours.

Warm the oil in a large skillet or deep sauté pan over medium-low heat. Add the onion and garlic, season lightly with salt and cook, stirring, until the onion is soft, about 5 minutes. Turn the heat up a little and pour in the wine. Cook, stirring, until it almost evaporates and then stir in the squid. Reduce the heat to low, season the squid lightly with salt and cook, stirring often, for 5 minutes. Add the tomatoes, herb sprigs and clam juice and increase the heat just enough to bring the mixture to a

simmer. Cover the skillet (use a baking sheet if you don't have a lid), turn the heat down low and let the squid cook, stirring only occasionally, for 30 minutes, until it is tender.

Remove the lid and simmer for another 20 minutes or so, again stirring now and then, until the sauce has reduced by about one third. Remove the herb sprigs. (*You can cover the pan and set the sauce aside for up to 2 hours, or refrigerate it overnight; bring to a simmer before continuing.*)

Bring a large pot of generously salted water to a boil. At this point, everything comes together quickly, so be prepared to have the dish on the table in less than 15 minutes. Make sure the sauce is at a simmer and, if you chilled it, that the squid is hot.

Add the pasta to the boiling water and set the timer for al dente.

Drop the fish pieces into the sauce. Then, 4 minutes before the timer is set to ring, add the shrimp and some pepper flakes — go easy, you can add more at the table. Scoop out 1 tablespoon of the pasta water, mix it together with the tomato paste and blend it into the sauce.

When the pasta is cooked, drain it, shaking off as much water as you can. Turn the pasta out into the skillet (if your skillet isn't large enough, turn the pasta out into a large bowl and stir the sauce into it) and stir to coat all the strands. Taste for salt and pepper flakes and add the butter and the lemon zest and juice, if you want some tang. Scatter over the chopped herbs, if using, and serve immediately.

———

STORING: This is a dish to be enjoyed as soon as it's made, but if you're the kind that likes to nibble on cold leftover spaghetti, I won't stop you.

# VEGETABLE GO-ALONGS & GO-ALONES

# MAPLE-SYRUP-AND-MUSTARD BRUSSELS SPROUTS

Makes 4 servings

I don't know when Brussels sprouts became a darling of the dinner table. You find them big and small everywhere now, and even corner greengrocers have pre-shredded sprouts and sprouts that have been separated into leaves. It's good news for all of us who love these mini-cabbages.

As big as Brussels sprouts' flavor is, it's a vegetable that mixes happily with other bold ingredients. For this dish, the sprouts are steamed, then seared, glazed with mustard and maple syrup and finished with bits of bacon. To build in even more flavor, they're steamed with slivers of garlic and shallot.

You can swap the maple syrup for balsamic vinegar, honey or brown sugar, in which case you may or may not want to ditch the mustard (I wouldn't).

1 pound (454 grams) Brussels sprouts, regular or mini, trimmed and, if large, cut in half from top to bottom

Fine sea salt and freshly ground pepper

1 to 2 garlic cloves (to taste), germ removed (see page 320) and cut into slivers

1 shallot, cut into slivers, rinsed and patted dry

6 strips thick-cut bacon

2 tablespoons pure maple syrup, or more to taste

1 tablespoon Dijon mustard (grainy, smooth or a mix, preferably French), or more to taste

1 tablespoon olive oil

Cider vinegar (optional)

**WORKING AHEAD**
You can steam the Brussels sprouts up to 1 day ahead and keep them covered in the refrigerator.

Set up a steamer. Season the Brussels sprouts with salt and pepper and toss them with the garlic and shallot. Steam the sprouts until the tip of a small knife can easily poke into but not completely pierce them, 8 to 10 minutes. (If your Brussels sprouts are large and/or older, they may take a bit more time.) Remove the sprouts (including the garlic and shallots) from the steamer and set them aside; if you are doing this ahead of time, dunk the Brussels sprouts in ice water or run cold water over them to stop the cooking, then pat them dry. (*You can cook the sprouts up to 1 day ahead and keep them refrigerated. Bring to room temperature or warm them by cooking gently before proceeding.*)

While the sprouts are steaming, cook the bacon in a large saucepan or high-sided skillet until crisp. Drain it between a triple thickness of paper towels, then coarsely chop into bite-sized pieces. Set the pan aside.

Mix the maple syrup and mustard together.

Pour off all but about 1 tablespoon of the bacon fat from the skillet and add the olive oil to the pan. Turn the heat to high, and when the oil is shimmering, add the Brussels sprouts. Cook, turning a few times, until the sprouts are charred here and there and crisp-tender. Lower the heat to medium and stir in the maple-mustard mixture. Cook, stirring, until the sprouts are uniformly glazed. Stir in the set-aside bacon, season with salt and pepper, then taste and add more syrup and/or mustard, if needed. If you'd like a touch of acidity, add a splash of vinegar.

Serve immediately.

STORING: Leftovers can be refrigerated and served in a salad the next day.

CHOICES: I often make the sprouts the main event, serving them over mashed sweet potatoes (you might want to double up on the glaze in that case, so the mixture is saucier) or, for something lighter, over a salad tossed with a vinaigrette that's heavy on the vinegar. If you opt for a salad, think about one that includes greens like kale or spinach.

# SWEET AND SMOKY ROASTED CARROTS

Makes 6 servings

¼ cup (60 ml) cider vinegar

1 tablespoon smoked paprika (see headnote)

1½ teaspoons fine sea salt

1¼ teaspoons ground cumin

¼ teaspoon cayenne pepper, or more to taste

3 tablespoons olive oil

2 tablespoons honey

2 pounds (907 grams) carrots, scrubbed, trimmed (see headnote) and patted dry

½ cup (120 ml) plain Greek yogurt

If you love smoked paprika, the odds are high that you'll love these carrots. They're roasted in a hot oven after they've been rolled around in a mix of honey, vinegar, cumin, cayenne and smoked paprika, which I consider a magical ingredient. I use it for its deep, almost sexy flavor and think of its beautiful rusty color as a bonus. However, smoked paprika is only magical if it's fresh. Give yours the once-over before you use it. Look at its color, which should be vibrant, then stir it or shake it and sniff — if it doesn't smell rich and smoky, you'll be disappointed in the dish.

Smoked paprika, which is also known as *pimentón*, can be either mild and sweet or *picante* (hot). I prefer to buy the sweet version and add cayenne or piment d'Espelette (see page 334) when I want some heat, but experiment and see what you like.

The carrots are good hot, at room temperature or cold, making them as right for dinner as for a summer picnic.

## a word on the carrots

If you have fresh carrots with their green tops, cut off the feathery tops but leave an inch or two of the green stems — they add to the dish's simple good looks. Similarly, if their taproots are still attached, trim them so that they, too, are just an inch or so long.

**WORKING AHEAD**
You can make the carrots up to 6 hours ahead and keep them at room temperature; the yogurt sauce can be made and refrigerated up to 2 days in advance.

Center a rack in the oven and preheat it to 425 degrees F. Line a baking sheet with a silicone baking mat or a double layer of parchment paper.

Whisk the cider vinegar, paprika, salt, cumin and cayenne together. When the spices are dissolved, whisk in the oil and honey and taste for cayenne.

Arrange the carrots on the baking sheet, pour over about ⅓ cup of the spice syrup you just made and turn the carrots until they're evenly coated. Set the remaining syrup aside.

Roast the carrots for 20 minutes, then flip them over, rotate the baking sheet and roast for another 20 to 30 minutes, until they are tender and browned — they might be a tad charred here and there and they'll probably be a bit wrinkled, and it's all good. Pull the sheet from the oven.(*The carrots can be made ahead to this point and kept at room temperature for up to 6 hours.*)

Stir a tablespoon of the leftover syrup into the yogurt, taste and add more, if you'd like. (*The yogurt sauce can be covered and refrigerated for up to 2 days.*)

Serve the carrots hot with the yogurt sauce spooned over them or spread under them as a base. Alternatively, cover the sauce and refrigerate it, then serve as a dipping sauce with the room-temperature carrots.

———

STORING: Leftover carrots can be covered and refrigerated for up to 2 days.

## SWEET AND SMOKY MAYO

Blend as much of the spice syrup from the carrots as you like into mayonnaise and use it for coleslaw or potato salad (thin with milk or buttermilk if needed). Or — and this is my favorite — use it when you're making chicken sandwiches.

## SWEET AND SMOKY GREEN SALAD

Think of the spice syrup as a vinaigrette and use it over kale or arugula. If you'd like, add a little more oil to the mix.

# SO-GOOD MISO CORN

Makes 4 servings

Many years ago, on a very cold afternoon in Kyoto, Michael and I warmed ourselves by eating grilled corn on the cob bought from a street vendor. The corn was sweet and salty and comforting and tasted different from any corn I'd ever had at home. I didn't try to figure out what made it so wonderful; I just assumed that, like everything else that we ate on that trip, it was touched by some kind of Japanese culinary wizardry. And then, one afternoon in Connecticut, I made this sautéed corn seasoned with miso, and Michael and I simultaneously declared it reminiscent of that by-now-mythical Kyoto corn. Was miso the secret? I don't know. What I do know is that it's wonderful in this dish.

I add za'atar to the corn. If you don't have it, you can use a mix of dried thyme, oregano, marjoram and, if you'd like, a few sesame seeds. Or, if you want to stay in Japan, sprinkle the corn with some furikake (a dried spice mixture often used to season rice) and swap togarashi (another Japanese blend) for the cayenne.

If you want to turn this into a main course, see page 217 for a version that includes quickly sautéed squid.

1 tablespoon light (white or yellow) miso

3 tablespoons hot water

4 teaspoons olive oil

4 ears corn, husked and kernels cut from the cobs (see opposite)

1 tablespoon unsalted butter

1 teaspoon za'atar (see headnote and page 336)

½ teaspoon fine sea salt

Pinch of cayenne pepper, piment d'Espelette (see page 334) or harissa powder (see page 334)

Snipped fresh chives and/or finely sliced scallions, chopped fresh cilantro and/or shredded fresh basil leaves (optional)

Freshly ground pepper (optional)

### WORKING AHEAD
The corn can be made up to a day ahead and kept covered in the refrigerator. Bring it to room temperature and reheat it with a little water in a skillet until the corn is hot and the water has evaporated. You could do this in the microwave, but the corn will become quite soft.

Mix the miso and water together to smooth and loosen the miso. You're unlikely to be completely successful, but that's fine.

Place a large skillet over high heat and add the olive oil. When the oil is hot, add the corn and cook for a minute, without stirring, then stir and cook for another minute, or until the kernels are charred here and there. Reduce the heat to medium-low, add the butter and miso mixture and cook, stirring and scraping up whatever you can of what's stuck to the pan, until the butter and miso melt and the water evaporates. Turn off the heat, add the za'atar, salt and hot pepper and stir to blend well.

Scrape the corn into a bowl and stir in the chives (and/or scallions and/or herbs), as well as the black pepper, if you're using them. Serve immediately or at room temperature.

## MAIN-COURSE MISO CORN AND SQUID

Cut 1 pound cleaned squid into rings about a scant ½ inch thick; pat dry. (I use bodies for this, but tentacles are fine too; if there are tentacles, cut them into bite-sized morsels.) Pour 1 tablespoon olive oil (in addition to what you need for the corn) into the skillet you'll use for the corn later and place over high heat. Add the squid and cook, turning, for about 30 seconds, until the rings are almost opaque all the way through — they'll finish cooking with the corn. (It's better to undercook than overcook squid.) Transfer the squid to a plate, season with salt and pepper — add a little hot pepper, if you'd like — and set aside. If any bits have stuck to the pan, wipe them out, then make the corn. When the corn is ready, add the squid and toss to reheat and finish cooking. Season as the recipe directs and then, just before serving, stir in some chopped sweet onion and halved cherry tomatoes. If you'd like, toss some mizuna, mustard greens and/or arugula with a bit of olive oil, salt and pepper and line the serving platter with this salad. Give the corn and squid a good squeeze of lime juice, toss once more and serve.

---

### cutting corn from the cob

Although you can use frozen or even canned corn (without sweeteners) for most recipes calling for corn, when it's the season for fresh corn, that's the hands-down best pick. And while it's a bit messy to cut the kernels from the cob, it's always worth the effort.

Husk the corn, pulling away the silk, and then cut off a slice from the bottom so that the cob will stand flat. Now here's the trick—I wish I could remember who taught me this, so that we could all thank him or her, but I don't: Put a small bowl upside down in a larger bowl. Stand the ear of corn up on the platform you've built and, using a chef's or other sturdy knife, and being careful to get a firm grip on the corn, start slicing from top to bottom, getting as close to the cob as possible, so that the kernels are released. At this point you'll realize why this trick is genius—the kernels (at least most of them) land in the larger bowl, not on your counter!

# BUTTER-POACHED CORN WITH EGG NOODLES

Makes 6 servings

4 ears corn, husked

1½ sticks (12 tablespoons; 6 ounces; 170 grams) unsalted butter, cut into chunks

¼ cup (60 ml) water

Fine sea salt

One 12-ounce (340-gram) package medium-width egg noodles

¾ cup (180 ml) crème fraîche or sour cream

About 1 tablespoon freshly squeezed lemon juice

Freshly ground pepper

½ cup (20 grams) snipped fresh chives or finely chopped or sliced other fresh herbs, such as parsley, basil and/or tarragon

**WORKING AHEAD**
You can poach the corn up to a day ahead.

My husband and I were on our way back to New York City, when our flight out of San Francisco was cancelled and we were put on a red-eye. While everyone else was complaining, Michael and I checked our bags and headed into town for dinner. Because it was very early, we were able to score a table at one of SF's beloved restaurants, Rich Table, named for the chefs, Evan and Sarah Rich, although it might just as well describe this dish.

At Rich Table, all of the pastas are homemade, and it was a thinnish egg noodle called *tajarin* that caught our eye. We were also intrigued by what it was served with: corn, pickled chanterelles and crème fraîche. My take on the dish is not as complex as the Riches', but the spirit is there, and the deliciousness too. The corn is butter-poached, as was theirs, but the pasta is store-bought egg noodles (if you make your own, you might want to do what I was told the Riches do: Add an extra egg yolk). Instead of including pickled chanterelles, I added a little lemon juice to the crème fraîche to up the acidity (I've also made this with sour cream and been very happy with it).

If you love this dish as much as I do, you'll be making it as often as I do when fresh local corn is available. Add it to the long list of "Reasons to Love Summer."

Cut the corn kernels off the cobs (see page 217 for a quick how-to).

Put the butter, water and ½ teaspoon salt in a large saucepan set over low heat. When the butter is melted, stir in the corn and cook, stirring now and then, for 5 to 8 minutes, until it is crisp-tender. Keep an eye on the pan — it's important that the butter doesn't boil and separate; the ideal is to see a few simmer-bubbles here and there. Turn the corn out into a bowl. (*You can cook the corn a day ahead and keep it covered in the refrigerator.*)

Bring a large pot of generously salted water to a boil and cook the noodles according to the package directions — you want them to be a little softer than al dente.

While the noodles are cooking, stir the crème fraîche or sour cream together with a little of the lemon juice and season with salt and pepper. Taste and add more juice until you get a cream that's slightly tart.

About 2 minutes before the noodles are ready, put the buttery corn in a skillet large enough to hold it and the noodles and warm over medium heat, stirring all the while, again being careful not to let the butter boil.

Drain the pasta, shaking off as much water as you can, and add it to the skillet. Turn everything around so that the pasta is evenly coated with butter. Taste for salt and pepper — you'll probably want pepper — and remove from the heat.

I like to divide the noodles and corn among individual bowls, top each serving with a couple of tablespoons of the cream and some herbs and let each person mix it up at the table. If you prefer family-style, turn the noodles and corn out into a large bowl, mix with the cream and scatter the herbs over the top.

STORING: Because of all the butter, the leftover pasta is not a great snack. You can reheat it gently, but the texture just won't be the same.

# POTATO TOURTE

Makes 6 main-course or 12 starter servings

A *tourte* is France's answer to our double-crusted pie, and if there were a beauty pageant for tourtes, I'd enter this one and expect it to win. It's gorgeous. And it's gorgeous even if you don't come to it with tourte-making experience — that's the magic of puff pastry baked in a pan. I build the tourte in a fluted tart pan with a removable bottom. You could make this in an all-American pie plate, but it's so beautiful that I think you'll want to serve it freestanding, and the tart pan makes that easy.

This very French tourte is filled with sliced potatoes, onions, garlic and herbs. After it's been baked to a lovely shade of bronze, you pour heavy cream into it, bake it some more and then allow it a short rest, so that the cream can be thoroughly absorbed by the already rich and tasty taters. The result is splendid enough to have you putting your fingers to your lips and kissing them in a gesture you'd have thought only a true French person could carry off.

## a word on timing

As tempting as it is to cut into the tourte as soon as it comes from the oven, don't! It has to sit for half an hour, because the cream needs time to "set," and besides, this is a dish that tastes better tepid. In fact, it's wonderful at room temperature, making it possible to enjoy it at any point in a meal — it can be a starter, a main or a side dish — and a picnic too.

## and a word on the herbs

There is hardly an herb that doesn't go well with potatoes, but I'm particularly fond of parsley, tarragon, dill and chives. And then there are the classics: rosemary and sage. If you're lucky enough to find or grow chervil, snip it into the mix.

Enough ready-to-use puff pastry, preferably all-butter, to make a double-crusted 9-inch pie

½ lemon

About ½ cup (20 grams) chopped fresh herbs (see headnote)

1 large spring onion or 1 bunch scallions, white and light green parts only, chopped

1¾ to 2 pounds (794 to 907 grams) Yukon Gold potatoes

Fine sea salt and freshly ground pepper

2 garlic cloves, germ removed (see page 320) and sliced paper-thin

4 tablespoons (2 ounces; 57 grams) unsalted butter, cut into bits

1 large egg yolk, lightly beaten with 1 teaspoon cold water

1 cup (240 ml) heavy cream

### WORKING AHEAD

The easiest way to construct this pie—and it is a construction project—is to get all of the components ready. Have one circle of puff pastry rolled out and fitted into the tart pan; have the other rolled out and covered in the refrigerator. Have the sliced potatoes rinsed and drying between cloth or paper towels, and the onion or scallions, herbs and lemon zest in a bowl. Slice the garlic and cut the butter into bits, ready to scatter. Then you can just layer the elements and finish the tourte with its top crust. You can wrap the tourte airtight and refrigerate it for up to 6 hours or freeze it for up to 1 month. Defrost it, still wrapped, in the refrigerator and then bake.

Position a rack in the lowest part of the oven and preheat it to 400 degrees F. Butter a 9-inch fluted tart pan with a removable bottom or a 9-inch pie plate. Place it on a baking sheet lined with parchment paper, a silicone mat or foil.

You need 2 sheets of pastry, so if necessary, cut the packet in half. Roll each piece on a lightly floured surface into a circle: Ideally, one circle should be between 11 and 13 inches (the bottom of the tourte) and the other should

be between 11 and 12 inches (the top). Fit the large circle of dough into the pan, pressing it lightly over the bottom of the pan and up the sides; allow the excess dough to hang over the edges. Prick the bottom of the dough all over with a fork, cover and slide the pan into the refrigerator. Slide the top circle onto a baking sheet, cover and chill it as well.

Using a vegetable peeler, remove the zest from the half lemon. If there's white pith on the back of any of the pieces, use a paring knife to remove it. Slice the zest into the thinnest strands you can and then cut the strands crosswise in half. Alternatively, if you have a zester that makes strands (if you make cocktails, you might have this tool), use it, then cut the strands into shorter lengths.

Put the zest in a bowl, add the herbs and onion or scallions and toss with your hands to mix.

Peel the potatoes and, using a mandoline (such as a Benriner) or a knife, cut them into thin slices. The slices should be about 1/16 inch thick — substantial enough to stand up straight when you hold them, but thin enough to be supple. If your potatoes are large, cut them lengthwise in half before you slice them. As you cut the potatoes, toss the slices into a bowl of cold water.

Drain the potatoes and dry them well (I pat them dry between kitchen towels).

Remove the pastry from the fridge. Sprinkle one third of the herb mix over the bottom crust and season

with salt and pepper. Place half of the potato slices over the herbs, spreading them out so that you get a reasonably even layer. Top with half of the garlic slivers and half of the remaining herb mix, then scatter over half of the butter bits and season with salt and pepper. Finish the filling with the rest of the potatoes, garlic, herbs and butter; season with salt and pepper.

Moisten the edge of the crust with cold water and place the top crust over the filling. Gently press the top and bottom overhang together to seal. Using scissors or a knife, cut away the excess dough, leaving 1/2 to 1 inch of overhang. Roll the overhang over on itself until it forms a rim just inside the tart pan's rim. Using a sharp cookie cutter, a metal piping tip or scissors, cut an air vent in the center of the top crust; the vent in the photo was made by cutting an X in the center and folding back the points. (*You can make the tourte to this point and cover and refrigerate it for up to 6 hours or freeze it for up to 1 month.*)

Brush the egg glaze over the crust, taking care not to let it drip down the sides — drips will glue the pastry's layers together and keep them from puffing to their max. Bake the tourte for 45 to 60 minutes, until a small knife or bamboo skewer poked through the center hole meets limited resistance; if at any point the tourte looks as though it's getting too brown (or soon will), cover the top loosely with a foil tent.

Remove the tourte from the oven; leave the oven on. Pour the cream into a microwave-safe container, cover and heat until it's just warm to the touch (or do this in a small pan on the stove).

If you can pour the cream into the tourte through the vent hole, do it. If not, using a sharp paring knife, cut a circle about 6 inches in diameter (use a plate as a guide) in the center of the top crust. Working gingerly, remove the circle, transferring it to a plate with the help of a wide spatula. Very slowly pour the warm cream over the potatoes — give it a chance to seep down through the potatoes before you add much more. If it looks as though the cream will overflow the crust, stop. (It's hard to give

## Playing Around

What doesn't go well with potatoes and cream? If you'd like, you can add finely sliced leeks to the mix; briefly steamed spinach, chard or kale; sautéed mushrooms (raw mushrooms give off too much liquid); cooked bacon bits or cubes of ham or prosciutto; or thin slices of truffles. And if you're lucky enough to have truffles for this, go all the way and serve the tourte with Champagne!

an exact amount here.) Carefully replace the crust circle, if you removed it, pressing it down gently to get a snug fit.

Return the tourte to the oven and bake for another 30 minutes, until the potatoes are tender, keeping the tourte tented if necessary. The cream will bubble and it may come through the vent or the seam where the circle was cut, and that's fine. Transfer the tourte, on the baking sheet, to a rack and let sit for at least 30 minutes before serving.

The tourte can be served warm or at room temperature.

STORING: The tourte is best eaten the day it is made; however, leftovers will keep, covered, for 1 day in the refrigerator. Allow the tourte to come to room temperature and then, if you'd like, reheat it in a 350-degree-F oven for about 15 minutes.

# PAPER-THIN
# ROASTED POTATOES

Makes 6 servings

3 tablespoons olive oil

1 small onion

2 pounds (907 grams) Yukon Gold or Idaho potatoes, peeled

8 sprigs fresh thyme and/or rosemary

Fleur de sel or flake salt, such as Maldon, and freshly ground pepper

About ½ cup (120 ml) crème fraîche, sour cream or plain Greek yogurt, for serving (optional)

Snipped fresh chives or dill (optional)

Somehow this dish manages to be both homey and rather elegant at the same time. Thinly sliced potatoes are interspersed with equally thin slices of onions in overlapping rows on a baking sheet, brushed with oil, strewn with herbs and roasted until their edges brown, crisp and curl upward. Once the potatoes are all in rows, you just wait for them to emerge from the oven, fragrant, tasty and beautiful. I think they're good just as they are, but if you'd like something tart to serve with them, go for crème fraîche, sour cream or yogurt.

## a word on shape

If you prefer, you can make the potato cake as a large round instead of a rectangular one. Start from the center and arrange the potatoes and onions in overlapping concentric circles.

Center a rack in the oven and preheat it to 425 degrees F. Line a baking sheet with parchment paper and, using a pastry brush, brush on a very light coating of the oil.

Both the onion and potatoes should be cut ⅛ inch thick, so if you have a mandoline or other slicer, use it. You can also use the slicing blade of a processor or a good old-fashioned chef's knife and some care. Cut the onion into rounds and set aside. Working with one potato at a time, cut them into rounds. Arrange the potato slices and, here and there, some slices of onion, slightly overlapping them, in rows down the length of the baking sheet. Overlap the rows as well to form a rustic slab. Brush the rows with oil, scatter the herb sprigs over the rows and season with salt and pepper.

Bake for 45 to 50 minutes, until the potatoes are crispy and deeply golden brown around the edges and cooked through at their centers — poke them with the point of a knife to be sure.

Serve hot or still warm, with or without the crème fraîche (or sour cream or yogurt) and snipped chives or dill on top or alongside. You can cut the slab into portions with a pizza wheel or knife or you can slide it onto a cutting board and let everyone pull off pieces. Served that way, it's like having hot potato chips.

STORING: The cake should be enjoyed very soon after it comes out of the oven. It loses its charm as it cools.

# BASTA PASTA
# POTATO SALAD

Makes 6 servings

Basta Pasta is the name of a New York City restaurant that is really Italian, slightly Asian and very happy to be indescribable, kind of like these potatoes. Seasoned with pickles and capers, wasabi, orange and saffron, there's surprise after surprise in this dish. In fact, the potatoes were such a surprise when I first had them that I can't remember what they were served with. Salmon tartare? Or smoked salmon? Or salmon burgers? They'd be good with those (page 174). Hamburger? They'd make a swell match. Grilled tuna? Something leafy and green? That would be nice.

When I put together this recipe, based on the flavors I remembered, I made a big bowl (I doubled this recipe; you can even triple it) and served the potatoes as one of many dishes in a buffet. The potatoes hold up well on the table, and any leftovers are delicious the following day, all of which means that this is a great party dish. Think of it the next time you're grilling. Or even the next time you want something to serve with hard-boiled eggs or a can of sardines.

**WORKING AHEAD**
This dish is best made a day ahead—you want to give all the disparate ingredients a chance to cozy up to one another.

STORING: The salad can be stored in a tightly covered container in the refrigerator for up to 2 days.

1½ pounds (680 grams) small potatoes, such as fingerlings, scrubbed or peeled

Kosher salt

1 orange

Pinch of saffron threads

⅔ cup (160 ml) mayonnaise

⅓ cup (80 grams) finely chopped sweet pickle, plus 2 tablespoons of the pickle juice

1 tablespoon capers, rinsed, patted dry and coarsely chopped if large

2 mini (Persian) cucumbers, peeled and finely diced (or 1 small regular cucumber, peeled, halved lengthwise, seeded and diced)

3 scallions, white and light green parts only, thinly sliced

1 teaspoon wasabi paste, or to taste

Fine sea salt and freshly ground pepper

Put the potatoes in a large pot, cover with cold water, add enough salt to make the water taste salty and bring to a boil. Lower the temperature so that the water's at a strong simmer and cook until the potatoes can be easily pierced with the point of a knife, 15 to 25 minutes, depending on the potatoes and their size; check early and often. Drain in a colander, rinse under cold water and leave the potatoes to dry in the colander.

Finely grate the zest of the orange into a large bowl, and squeeze 2 tablespoons of the juice into a small bowl. Add the saffron to the juice, rubbing it between your fingers as you do, and let it soften in the juice.

Put the mayo, pickle and juice, capers, cucumbers, scallions and wasabi into the bowl with the zest and stir to mix. Cut the potatoes into small chunks and add them to the bowl, along with the orange juice. Stir gently to coat the potatoes. Add sea salt and pepper. Though there are many salty ingredients, I find it still needs a generous bit of salt.

You can serve the dish now, but it's best if covered and refrigerated overnight. If it's cold, taste again for salt.

# MISO-MAPLE-JAMMED SWEET POTATOES

Makes 4 servings

4 medium sweet potatoes or yams (see headnote), scrubbed

2 tablespoons unsalted butter

2 tablespoons light (white or yellow) miso

2 tablespoons maple syrup

1 tablespoon ponzu sauce (see page 334)

Sriracha

Fine sea salt and freshly ground pepper

You could probably just lick this miso-maple jam off a spoon and be happy, but happiness is multiplied many-fold when you spread it generously over steaming-hot sweet potatoes. The jam, a mix of melted butter, miso, maple syrup, Sriracha and ready-made ponzu sauce, is just a touch sweet; mainly it's spicy, salty and, because of the miso, hard to describe, as so many umami-rich foods are. If you like the jam as much as I do, keep some in the fridge to use on roasted carrots or squash, steamed cauliflower or seared salmon, halibut or scallops.

## a word on the potatoes

The jam will be luscious on any type of sweet potato — it's not bad on white potatoes either — but my preference is for Garnet sweet potatoes. You could use Japanese yams — the ones with white flesh — but they're so inherently sweet that they tend to mute the complexity of the jam.

**WORKING AHEAD**
The jam can be made up to 3 days ahead and kept tightly covered in the refrigerator.

Center a rack in the oven and preheat it to 400 degrees F. Line a baking sheet with foil.

Using a paring knife, poke a few holes in each potato. Place the potatoes on the baking sheet and roast for about 1 hour, until they give when prodded or squeezed.

Meanwhile, melt the butter in a small saucepan over low heat. Turn off the heat and gently whisk in the miso until fully incorporated. Whisk in the maple syrup, ponzu, 1/4 teaspoon Sriracha, a big pinch of salt and a few grinds of black pepper. Even though the miso and ponzu are salty, you need more salt to counterbalance the syrup and enliven the jam. Taste and add more Sriracha, salt and/or pepper, if you'd like. (*You can pack the jam airtight and keep it in the refrigerator for up to 3 days.*)

The simplest way to serve this dish is to let everyone split their potatoes and slather on some of the miso jam. Alternatively, line the baking sheet that the potatoes roasted on with clean foil and lightly butter or oil it. Cut the potatoes into chunks and place them flesh side up on the sheet. Press them down with a fork — don't overdo it, you just want to create a few grooves — and spread some jam over each chunk. Return the potatoes to the oven for another 10 minutes.

Pass the rest of the maple-miso jam at the table, so that everyone can have a little more.

STORING: The potatoes are meant to be served as soon as they're roasted. However, if you have leftovers, you can remove them from their skins, mash them with some miso jam and reheat them in a 350-degree-F oven.

# BUTTER-GLAZED TURNIPS

Makes 4 servings

2 tablespoons unsalted butter

¼ cup (60 ml) water

2 teaspoons sugar

About ½ teaspoon fine sea salt, or more to taste

1 pound (454 grams) turnips (purple-top, white or other), peeled and cut into 2-inch cubes

1 teaspoon honey

Freshly ground pepper

I love this technique for cooking and lightly glazing vegetables at the same time. The glazing ingredients — butter and sugar — go into the pan with the cooking water. By the time the water has boiled away, the vegetables are cooked and then the glazing begins automatically. I particularly like this tandem technique for turnips, which have a big personality that can always use a little tamping down and a touch of sweetness, both of which it gets here. Cut the turnips into chunks so that they cook quickly and evenly. When you want something different, use the same process for carrots.

Put the butter, water, sugar and salt in a medium to large skillet over medium heat and bring to a boil, stirring to dissolve the sugar and salt. Drop in the turnips, turn them around in the mixture, cover the pan and cook over medium-low heat until they're almost tender, about 8 minutes, turning them occasionally and checking that there's enough water in the pan to bubble around them; add more if needed. Remove the cover, turn up the heat a tad and finish cooking the turnips (you'll boil away whatever water remains). Don't flip them too often — you want to get a little color here and there.

When the turnips are cooked through but still al dente, drizzle over the honey and stir them for a minute. Taste for salt and pepper and serve.

STORING: It's best to serve the turnips as soon as they're ready, but they're nice at room temperature. If you have leftovers, you can keep them covered in the refrigerator for a day or two and reheat them.

# ROASTED ACORN SQUASH WEDGES

Makes 4 servings

I had always played to squash's sweet side. But in a wild and crazy moment, when I opened the kitchen cabinet and saw pomegranate molasses (a delicious, oddly sour syrup) and za'atar (a seasoning mix based on thyme and oregano) not far away, I grabbed them. The result was wedges of roasted squash, its dense, naturally sweet flesh herb-accented from the za'atar and slightly tart from the molasses. And the skin — my favorite part — had spots of tasty char and, where the oil mixture had puddled, patches of bright flavor.

**WORKING AHEAD**
The squash can be kept at room temperature for about 6 hours.

STORING:  Leftover squash can be refrigerated, covered, for up to 2 days. Bring to room temperature or reheat before serving.

CHOICES:  This squash is great mixed into salads, tossed into pasta or served alongside grilled meat or fish. It's also nice on a bed of bitter greens with a drizzle of olive oil or a dollop of spiced yogurt.

2 medium acorn squash, about 1½ pounds (680 grams) each

¼ cup (60 ml) extra-virgin olive oil

2 tablespoons pomegranate molasses (see page 334)

2 teaspoons za'atar (see page 336)

2 teaspoons freshly squeezed lemon juice, plus (optional) more for serving

1 teaspoon fine sea salt

Pinch of cayenne pepper

Fleur de sel or other coarse sea salt

Harissa Yogurt (page 313), for serving (optional)

Center a rack in the oven and preheat it to 425 degrees F. Line a baking sheet with foil, a double layer of parchment paper or a silicone baking mat.

Scrub the squash well — you're going to want to eat the skin. Cut each one in half from top to bottom, scoop out the seeds and strings (discard the seeds or clean and roast them) and cut each half into 4 wedges. Stand the wedges up on the baking sheet skin side down.

Whisk together the remaining ingredients *except* the fleur de sel and yogurt in a bowl or put them in a jar, cover and shake to blend. Taste and adjust the seasoning, if you'd like, keeping in mind that the sourness of the molasses won't be as pronounced against the roasted squash. Brush some of the flavored oil over the wedges, moistening the flesh and leaving the skin as is.

Roast the wedges for 25 to 35 minutes, until they can be pierced easily with the tip of a paring knife.

(*You can serve the squash now or allow it to cool until it is just warm or reaches room temperature.*)

Sprinkle the squash with fleur de sel and, if you'd like, give each wedge a splash of lemon juice right before serving. The Harissa Yogurt is good with the squash no matter its temperature.

# GRANOLA-TOPPED SQUASH AND ROOT VEGETABLE GRATIN

Makes 4 to 6 servings

During the long winter stretch, when the only color in the green market is citrus, it's a challenge to find new ways to zhoosh up the season's stalwarts, root vegetables and squash. It was then that I first made this gratin. The vegetables in the dish include potato and celery root as well as squash. This triumvirate is cubed, quickly steamed and then roasted with maple syrup and a few spoonfuls of cream. The twist is the topping: homemade granola. You can use store-bought, but homemade (page 323) always wins. And because it's sprinkled over the vegetables and roasted for only 5 minutes, essentially just warmed through, it retains its crunch.

This is a truly simple dish, but not to be overlooked. You'll be happy to serve it alongside anything from an omelet or a salad to a roast or a chicken.

¾ pound (340 grams) russet potatoes, peeled and cut into bite-sized pieces

¾ pound (340 grams) peeled winter squash, such as butternut, cut into bite-sized pieces

¾ pound (340 grams) celery root, trimmed, peeled and cut into bite-sized pieces

Fine sea salt and freshly ground pepper

2 tablespoons maple syrup, honey or hot (spicy) honey

1 tablespoon olive oil

¼ cup (60 ml) heavy cream or vegetable or chicken broth

½ cup (about 65 grams) granola, preferably Not-So-Sweet Granola (page 323)

Hot sauce, for serving (optional)

**WORKING AHEAD**
You can steam the vegetables ahead of time and refrigerate them for up to 1 day; bring them to room temperature before you roast them.

Center a rack in the oven and preheat it to 400 degrees F. Lightly oil or butter a rectangular baking pan that holds at least 2 quarts (such as a 9-by-13-inch Pyrex pan).

Choose a pot that can hold a steamer basket, add some water and salt and bring to a boil. Toss the cubed vegetables together with salt and pepper, transfer them to the basket and set it in place. Cover and steam the vegetables for about 10 minutes, until a knife poked into them meets some resistance — this is just a precooking.

Lift the basket out of the pot, let the vegetables drain and turn them out into the baking pan. (*You can cool, cover and refrigerate the vegetables for up to 1 day. Bring to room temperature before continuing.*) Taste a morsel and decide if the mix needs more salt and pepper — it probably will. Drizzle the maple syrup or honey over the vegetables, followed by the oil and the cream or broth, then give everything a few good turns.

Roast the vegetables for 35 minutes, until they are tender and have some color — no need to do anything, just let them be. Sprinkle the granola over the vegetables and roast for another 5 minutes. Serve immediately, passing hot sauce, if you'd like.

———————

STORING: The gratin is best served soon after it's baked. If you want to reheat it, give it a few minutes in a hot oven.

## Playing Around

The gratin welcomes substitutions—use what you've got; it's meant to be easy. I'm saying ¾ pound of each vegetable, but there's no need to be exact, and the gratin will be tasty even if you use just one vegetable. I often add ⅓ cup shredded cheese, such as Asiago or sharp cheddar, stirring it in after the vegetables have roasted for 10 minutes. However, if your granola includes sweet spices, like cinnamon, you probably shouldn't do that.

# PASTA WITH CABBAGE, WINTER SQUASH AND WALNUTS

Makes 4 servings

½ pound (227 grams) winter squash, such as Delicata, Kabocha, acorn or butternut, scrubbed or peeled, as you like

¼ cup (60 ml) extra-virgin olive oil, or a little more

Fine sea salt and freshly ground pepper

2 tablespoons cider vinegar

1½ teaspoons honey

½ pound (227 grams) linguine or other long pasta

¼ cup (30 grams) dried cranberries

½ pound (227 grams) green cabbage, trimmed, cored and shredded (about 2 lightly packed cups)

¼ cup (30 grams) walnut pieces, toasted, if you'd like

Freshly grated Parmesan, for sprinkling

Some dishes take days of planning and some just pop into your head while you're fretting that there's nothing in the house for dinner. This was such a dish. I'd left planning to well after the last minute, so I had to scramble and make do with whatever I could forage in the fridge. It turned out there were hunks of cabbage and squash and a piece of Parmesan. Since there's always pasta, there was dinner, a scrambler's dinner that turned into a dish worthy of being made "on purpose."

This is a good dish to prep with a mandoline, like a Benriner, or the slicing blade of a food processor, although you can cut the cabbage into shreds by hand and, if you'd like, you can cut the squash into small cubes instead of slicing it. I've given you measurements, but there's no need to be precise — a little more or a little less doesn't matter. As for the pasta, go with what you've got.

The secret to the dish's flavor is the vinegar. Cider vinegar is best, but again, this is a pickup dinner, so pick up what you've got. Just make sure to cook it down so that you get its flavor, not its bite. Oh, and there's another surprise ingredient: dried cranberries — there for tartness, color and chew.

Bring a large pot of generously salted water to a boil.

Meanwhile, cut the squash in half and remove the seeds and strings (discard the seeds or clean and roast). Thinly slice or cut into cubes (see headnote). You'll have about 2 lightly packed cups.

Warm 2 tablespoons of the oil in a large high-sided skillet, preferably nonstick, over medium-high heat. Toss in the squash, season with salt and pepper and cook, stirring, until it is almost tender, about 8 minutes. Stir in 1 tablespoon of the vinegar and cook until it is absorbed by the squash — this is quick. Add the honey and stir to coat, then scrape the squash into a bowl and set aside.

Cook the pasta according to package directions. About a minute before the pasta is ready, toss the dried cranberries into the pot. When the pasta is cooked, scoop out ¼ cup of the cooking water and set aside, then drain the pasta, leaving a little water clinging to the strands.

Return the skillet to medium-high heat, add 1 tablespoon of the remaining oil, toss in the cabbage and season with salt and pepper. Cook, stirring, for a minute or two, then add the remaining 1 tablespoon vinegar and cook, stirring, until it is absorbed. Pour in the reserved

*(Recipe continues on facing page)*

pasta water and cook for a minute, then add the pasta and cranberries and stir it all around. Mix in the squash and the remaining 1 tablespoon oil. Taste for salt and pepper and see if you want to add a bit more oil.

Transfer to a warm bowl or leave the pasta in the skillet to serve, topped with the walnuts and Parmesan.

STORING: The dish is really best served as soon as it's made.

# SUMMER VEGETABLE TIAN

Makes 4 servings

*Tian* is the word for both the pottery casserole in which this dish is cooked and the dish itself. I always think of a tian as having a mélange of tomatoes, onions, zucchini and sometimes eggplant (like ratatouille), but I think that's because I've taken my notion of a tian from Roger Vergé, the late Provençal chef who popularized the slow-roasted dish. My friend, the cookbook author Lucinda Scala Quinn (*Mad Hungry*), summed up the dish perfectly: She said the best ones should have too much oil, enough salt and a long cooking. In other words, if your vegetables melt and border on jam, you've made a good tian.

I'm giving you a range on the oil. Use the lower amount, and you'll have a flavorful tian with just enough "sauce" to keep the vegetables moist; use the higher amount, and you'll have enough oil to use as a dunk for bread.

This way of cooking makes even less-than-wonderful vegetables taste good. Since the eggplant will soak up more juice than it will give off, it's good to bookend it with slices of tomato. It's also nice to put the zucchini and onions together. Use whatever herbs you have and use them abundantly, and don't be afraid of salt, pepper and garlic. If you've got a mandoline (such as a Benriner), use it for the garlic — it's nice to stud the dish with slivers of garlic.

## a word about the baking pan

I use a 9-inch pie plate to make my tian, but you can use any ovenproof casserole of a similar size. If you have a bigger or smaller pan, just multiply or divide the recipe — it's completely flexible.

5 to 9 tablespoons (75 to 135 ml) extra-virgin olive oil

3 garlic cloves, germ removed (see page 320) and thinly sliced (see headnote)

About 10 sprigs fresh herbs, such as parsley, thyme, rosemary, tarragon and/or basil

Fine sea salt and freshly ground pepper

1½ pounds (680 grams) tomatoes

½ pound (227 grams) zucchini, green and/or yellow, scrubbed and trimmed

¼ pound (113 grams) eggplant, washed and trimmed

¼ pound (113 grams) red onion(s)

Good bread, for serving

Center a rack in the oven and preheat it to 400 degrees F. Pour 2 tablespoons of the oil into the baking dish (see headnote), tilting it so the oil coats the sides. Scatter over half of the garlic and a little more than half of the herbs and season generously with salt and pepper.

Slice the vegetables: They should be cut about ¼ inch thick. Ideally they should all be about the same size, so if any are particularly large, you might want to cut them in half the long way before slicing them. This is a nicety, not a necessity.

Arrange the vegetables in the dish in tightly overlapping circles. Try to squeeze the eggplant between slices of tomato and get the zucchini and onions to cuddle up to one another. Keep the circles tight, since the vegetables will soften and shrink in the oven. Season generously with salt and pepper, tuck the remaining slivers of garlic in among the vegetables, top with the remaining herbs and drizzle over as much of the remaining oil (3 to 7 tablespoons) as you'd like. Place the tian on a baking sheet lined with foil, parchment or a silicone baking mat.

Bake the tian for 70 to 90 minutes, until the vegetables are meltingly tender and the juices are bubbling.

*(Recipe continues)*

Serve the tian a few minutes out of the oven or allow it to cool to room temperature. Either way, you'll want bread . . . a lot of it.

———————

STORING: The tian is best the day it is made, but leftovers can be kept covered in the fridge for a day. Pull it out a few hours before serving or, if you'd like, warm it gently in a microwave or a 350-degree-F oven.

CHOICES: You can reheat the tian, but you can also repurpose the vegetables. They make wonderful bruschetta and tartines — top the vegetables with a little ricotta, season and drizzle with oil. They're terrific as a topping for homemade pizza. Chopped, they make a really nice base for a pasta dish — toss the pasta with the vegetables and oil, add some fresh oil and pepper flakes and dinner is done.

# SAVORY BREAD PUDDING

Makes 8 to 10 servings

When you're married to a man who makes two dozen loaves of bread every couple of weeks, as I am, you're wise to have some great stale-bread recipes tucked away, like this bread pudding. In it, onions, slowly cooked in butter until they're deeply sweet and caramelized, take the lead. Don't look for shortcuts. It's time — and butter — that brings out their flavor and makes them distinctive enough to hold their own against the rich custard and cheese that bind the pudding. If you can, do add the Calvados and pancetta — they're little extras that make a difference.

## a word on the bread

Most often, I use a baguette for the pudding, leaving the crust in place and cutting the bread into cubes. However, challah or another egg-rich bread is also a good choice. If all you've got is a sandwich loaf, use it. Finally, while stale bread is best, you can always "stale" it yourself in the oven. In fact, I usually oven-stale even already stale bread, insurance against it falling apart in the pudding.

## and a word on skillet size

The onions are voluminous until they begin to soften. If you can't get all of them into your favorite large skillet with room to turn them around, start with half the onions and then, when they settle down, add the remainder. You'll be cooking the onions for a long time, so the fact that some will have a head start over others won't matter.

4 tablespoons (2 ounces; 57 grams) unsalted butter

2 pounds (908 grams) onions (about 3 large), coarsely chopped, rinsed and patted dry

2 garlic cloves, germ removed (see page 320) and minced, or to taste

1 teaspoon sugar

Leaves from 3 sprigs fresh thyme

1 to 2 tablespoons Calvados, cognac or bourbon (optional)

¼ cup (40 grams) diced pancetta or cooked ham (optional)

Fine sea salt

Freshly ground pepper

½ pound (227 grams) baguette or egg-rich bread (see headnote), preferably stale, cut into 1- to 2-inch cubes

1½ cups (360 ml) whole milk

1½ cups (360 ml) heavy cream

4 large eggs

2 large egg yolks

2 tablespoons snipped fresh chives (optional)

⅓ cup (37 grams) coarsely grated cheese, such as cheddar, Swiss or either of these mixed with Parmesan

**WORKING AHEAD**
You can make the onions up to 3 days ahead and refrigerate them, covered. You can refrigerate the bread-and-custard mixture overnight.

If you need to dry the bread (see headnote), center a rack in the oven and preheat it to 350 degrees F.

Melt the butter in a large skillet, preferably nonstick, over medium heat. Add the onions and garlic, stirring to coat with butter, and cook, stirring, for 5 to 10 minutes, until they soften. Mix in the sugar and thyme, then pour in the alcohol, if you're using it. Cook until it's almost evaporated, then turn the heat to low. Stir in the pancetta, if you're using it (if you've got cooked ham, hold on to it for now), and cook, stirring often, until the onions caramelize and turn the color of maple syrup. This could take about 40 minutes, but it's the color that will determine their flavor, so stay with it. Season the onions with 1 teaspoon salt and some pepper, and if you've got cooked ham, stir it in. Remove from the heat. (*You can prepare the onions up to 3 days ahead and keep them covered in the refrigerator.*)

Meanwhile, if your bread needs drying, spread the cubes out on a baking sheet and stale them for about 10 minutes in the oven; stir them around after 5 minutes. Toss the bread into a large bowl. (Turn off the oven — you won't need it for another hour or so.)

Heat the milk and cream in the microwave or a saucepan until they come almost to a boil.

Whisk the eggs and yolks together and season with salt and pepper. Slowly whisk in the warm milk and cream. Pour the custard over the bread cubes and stir. When the onions are ready, add them to the bread mixture, stirring so that everything is well blended. Cover the bowl and leave the bread to soak and absorb the custard for about 1 hour, poking the bread down now and then. (*If it's more convenient, you can refrigerate the setup for as long as overnight.*)

When you're ready to bake, preheat the oven to 350 degrees F. You can bake the pudding in a 9-inch round or square pan. It will cook in a water bath, so line a roasting pan that will hold it with a double thickness of paper towels (they'll keep the baking pan from jiggling).

Stir the chives, if using, and all but a tablespoon or so of the cheese into the bread mixture, then scrape it into the baking pan. Smooth the top and sprinkle over the remaining cheese. Set the pan in the roaster and fill it with enough hot water to come halfway up the sides of the baking pan.

Bake for 50 to 60 minutes, until the pudding is golden brown (if it's browning too quickly, cover it loosely with a foil tent) and puffed all the way to the center; a knife poked into the pudding should come out clean. Carefully transfer the pudding to a rack and let cool until just warm or at room temperature before serving.

STORING: Once cooled, leftover pudding can be covered tightly and kept in the refrigerator for up to 4 days. Bring it to room temperature before serving or warm it, covered, in a 350-degree-F oven.

CHOICES: Sometimes I serve small pieces of the pudding with a green salad as a starter, but more often I serve it alongside grilled fish or steak, chicken (page 128 or page 131) or the Thanksgiving turkey.

# GINGER FRIED RICE

Makes 6 servings

For all the years that I've been frying rice, I'd never written a recipe for the dish — it was always something I'd make up as I went along. And it was never the same dish twice, because it always depended on what was in the fridge. I love cabbage in fried rice, but if I didn't have it, I'd use spinach or odd salad greens. Carrots are a favorite, but sometimes celery stood in for them. At times there were scallions, peppers and mushrooms, and on good days, bok choy. On the best days, there were shreds of cooked chicken, cubes of leftover pork, diced cooked shrimp or squares of tofu. The fun of corralling all of this into a recipe was coming up with a dish I really liked that I could replicate . . . or not: Once a fridge-raider, always a fridge-raider.

As for the flavoring sauce — if you don't have ponzu, a mix of citrus and soy, use regular soy sauce and, if you'd like, splash the rice with some lemon juice. If you don't have gochujang, use Sriracha or another hot sauce (or skip it). The only thing you don't want to skip is the ginger. Ginger is the liven-upper ingredient you count on here to make the dish taste fresh, bright and not at all like the toss-up of leftovers it really is.

3 tablespoons ponzu sauce (see page 334) or soy sauce

1 teaspoon gochujang (see page 334)

1 teaspoon honey

½ large bok choy, trimmed and sliced crosswise into ½-inch-wide strips, or 4 to 6 baby bok choy, halved or quartered lengthwise

½ Napa (or other) cabbage, trimmed and sliced into ½-inch-wide strips

2 carrots, peeled, halved lengthwise and thinly sliced

1 medium onion, coarsely chopped, rinsed and patted dry

1 to 1½ tablespoons finely chopped peeled fresh ginger (to taste)

1 to 2 garlic cloves, germ removed (see page 320) and finely chopped (to taste)

2 to 3 tablespoons peanut, grapeseed or canola oil (you need an oil with a high smoke point)

Fine sea salt

About 3 cups (about 510 grams) cold cooked rice; break up any clumps

Chopped or diced cooked chicken, pork, shrimp or (uncooked) firm tofu, for add-ins (optional)

Freshly ground pepper

### WORKING AHEAD

You'll need to have leftover rice—cooked rice is best if it's had a little time in the refrigerator, so that it's dry. You can use any kind of rice you've got, white or brown, long- or short-grained.

Mix the ponzu or soy, gochujang and honey together. Do the same with the vegetables, ginger and garlic.

Heat 2 tablespoons of the oil in a wok or a large skillet, preferably one with high sides, over high heat. When the oil is hot, add half of the vegetables and toss until some of the vegetables are charred, about 3 minutes (go by color, not time). This high-heat, high-color step is what gives the dish full flavor. Season with salt, add the rice and keep tossing, turning and stirring. If the rice sticks to the pan — and it probably will — add more oil as needed and/or add water, tiny splashes at a time. When the rice is hot all the way through, stir in the rest of the vegetables and pour over the ponzu mixture. If you've got add-ins, now's the time to stir them in. Cook to get everything really hot, then taste for salt and pepper and serve immediately.

STORING: Fried rice is best the instant it's made, but it takes well to reheating. You can sprinkle water over it, cover it and reheat it in a microwave, but the best method is to refry it briefly in a little oil over high heat. Cooled and covered, leftovers will keep for about 3 days in the refrigerator.

# SOY-SAUCE EGGS AND STICKY RICE

Makes 3 to 6 servings

There is so much to love about this dish, including how I came to make it. I first heard about it during a chance meeting at the market with a Korean woman who introduced herself as Nicole. She told me that even though she lives in exurban Connecticut, she continues to cook traditional Korean foods for her family. We'd only spoken for a few minutes before she asked if I'd ever made soy sauce eggs. I hadn't, so she proceeded to tell me the recipe: Put egg yolks in a bowl with soy sauce, cover and refrigerate overnight. When you're ready to serve, cook sticky rice, mix the rice with butter and a little sesame oil and top with some of the egg yolks. "You'll want it every day," she said, and she was right. Then she gave me a last tip: If you know kids who are picky eaters, make them this. Children love it!

Never having heard of soy-sauce eggs, I was delighted to find a story about them in the *New York Times* just two days later. The *Times* story was titled "Drinking Food," and the dish, made by a Japanese bar owner, was served with plenty of sake and beer.

It's an all-things-to-all-people dish! And, yes, young picky eaters with a bent for Asian flavors do, indeed, love this, as do grown-ups with a thirst for sake and beer.

## a word about serving size

It would be easy to eat several eggs at a sitting — the umami factor here is high — but it wouldn't be wise; in its own simple way, the dish is rich. I like to serve a small bowl of rice with one egg yolk as an appetizer or a slightly bigger portion of rice with a couple of yolks if I'm also serving a salad. If you're serving this as "drinking food," I leave it to you to decide how much each drinker needs.

### For the eggs

½ cup (120 ml) soy sauce

1 tablespoon mirin (optional)

6 impeccably fresh egg yolks, preferably organic local eggs (size doesn't matter)

### For the rice

1½ cups (270 grams) short-grain sushi rice or other sticky rice

3 cups (720 ml) water

½ teaspoon fine sea salt

1 to 3 tablespoons unsalted butter (to taste)

Asian sesame oil

**WORKING AHEAD**
Start the egg yolks at least 5 hours and up to 1 day ahead.

TO MAKE THE EGGS: At least 5 hours ahead, pour the soy sauce and mirin, if you're using it, into a small deep bowl or a Pyrex measuring cup. Add the yolks, cover tightly and refrigerate. Don't "baste" the eggs during this time; they'll pickle nicely bobbing in the soy. (*The yolks can be refrigerated for up to 1 day.*)

TO MAKE THE RICE: Put the rice in a strainer or colander and run cold water over it until the water runs clear, a minute or so. Stir the rice, water and the salt together in a medium saucepan and bring to a boil, then stir, cover the pan, reduce the heat to low and cook until the water is absorbed and the rice is tender, usually 14 to 18 minutes (although it can take longer). Remove the pan from the heat.

To serve, spoon the rice into bowls and stir in as much butter as you'd like. (I find the eggs and rice fairly rich and so only gloss the top of the rice, but many people like a real pat of butter.) Sprinkle the rice sparingly with sesame oil. Spoon an egg yolk or two into each bowl, followed by as much of the soy sauce as you'd like.

You can eat this with a spoon, but I think chopsticks

are best. Poke the yolk with a chopstick, stir to mix everything lightly and enjoy.

STORING: You can keep the soy-sauce eggs in the refrigerator for longer than a day, but they'll get firmer. For me, part of the lusciousness of the dish is the unctuousness of the yolk, which is lost after a day.

## Playing Around

There are no laws that say that you can't build on the dish. I like to add sliced scallions, chopped fresh cilantro, finely chopped toasted peanuts and/or slivers of dried seaweed. A sprinkling of furikake (see page 333) is also nice.

# DESSERTS

# CHEWY CHOCOLATE CHIP COOKIES

Makes about 35 cookies

I can't imagine a time when I won't be creating new chocolate chip cookies. This latest addition to my collection is chewy and a bit crunchy on the edges. That it's got oatmeal is almost a secret — there's not much, it's not really visible and until the cookie's a day old, its taste is in the background — but it's part of what makes the chewiness so winning.

I've kept the sugar to a minimum — less sugar means more chocolate flavor. If you want to increase it, though, I've given you options, but I'd suggest that you make a choice: Increase either the granulated or the brown sugar — don't up both of them at the same time. The one absolute in this cookie is the chocolate: Use good chocolate and chop it yourself. Chips will work, but they won't give you great flavor, they won't melt into the cookie the way chopped chocolate does and they won't give you the tweedy look that you get when you chop chocolate and then include the "dust."

## a word on chubbiness

If you bake these cookies straight from the mixing bowl, they'll spread. If you chill or freeze the dough, they'll be chubbier. They're very good both ways.

1⅔ cups (227 grams) all-purpose flour

1 cup (80 grams) rolled oats (not instant)

½ teaspoon baking soda

¾ to 1 cup (150 to 200 grams) sugar (see headnote)

½ to ¾ cup (100 to 150 grams) packed light brown sugar (see headnote)

1 teaspoon fleur de sel or ¾ teaspoon fine sea salt

½ teaspoon ground cinnamon (optional)

2 large eggs, at room temperature

1½ teaspoons pure vanilla extract

1¾ sticks (14 tablespoons; 7 ounces; 198 grams) unsalted butter, melted and still warm

¾ pound (340 grams) semisweet or bittersweet chocolate, chopped into irregular bits

**WORKING AHEAD**
The dough can be made ahead and kept covered in the refrigerator for up to 5 days or frozen for up to 2 months. If you'd like, freeze scoops of dough and then bake directly from the freezer, adding a couple of minutes to the baking time.

Position the racks to divide the oven into thirds and preheat it to 375 degrees F. Line two baking sheets with parchment paper or silicone baking mats.

Whisk together the flour, oats and baking soda.

Working in a large bowl with a flexible spatula, stir together both sugars, the salt and cinnamon, if you're using it. Drop in the eggs one at a time and beat with the spatula to blend, then stir in the vanilla. Pour in the melted butter — do this in two or three additions — and stir until you have a smooth, shiny mixture. Add the flour and oats all at once and stir gently until they're almost incorporated. Add the chocolate bits and stir until the dry ingredients are fully blended into the dough. (*You can wrap the dough and refrigerate it for up to 5 days or freeze it for up to 2 months.*)

Portion out the dough using a medium cookie scoop (one with a capacity of 1½ tablespoons), or use rounded tablespoons of dough, and place about 2 inches apart on the sheets — these are spreaders.

Bake for 10 to 12 minutes, rotating the sheets from front to back and top to bottom, until the cookies are golden and somewhat firm around the edges but still soft in the center — they'll set as they cool. Let the cookies rest on the baking sheets for about 3 minutes before carefully transferring them to racks to cool to just warm or room temperature.

Repeat with the remaining dough, always using a cool baking sheet.

STORING: The cookies can be kept at room temperature for about 5 days or frozen for up to 2 months.

# CHOCOLATE-COVERED CHAI-TEA BARS

Makes 16 bars

The warm flavors of chai tea, at once exotic and familiar, are the perfect base for these slim bars. There's no standard for which spices are included in chai or in what proportions, but you usually look forward to pepper, cardamom, cloves, cinnamon and ginger. I mix the chai with melted butter to distribute its linchpin flavors evenly throughout the dough, and I add extra ginger and cinnamon as well as honey, which you'd want with your chai, and orange zest, which is so right with the tea. The bars can be left plain — they've got enough flavor to stand happily on their own — or slicked with a little melted milk chocolate. I always go for the chocolate.

1 cup (100 grams) almond flour

⅓ cup (45 grams) all-purpose flour

¼ cup (50 grams) sugar

¼ teaspoon ground ginger

¼ teaspoon ground cinnamon

¼ teaspoon fine sea salt

Finely grated zest of 2 clementines, 1 tangerine or 1 orange

3 large egg whites, at room temperature, lightly beaten with a fork

1 tablespoon honey

1 teaspoon pure vanilla extract

1 tablespoon chai tea (from 3 teabags)

1 stick (8 tablespoons; 4 ounces; 113 grams) unsalted butter, melted and still warm

3 ounces (85 grams) milk chocolate, for the glaze (optional)

## WORKING AHEAD

You can wrap the unglazed cake (or bars) in plastic wrap and keep it at room temperature for up to 4 days or freeze it for up to 2 months.

Center a rack in the oven and preheat it to 350 degrees F. Butter an 8-inch square baking pan and line the bottom with parchment paper.

Put both flours, the sugar, ginger, cinnamon and salt in a large bowl and whisk (or stir with a fork) to blend and work out any clumps of almond flour. Stir in the zest. Pour the whites over the dry ingredients and mix them in with a flexible spatula. It takes a minute or so to blend in the whites; when they're in, you'll have a thick batter. Stir in the honey and vanilla. Stir the tea into the warm melted butter and pour the butter over the batter. Working patiently (you'll think there's too much butter, but there isn't), stir and fold the batter until the butter is fully incorporated. You'll have a beautiful, smooth batter with a silky sheen. Scrape it into the pan — it will be a thin layer — and use the spatula to even the top.

*(Recipe continues)*

Bake for 25 to 27 minutes, until the cake is a deep golden brown and just starting to pull away from the sides of the pan. Poke the top, and it will feel firm and just a bit springy; a tester inserted into the center of the cake will come out clean. Transfer the pan to a rack and wait for 3 minutes, then run a table knife between the cake and the sides of the pan. Invert the cake onto the rack, peel away the paper, invert onto another rack and allow to cool to room temperature.

If you'd like to glaze the bars, melt the chocolate in a heatproof bowl over barely simmering water or in the microwave. However you do it, melt it slowly and carefully — milk chocolate has an unpleasant way of going from smooth to grainy and then burnt; baby it. Pour the chocolate over the top of the cake and spread it evenly over the surface. Slide the glazed cake, on the rack, into the refrigerator for about 30 minutes to set the chocolate.

Cut the cake into 16 bars or, if you're not using the entire cake, into only as many bars as you need; the rest of the cake will keep better if it's in a larger piece. If the cake was glazed and refrigerated and the bars are still cold, let them sit until they come to room temperature.

———

STORING: Kept in a covered container, glazed bars will hold for about 2 days at room temperature; unglazed bars will be good for up to 4 days. Glazed or not, the bars can be wrapped airtight and frozen for up to 2 months. It's easiest to put the glazed bars in the freezer uncovered and then wrap them when they're frozen.

# LAST-OF-THE-BUNCH BANANA BUNDT

Makes 12 servings

'Twas the night before a cross-country flight and all through the kitchen I was picking up leftovers and deciding what I should toss, when my husband, spying mottle-skinned bananas, said, "You could make a banana cake to take on the plane." Yeah, I could, but we'd set the alarm for 3:30 a.m. and I had bed, not baking, in mind. Still, I turned on the oven, pulled out the last of the eggs, measured the flour and set to work, realizing that this cake was also a good opportunity to finish up the yogurt and the half cup of coconut that was in the cupboard.

In case you're wondering, this clear-the-fridge cake was great on the plane and for days after.

## a word on the butter and coconut oil

You can make this cake with all butter, if you'd like, but given that the cake has coconut in it, and that bananas and coconut are such a good combo, I think it's nice to use some coconut oil too.

## and a word on icing

Icing a Bundt cake takes an everyday cake to a party. Ice the cake if you don't expect to be keeping it for long. If you'd like a more generous coating of icing, increase the amount of confectioners' sugar and add as much additional milk as needed to get the right texture.

### For the cake

3 cups (408 grams) all-purpose flour

2 teaspoons baking soda

½ teaspoon freshly grated nutmeg

1 stick (8 tablespoons; 4 ounces; 113 grams) unsalted butter, cut into chunks, at room temperature

½ cup (113 grams) coconut oil, at room temperature, or another stick (113 grams) butter

1 cup (200 grams) sugar

1 cup (200 grams) packed light brown sugar

½ teaspoon fine sea salt

2 large eggs, at room temperature

1 tablespoon dark rum (optional)

1 tablespoon pure vanilla extract

3 to 4 ripe bananas, mashed to a puree (about 1¾ cups; 360 ml)

1 cup (240 ml) plain yogurt (Greek or regular)

3 ounces (84 grams) chocolate (milk, semisweet or bittersweet), finely chopped

½ cup (60 grams) sweetened flake coconut

### For the icing (optional)

¾ cup (90 grams) confectioners' sugar

1 to 1½ tablespoons milk

Sweetened flake coconut, toasted, for sprinkling (optional)

**WORKING AHEAD**

I think the taste and texture of this cake are better after an overnight rest.

TO MAKE THE CAKE: Center a rack in the oven and preheat it to 350 degrees F. Generously butter a Bundt pan, dust with flour and tap out the excess (or coat with baker's spray). Do this even if your pan is nonstick.

Whisk together the flour, baking soda and nutmeg.

Working in a stand mixer fitted with a paddle attachment, or in a large bowl with a hand mixer, beat the butter, coconut oil, if you're using it, both sugars and the

salt together at medium speed for 3 minutes, or until well blended, scraping down the bowl as needed. Add the eggs one by one, beating for 1 minute after each egg goes in, then beat in the rum, if you're using it, and the vanilla extract. With the mixer on low, beat in the mashed bananas; don't worry about how curdled the batter looks.

Still working on low, add half of the flour mixture. When it's almost incorporated, beat in all of the yogurt, and when that is almost in, add the rest of the flour and mix until blended. Switch to a flexible spatula, scrape down the bowl and mix in the chocolate and coconut.

Spoon the batter into the pan, smoothing the top and swiveling the pan from side to side to even the batter and get it into all of the pan's curves.

Bake for 65 to 75 minutes, until the top is brown and the sides of the cake pull away from the pan when gently nudged; a skewer inserted into the center of the cake will come out clean. Transfer the cake to a rack and let it rest for about 5 minutes, then unmold it onto the rack. Let cool to room temperature. If you have patience, wrap the cake once it cools and let it "ripen" overnight.

TO ICE THE CAKE (OPTIONAL): Put the confectioners' sugar in a small bowl and stir in 1 tablespoon milk. Add more milk if necessary, a drop at a time, stirring until you have an icing that falls easily from the tip of the spoon.

Drizzle the icing over the cake and sprinkle over some toasted coconut, if desired. Let the cake sit for at least 20 minutes, or until the icing is set, before you serve or store the cake.

___

STORING: Covered, the cake will keep for up to 5 days at room temperature. Without the icing, it can be wrapped airtight and frozen for up to 2 months.

# BLUEBERRY-BUTTERMILK BUNDT CAKE

Makes 12 servings

Whenever I make this cake — which is just about weekly during blueberry season — I read over the ingredients and think, maybe I should jazz them up with spice or nuts or different kinds of berries. And then I come to my senses and follow the recipe, keeping it simple and adding nothing but the standards — vanilla, citrus zest and salt — to bolster the berries' flavor, not change it in any way.

The oil in the batter makes the cake moist and the texture resilient; the buttermilk makes it tender. Since there's not much in the way of flavoring, be sure your berries are plump, juicy and sweet. They may only speckle this big cake, but they're its true stars.

2 cups (272 grams) plus 1 tablespoon all-purpose flour

1¼ teaspoons baking powder

¼ teaspoon baking soda

1 pint (340 grams) blueberries

1¼ cups (250 grams) sugar

1 lemon or lime (you'll use just the zest)

1 stick (8 tablespoons; 4 ounces; 113 grams) unsalted butter, cut into chunks, at room temperature

¼ teaspoon fine sea salt

3 large eggs, at room temperature

1½ teaspoons pure vanilla extract

½ cup (120 ml) neutral oil, such as canola

½ cup (120 ml) buttermilk (well shaken before measuring), at room temperature

Confectioners' sugar, for dusting (optional)

**WORKING AHEAD**
The cake's flavor improves after an overnight rest.

Center a rack in the oven and preheat it to 350 degrees F. Generously butter a Bundt pan, dust with flour and tap out the excess. Or coat with baker's spray and then dust with flour — this cake can be a sticker. Do this even if your pan is nonstick.

Whisk together 2 cups of the flour, the baking powder and baking soda.

Toss the remaining 1 tablespoon flour with the blueberries (this will help keep the berries from sinking to the bottom of the cake).

Put the sugar in the bowl of a stand mixer, or in a large bowl if you're using a hand mixer. Grate the zest of the lemon or lime over the sugar and, with your fingertips, rub them together until the sugar is moist and fragrant. If you're using a stand mixer, attach the bowl and fit it with the paddle attachment.

Add the butter and salt to the sugar and beat on medium speed until well blended, about 3 minutes. Reduce the speed to low and add the eggs one by one, beating for a minute after each egg goes in. Beat in the vanilla extract, then the oil. You'll have a glossy mixture with the creamy smoothness of mayonnaise. On low speed, beat in the buttermilk. Turn the mixer off, add the flour mixture all at once, then pulse the mixer just to begin the blending. Beat on low speed only until the dry ingredients disappear and the batter is smooth. Using a flexible spatula, fold in the berries.

Spoon the batter into the pan, smoothing the top and swiveling the pan from side to side to even the batter and get it into all the curves.

Bake for 55 to 60 minutes, until the top is brown and the sides of the cake pull away from the pan when gently nudged; a skewer inserted into the center of the cake will come out clean. Transfer the cake to a rack and let it rest for 15 minutes, then unmold it onto the rack. Be gentle with the cake — it's delicate. Cool completely before dusting with confectioners' sugar, if using, and serving.

———

STORING:  Covered, the cake will keep for up to 4 days at room temperature. It can be wrapped airtight and frozen for up to 2 months.

# BROWN SUGAR–SPICE CAKE

Makes 10 servings

1 cup (136 grams) all-purpose flour

¼ cup (38 grams) yellow cornmeal

1 teaspoon baking powder

½ teaspoon ground ginger

¼ teaspoon ground cardamom

¼ teaspoon ground cinnamon

¼ teaspoon ground coriander

3 large eggs, at room temperature

¾ cup (150 grams) packed light brown sugar

¼ teaspoon fine sea salt

2 teaspoons pure vanilla extract

½ cup (120 ml) neutral oil, such as canola

9 to 11 Italian plums, preferably small, halved and pitted

¼ cup (60 ml) honey, for the glaze

Lightly whipped cream, sweetened or not, for serving (optional)

If there were a kind of cake called "snackable," this would be it. It's a cake you enjoy when it's served to you on a plate, with or without whipped cream, and then you go back into the kitchen and polish it off, one thin slice at a time. The combination of brown sugar, warm spices, cornmeal and plums marks it for fall, but its tender crumb and appealing fragrance can stretch into spring. You can keep the spices and swap the plums for apples or pears in late fall through winter and then, when spring is just beginning to show its colors, you can top the cake with rhubarb and strawberries. For those two fruits, I'd omit all the spices except the ginger.

Center a rack in the oven and preheat it to 350 degrees F. Generously butter a 9-inch round cake pan with 2-inch-high sides (use a springform if you don't have a tall regular cake pan), dust with flour and tap out the excess. Line a baking sheet with parchment paper or a silicone baking mat.

Whisk the flour, cornmeal, baking powder and spices together.

Whisk the eggs, brown sugar and salt together in a large bowl until the sugar dissolves and the mixture is smooth. Whisk in the vanilla. Pour in the oil and whisk until the batter is shiny and homogeneous. Add the dry ingredients all at once and stir with the whisk until thoroughly blended.

Pour the batter into the pan. Arrange the plums cut side down over the batter in whatever pattern you like and place the pan on the baking sheet.

Bake the cake for 23 to 26 minutes, until it's golden brown, slightly springy to the touch and just starting to pull away from the sides of the pan; a skewer inserted into the center of the cake should come out clean. Transfer the cake to the rack and cool for 5 minutes, then run a table knife around the sides of the pan, very carefully unmold the cake onto a rack and invert it onto another rack so that it is plum side up. Or, if you used a springform, simply remove the sides of the pan.

Put the lined baking sheet under the rack with the cake and have a pastry brush at hand. Place a skillet over medium-high heat, pour in the honey and boil for 1 minute, just until it colors lightly. Carefully pour the honey over the hot cake, using the pastry brush to gently spread it over the surface — a light touch is important here, because the cake is tender.

Allow the cake to rest until it is only just warm or reaches room temperature before serving, with whipped cream, if you'd like.

STORING: Once cooled, the cake can be covered and kept at room temperature for up to 2 days.

# CARAMEL-PEAR AND FIVE-SPICE UPSIDE-DOWN CAKE

Makes 10 servings

When I was a kid, upside-down cakes came one way: topped with canned pineapple rings and maraschino cherries the color of a clown's nose. I didn't like them as a child, and I didn't make them as a baker . . . at least not with pineapple. My current favorite upside-downer is this one, where the fruit is fresh pears and the batter is flavored with lemon, ginger and Chinese five-spice powder, a blend that swings savory and sweet (you can substitute cinnamon if you prefer).

The cake is a beacon of warmth and welcome. Who wouldn't want to come home to a slice of cake, its top the color of mahogany, its fruit translucent and candied and its texture between the spring of a sponge cake and the sturdiness of a farmstead loaf cake? And I haven't even mentioned that the batter is whirred in a food processor, so it comes together in seconds, not minutes.

The minutes, about ten of them, are reserved for the caramel. Because this caramel starts with sugar and water, not just sugar, it's a great one if you're a novice or a nervous carameler. Adding the water slows down the whole process and gives you plenty of time to judge the color. (Keep a white plate nearby so that you can drop a little caramel on it — it's easier to see the color on a plate than it is in a dark skillet.) The squirt of lemon juice flavors the caramel and, more important, keeps the sugar from hardening too quickly. And — this is the best trick! — preheating the cake pan makes it simple to swish the caramel over its bottom and up its sides.

## For the caramel

1 lemon

¾ cup (150 grams) sugar

⅓ cup (80 ml) water

## For the cake

2 firm, not very ripe pears, any variety

1¼ cups (170 grams) all-purpose flour

¼ cup (25 grams) almond flour or 3 tablespoons (25 grams) additional all-purpose flour

2 teaspoons baking powder

1 teaspoon Chinese five-spice powder (or ground cinnamon)

½ teaspoon ground ginger

¼ teaspoon baking soda

¼ teaspoon fine sea salt

¾ cup (150 grams) sugar

¼ cup plus 2 tablespoons (90 ml) neutral oil, such as canola

3 large eggs

2 tablespoons plain yogurt or sour cream

2 teaspoons pure vanilla extract

Center a rack in the oven and preheat it to 375 degrees F. Place a 9-inch round cake pan with 2-inch-high sides (if you've got a nonstick pan, use it) on a baking sheet lined with parchment paper or a silicone baking mat. When you start to make the caramel, put the empty pan, on the sheet, in the oven.

TO MAKE THE CARAMEL: Grate the zest of the lemon and set it aside. Cut the lemon in half; set one half aside for the cake and the other for the caramel. Have a white plate at the side of the range as well as a bowl of water and a pastry brush (preferably silicone), which you'll use to brush down the sides of the skillet.

Put the sugar in a medium skillet (nonstick is good here), pour over the water to moisten the sugar and place the skillet over medium-high heat — caramel does

best over real heat, so don't wimp out. And don't leave the stove — things move quickly with caramel! As the water boils away and the sugar dissolves, there may be spatters on the sides of the skillet — brush these down with water. The bubbles in the pan will get bigger and slower and the sugar will start to color. Don't stir; instead, swirl the pan gently to even out the color, and when the color is amber — you may see a few wisps of smoke — remove the pan from the heat, stand away and squeeze in the juice from the lemon half. If it looks as though you've got a few lumps, put the pan back over the heat for a few seconds.

Remove the cake pan from the oven and pour in the caramel. Grab the pan with pot holders and swirl it so that the caramel covers the bottom and sides. The bottom will grab the lion's share of the caramel, but try to get a slick on the sides. Return the pan to the baking sheet and set aside.

TO MAKE THE CAKE: Peel the pears, cut them in half the long way and remove the cores. Cut the halves into long slices about a scant ½ inch thick. Arrange them on top of the caramel in a single layer, making whatever pattern pleases you.

Put all the dry ingredients in a food processor and pulse a couple of times to blend. Add the rest of the ingredients, squeeze in the juice from the remaining lemon half and toss in the zest. Pulse, scraping down the sides and bottom of the bowl, until you have a smooth batter. Don't overdo it — it will take fewer than 10 pulses to blend the ingredients. Pour the batter over the fruit and swivel the pan to level it. You'll have a thin layer of batter.

Bake the cake for 35 to 38 minutes, until it's a deep golden brown. Pull an edge of the cake gently, and it will release from the pan; a tester inserted into the center of the cake will come out clean. Transfer the cake to a rack and let rest for 5 minutes, then run a table knife around the sides of the cake. Invert the pan onto a serving plate and lift off the pan. If any fruit has stuck to the pan, use a spatula to carefully return it to the cake.

Let the cake cool until it is just warm or reaches room temperature before cutting and serving.

———

STORING: The cake is best served the day it is made, but leftovers will keep for another day at room temperature. Press a piece of plastic wrap against the cut edges and cover the cake with a cake keeper or a big bowl.

# MOLASSES
# COFFEE CAKE

Makes 8 to 10 servings

There's no reason not to have this cake year-round, but there are many reasons to have it all through the fall, the holiday months and into late winter, when soft spice cakes seem as cozy as fuzzy slippers. The cake reminds me of gingerbread, but its texture is lighter and its flavor more complex. The spices, a mix of ginger and cinnamon along with Chinese five-spice powder, a blend that brings depth to the cake as well as a spot of mystery: They're not easy to place. But it's the coffee that will surprise you. You add it when it's hot, so it thins and smooths the batter, and you think that it might be the cake's strongest flavor, but it plays hard to catch. In the end, it's the ease with which the ingredients coalesce that makes the cake so good. You don't have to glaze it — it's fine plain and so good plain with a scoop of vanilla, chocolate or coffee ice cream — but the glaze, a mixture of white chocolate, cream and coffee, is a beautiful finish. Glaze it, put it on a pretty plate and you've got a party cake. That the cake, baked and prettily glazed, can be kept in the freezer for a couple of months, waiting for a birthday or Thanksgiving, puts it at the top of my bake-often list.

## a word on the glaze

The recipe for the glaze makes about 1 cup, which is more than you'll need for the cake. However, making less is fussy and not always successful. You can store the excess glaze in the refrigerator and warm it very gently in a microwave when you want to use it again — it makes a good dip for cookies, it's fun over ice cream and it's nice to pass at the table with the cake.

### For the cake

1½ cups (204 grams) all-purpose flour

1 teaspoon baking powder

½ teaspoon baking soda

½ teaspoon fine sea salt

1 teaspoon ground ginger

1 teaspoon Chinese five-spice powder

½ teaspoon ground cinnamon

¼ teaspoon freshly ground pepper

1 stick (8 tablespoons; 4 ounces; 113 grams) unsalted butter, at room temperature

⅔ cup (132 grams) packed brown sugar

⅓ cup (80 ml) unsulfured molasses

1 large egg, at room temperature

1 teaspoon pure vanilla extract

⅓ cup (80 ml) hot coffee or espresso (can be made with instant coffee or espresso powder)

### For the coffee glaze (optional)

1½ teaspoons instant espresso powder, plus (optional) more for decoration

1 tablespoon boiling water

5 ounces (142 grams) best-quality white chocolate, finely chopped

⅓ cup (80 ml) heavy cream

2 teaspoons unsalted butter, cut into 2 pieces, at room temperature

Whipped cream, for topping

**WORKING AHEAD**
This cake is even better on the second day—the spices have more time to ripen.

TO MAKE THE CAKE: Center a rack in the oven and preheat it to 350 degrees F. Butter a 9-inch round cake pan that's at least 2 inches high (use a springform if you don't have a regular cake pan that's tall enough), fit a round of parchment paper into the bottom of the pan, butter the paper and dust the interior with flour; tap out the excess.

Whisk together the flour, baking powder and soda, salt, ginger, five-spice powder, cinnamon and pepper.

Working in a stand mixer fitted with a paddle attachment, or in a large bowl with a hand mixer, beat the butter and brown sugar together on medium speed for about 2 minutes. Add the molasses and beat for 2 minutes more, scraping the bowl as needed. Add the egg and beat for 2 minutes, then beat in the vanilla. Turn the mixer off, add the flour mixture and pulse to begin incorporating it. Then beat on low speed only until the dry ingredients disappear into the batter. With the mixer on low, add the hot coffee, again mixing only until it is incorporated. Scrape the batter into the pan and swivel the pan to even it.

Bake for 28 to 33 minutes, until the cake is beautifully browned and has risen uniformly. It will pull away from the sides of the pan if gently tugged and a tester inserted into the center of the cake will come out clean. Transfer the pan to a rack and let the cake rest for 5 minutes, then run a blunt knife around the sides of the cake. Turn the cake out onto the rack, gently peel off the parchment, invert onto another rack and cool to room temperature; or, if you used a springform, simply remove the ring. The cake may develop a little dip in the center — that's its personality.

TO MAKE THE OPTIONAL GLAZE: Dissolve the instant espresso in the boiling water. Put the chopped chocolate in a small heatproof bowl.

Bring the cream to a boil (you can do this in a microwave oven), stir in the espresso extract that you made and pour the cream over the chocolate. Let sit for 30 seconds and then, using a whisk or small heatproof spatula, stir until the mixture is smooth. Add the butter one piece at a time, stirring until it is melted and incorporated.

Set the cake, on the rack, on a piece of foil to catch drips. Pour as much of the glaze as you want over the cake and use a long spatula or a table knife to spread it. I like it when the glaze drips down the sides of the cake unevenly; if you want to smooth it, you can, of course. Sprinkle with a little instant espresso powder to decorate, if you'd like.

Put the cake in the refrigerator for about 20 minutes to set the glaze, then return it to room temperature for serving. Pass any remaining glaze at the table.

———

STORING: Wrapped well, the cake can keep at room temperature for up to 3 days. Wrapped airtight, it can be frozen for up to 2 months, glaze and all.

# CORNMEAL-BUTTERMILK LOAF CAKE, WITH OR WITHOUT BERRIES

Makes 8 servings

1¼ cups (170 grams) all-purpose flour

½ cup (76 grams) yellow cornmeal

1 teaspoon baking powder

¼ teaspoon baking soda

¼ teaspoon fine sea salt

2 large eggs, at room temperature

1 cup (200 grams) sugar

2 teaspoons pure vanilla extract

½ cup (120 ml) buttermilk (well shaken before measuring), at room temperature

1 stick (8 tablespoons; 4 ounces; 113 grams) unsalted butter, melted and cooled

About 1 cup (240 ml) blueberries or raspberries (optional)

When you bake as much as I do, which is just about daily, it's hard to have favorites, and harder to bake those favorites often. But I always find time for this cake. It's one of the simplest, plainest cakes I make, and yet its appeal is so strong that it's become a standard. It's a great weekend cake — it'll last the weekend and beyond; it's a terrific cake to take anywhere as a host/house gift; and, if you're like my husband and son, you'll love the cake cut into thick slices and toasted. They slather it with butter — so unnecessary, but so good; I sometimes pile it with jam (also unnecessary).

The cornmeal in the batter adds a slight roughness to the texture and a beautiful sunny color, and the buttermilk moderates the sweetness and saves the cake from being too rich for breakfast. If you want, add the finely grated zest of a lemon, a lime or half an orange to the batter (rub the zest into the sugar before you beat in the eggs).

This recipe started its happy life as a skillet cake (see opposite), and it's still the version I make most often for brunch, cutting the cake into wedges and turning it into a kind of shortcake. But if you're looking for portability, this loaf's the way to go.

STORING:  Wrapped in plastic, the cake will keep at room temperature for at least 3 days; if it stales, toast the slices. Wrapped airtight, the cake can be frozen for up to 2 months; defrost it in its wrapping.

Center a rack in the oven and preheat it to 350 degrees F. Butter a 9-inch loaf pan, dust with flour and tap out the excess; or use baker's spray.

Whisk together the flour, cornmeal, baking powder, baking soda and salt.

Whisk the eggs and sugar together in a large bowl until well blended, a minute or two. Whisk in the vanilla. Switch to a flexible spatula and gently stir in half of the dry ingredients. Blend in the buttermilk and then add the rest of the dry ingredients, mixing gently until fully incorporated. Gradually stir in the melted butter. It may look as if you've got more butter than the batter will absorb, but if you work slowly, gently and patiently, it will be just right. Carefully stir in the berries, if you're using them. Scrape the batter into the pan, then smooth the top.

Bake the cake for 50 to 55 minutes, until the top is lightly browned (the center will crack, which is pretty) and, most important, a skewer inserted deep into the center of the cake comes out clean. Transfer the pan to a rack and let it sit for 5 minutes, then run a table knife between the cake and pan, turn the cake out onto a rack, invert onto another rack and cool to room temperature.

# CORNMEAL SKILLET CAKE

Butter a 10-inch skillet or use baker's spray. Make the batter, but don't stir in the berries. Scrape the batter into the skillet and use a spatula to spread it evenly. Scatter over the berries, if using. Bake for 30 to 33 minutes, until the cake is golden brown, particularly around the edges, and starting to come away from the sides of the skillet; a skewer inserted into the center should come out clean. Transfer the cake to a rack and let cool. To serve, cut the cake into wedges. If you haven't topped the cake with berries, you might want to slice each wedge in half horizontally, pile the bottom slice with whipped cream and berries and then lean the top slice against the cream and fruit to make a shortcake.

# TRIPLE-LAYER PARSNIP AND CRANBERRY CAKE

Makes 16 to 18 servings

A layer cake is like a fanfare: It blares "Celebration!" This cake is meant for birthdays and anniversaries, graduations, holidays — I love it for Thanksgiving — house parties and any time you want to make a big group of people happy. Full of flavor, it's based on nuts, cranberries and grated parsnips, a vegetable that might not spring to mind immediately when you're thinking cake. I'm sure that's how people felt when carrot cakes were new. In fact, this is very much like a carrot cake — complete with cream cheese frosting — and if you wanted to swap the sweet, earthy parsnips for sweet, earthy carrots, or combine the two, that would be fine.

The cake is double-filled — it gets a layer of cream cheese frosting and then one of gingered-cranberry jam, made lickety-split. It's a fabulous combo, and the brilliant color of the cranberries makes the cake that much more of an occasion. I've given you a recipe for enough frosting to completely cover the cake, but whether you do or don't is your decision. I love the look of the cake with bare sides, so that you can see the double-decker filling, or with just a thin swipe of frosting for a skim coat. So many choices. All delicious.

### For the cake

2 cups (272 grams) all-purpose flour

2 teaspoons ground coriander

2 teaspoons baking powder

1 teaspoon baking soda

1 teaspoon fine sea salt

1 cup (200 grams) plus 2 teaspoons sugar

1 tablespoon minced peeled fresh ginger

Finely grated zest of 1 small orange or 1 tangerine

1 cup (240 ml) neutral oil, such as canola

½ cup (100 grams) packed light brown sugar

4 large eggs, at room temperature

1½ teaspoons pure vanilla extract

1 pound (454 grams) parsnips, trimmed, peeled and grated (3 cups)

1 cup (120 grams) chopped pecans or other nuts, toasted or not

½ cup (50 grams) chopped fresh cranberries

### For the cranberry filling

One 12-ounce (340-gram) bag cranberries (if frozen, don't defrost)

¾ cup (150 grams) sugar

½ cup (120 ml) freshly squeezed orange juice (or water)

1 teaspoon minced peeled fresh ginger

### For the frosting

¾ pound (340 grams) cream cheese, cut into chunks, at room temperature

1½ sticks (12 tablespoons; 6 ounces; 170 grams) unsalted butter, cut into chunks, at room temperature

6¼ cups (750 grams) confectioners' sugar

½ teaspoon fine sea salt

4 teaspoons pure vanilla extract

### WORKING AHEAD

You can make the filling up to 3 days ahead and refrigerate it. You can make the cake layers a day ahead and keep them wrapped airtight. The cake slices better if it is refrigerated for an hour or two.

*(Recipe continues)*

TO MAKE THE CAKE: Center a rack in the oven and preheat it to 325 degrees F. (If your oven can't hold three 9-inch cake pans on one rack, position the racks to divide the oven into thirds.) Butter three 9-inch round cake pans, dust the interiors with flour and tap out the excess; or use baker's spray.

Whisk the flour, coriander, baking powder, baking soda and salt together.

Put 2 teaspoons of the sugar in a small bowl and stir in the minced ginger and zest.

Working in a stand mixer fitted with a paddle attachment, or in a large bowl with a hand mixer, beat the oil, the remaining 1 cup sugar and the brown sugar together on medium speed for about 2 minutes. The mixture might look grainy, but that's fine. One by one, beat in the eggs and then continue to beat until the mixture is smooth and velvety. Beat in the vanilla, followed by the ginger-zest mixture and any syrup that might be in the bowl. Turn off the mixer and add the flour mixture all at once. Pulse the mixer to start incorporating the flour, then mix on low just until the dry ingredients almost disappear. Add the parsnips and nuts and mix to incorporate. Switch to a flexible spatula and gently fold in the cranberries. Divide the batter evenly among the three pans and smooth the tops.

Bake for 33 to 37 minutes, until the cakes are golden and just starting to pull away from the sides of the pans; the tops will feel springy to the touch and a tester inserted in the center will come out clean. If you're baking on two racks or your oven has hot spots, rotate the pans from front to back and top to bottom after 18 minutes. Transfer the cakes to racks and cool for 5 minutes, then run a table knife around the sides of the pans and turn the cakes out onto racks to cool to room temperature. (*You can make the cakes a day ahead — wrap them well and keep them at room temperature.*)

TO MAKE THE FILLING: Put all the ingredients in a medium saucepan, stir and cook over medium heat, stirring, until the mixture bubbles, many of the cranberries pop and the sauce starts to thicken, about 10 minutes. The filling will thicken more as it cools. Scrape the filling into a bowl and cool to room temperature, then cover and refrigerate if you're not using immediately. (*The filling can be made up to 3 days ahead and kept in the fridge.*)

TO MAKE THE FROSTING: Working in a stand mixer fitted with the paddle attachment, or in a large bowl with a hand mixer, beat the cream cheese, butter, confectioners' sugar and salt together on medium speed until very smooth; scrape the beater and bowl down frequently. Add the vanilla and beat to blend.

TO ASSEMBLE THE CAKE: If the tops of the cakes have mounded (these usually bake pretty flat), you can slice away the crowns to even them. Place one layer bottom side down on a cake plate. Using an offset spatula or a table knife, generously cover the top of the layer with frosting. Spoon half of the cranberry filling into the center of the frosting and spread it so that it comes to about an inch or two shy of the edges of the cake. Place the second layer on the cake, top side down. Cover with frosting and spread the remaining filling over it. Finish by placing the last layer on the cake, bottom side up. Cover the top layer with frosting, adding some swirls and whorls, if you'd like. If some of the cranberry filling oozed to the edges or maybe even spilled over a little, celebrate it! I love the casual look of this cake.

You'll have frosting left over, so you can frost the sides of the cake, if you'd like. I like to leave the sides bare or run just a very thin layer of frosting around them, a layer that looks almost sheer, kind of naked, but not quite.

The cake can be served as soon as it's assembled, but it's easier to slice if you give it an hour or two in the fridge.

STORING: You can keep the cake at room temperature (not hot or humid) for a couple of days or, wrapped, in the refrigerator for at least 5 days. You can also freeze the cake. Freeze it, then wrap airtight; if you can manage it, defrost it overnight in the refrigerator.

## SUGARED CRANBERRIES

For an even more festive cake, crown it with sugared cranberries — finishing it like this is beautiful for the holidays. Make a simple syrup by boiling ½ cup sugar and ½ cup water together, stirring, for 3 minutes. Remove from the heat, drop in as many fresh cranberries as you'd like and roll them around to coat with syrup, then lift them out with a slotted spoon or mesh spider and transfer them to a rack. Let them set for about 1 hour — they'll be sticky and tacky, and that's what you want. Roll the cranberries around in a cup of sugar and then let them dry on a clean rack for another hour. Sugared berries are meant for the last minute — they'll get syrupy in the refrigerator and won't survive freezing.

# TANGERINE-TOPPED CHEESECAKE

Makes 16 servings

Aside from the many qualities that make cheesecake beloved — among them, its velvety texture, the way it tag-teams sweet and tangy and the nonchalance with which it announces itself as something special — it has convenience on its side. It takes less than thirty minutes to prepare the batter and then the cake spends a long time in the oven, during which you're not on duty. After that, it goes into the refrigerator (or the freezer), where it's happy to rest until you decide to have a party and bring it out on a big platter. It's a splendid cake for a celebration or an everyday dinner when you've got lots of people around the table. The base of this cake is made with crushed cookies or bread crumbs, but it's more a dusting to keep the cake from sticking to the pan than it is a crust. The heart of it is a blend of ricotta and cream cheese that's beaten for about 10 minutes to ensure that it will bake to a beautiful smoothness. I use the finely grated zest of two or three tangerines to flavor the batter just enough so that you get the citrus, but not so much that you miss the flavors of the cheese. If you want more orange flavor, you can add some orange extract or orange oil to the batter. And if you'd prefer lemons or oranges to the tangerines, make the swap. I like to finish the cake with slices of tangerine and brush over honey for shine.

## a word on the ricotta

If your ricotta has liquid around it or if it seems loose in any way, it's best to spoon it into a cheesecloth-lined strainer set over a bowl, fold the cloth over the cheese, place a weight, like a can of beans, on top and put the setup in the fridge to drain for about 3 hours. If you use a brand like Polly-O, this is unnecessary.

About 3 tablespoons cookie or graham cracker crumbs or dried bread crumbs

1 cup (200 grams) sugar

2 or 3 tangerines (or 2 or 3 lemons or 2 oranges)

1½ pounds (681 grams) cream cheese, cut into chunks

½ teaspoon fine sea salt

2 pounds (908 grams) whole-milk ricotta (see headnote)

¼ cup (32 grams) cornstarch

3 large eggs

2 teaspoons pure vanilla extract

½ to 1 teaspoon pure orange extract or oil (optional)

Honey, for the glaze and serving (optional)

**WORKING AHEAD**
The cake must be refrigerated for at least 8 hours, or overnight.

Center a rack in the oven and preheat it to 325 degrees F. Butter a 10-inch springform pan, dust it with the cookie or bread crumbs and knock out the excess. Set the pan on a baking sheet.

Put the sugar in the bowl of a stand mixer, or in a very large bowl if you're using a hand mixer. Grate the tangerine zest (to taste) over the sugar and, using your fingers, rub the two together until the sugar is moist and very fragrant — it might even turn orange. If you are going to serve the tangerines or oranges with the cake, wrap them in plastic and refrigerate until needed. If you're using a stand mixer, attach the bowl and fit it with the paddle attachment.

Add the cream cheese and salt to the bowl and beat on medium speed, scraping the bowl often, for 4 minutes. Spoon in the ricotta and beat and scrape for another 4 minutes — all this beating is what will give you the creamy texture you'll love. Turn off the mixer, add the cornstarch and then mix on low speed to incorporate it. One by one, add the eggs, mixing on medium speed for 1 minute after each egg goes in. Beat in the vanilla

extract and orange extract, if you're using it. Scrape the batter into the pan and swivel the pan to level it.

Bake the cake for 90 minutes without opening the oven door. The cake may crack, but that's normal. The top may have risen above the rim of the pan and it will have browned. Turn the oven off and open the door a little — prop it open with a wooden spoon, if necessary — and let the cake rest in the oven for 1 hour.

Transfer the cake to a rack and let it cool to room temperature, then refrigerate for at least 8 hours, or, better, overnight.

When you're ready to serve the cake, run a table knife between the cake and the sides of the pan and remove the springform ring. If it looks as if the cake has stuck (unusual, but possible), warm the sides of the pan with a few puffs of hot air from a hairdryer or moisten a dish towel in hot water, wring it out and wrap it around the pan, then remove the ring.

To glaze the cake — optional but nice — warm about 3 tablespoons honey in a saucepan or microwave just until it's liquid. Brush it over the top of the cake. You can pass more honey at the table, if you'd like.

If you are serving with tangerines or oranges, working with one at a time, stand the fruit up on a cutting board and, using a sharp knife, slice away the rind and white pith, cutting so that you remove a thin layer of the fruit as well; it's important to expose the fruit. Now, working over a bowl, cut between the fruit and the membranes to release the segments; remove any seeds. Squeeze the membranes to release whatever juice remains and stir it into the fruit. If not using immediately, cover and refrigerate until needed (they'll be fine for up to 6 hours).

Use a long knife to cut the cake, running the blade under (or dipping it into) hot water and wiping it dry between cuts. If you're using the tangerines, either spoon some fruit and juice over each slice or pass the fruit at the table.

———

STORING: Wrapped well, the cake will keep in the refrigerator for up to 5 days, although the glaze might not fare as well as the cake. Unglazed, the cake can be wrapped airtight and frozen for up to 2 months; defrost overnight in the refrigerator.

# DROP-BISCUIT
# PEACH COBBLER

Makes 6 servings

A cobbler is the dessert of choice when the season brings soft fruits with lots of juice. The sweet-biscuit topping for this one is light and cakey and just about begs to be soaked with the flavorful syrup that comes with cooked fruits. To make the topping, you stir the ingredients together with a fork and drop the batter over the fruit — it's a biscuit recipe for a beginner, no cutting in butter, no fretting over working the dough too much or too little. As with so many of the best homemade classics, this is less a formula than a construct — one 9-inch deep-dish pie plate and this recipe, and you're on your way to a lifetime of cobblers.

## a word on serving

I like to spoon the cobbler out of the dish and serve it in bowls, with some of the fruit juices around it, but some people like the cobbler upside down, biscuit on the bottom, the fruit on top and the juice soaking into the biscuit. Ice cream or whipped cream is a good move no matter how you serve it.

### For the fruit

3 pounds (about 1½ kg) peaches

¼ cup (50 grams) sugar, or to taste

Freshly squeezed lemon juice (optional)

1 cup (150 grams) blueberries (optional)

2 teaspoons cornstarch (optional)

### For the biscuit topping

1½ cups (204 grams) all-purpose flour

3 tablespoons sugar

2 teaspoons baking powder

½ teaspoon fine sea salt

¼ teaspoon baking soda

1 cup (240 ml) cold heavy cream

½ cup (120 ml) cold buttermilk (well shaken before measuring)

Ice cream or whipped cream, for serving (optional)

Center a rack in the oven and preheat it to 350 degrees F. Line a baking sheet with parchment paper or a silicone baking mat. Butter a 9-inch deep-dish pie plate and put it on the baking sheet.

TO MAKE THE FRUIT: I know this may sound sacrilegious, but I no longer peel peaches for cobblers, crisps or pies — I actually like the extra bit of chew that you get with the skins and it speeds up the prep. But if you want to peel them, cut a shallow X in the base of each peach. Bring a pot of water to a boil. Drop in the peaches a few at a time, leave for about 15 seconds, lift out and transfer to a bowl filled with very cold water and ice cubes. Leave for a couple of minutes, then drain and peel.

Cut the peaches into bite-sized chunks or slices and toss them into the pie plate. Taste and decide how much sugar you want and then, if you'd like, add some lemon juice. Add the blueberries, if you're using them, and then make a decision about the cornstarch: It's only a tiny bit,

You can vary the cobbler according to what fruits are in season and within reach. Just know that you need a scant 6 cups cut-up fruit, sugar to taste and, if you'd like, lemon juice. I love an all-berry cobbler—mix whatever berries you can get and, if you want, cut in some ripe mango; add 1 to 2 tablespoons cornstarch to the berries—they're very juicy. Plums make a pretty cobbler and are nice in combination with peaches or nectarines. I adore apricots, though it can be hard to find good ones—but when you bake them in a cobbler, even so-so apricots can shine. In spring, go with rhubarb and strawberries (and some cornstarch).

but it will thicken the juices a little. If your peaches are very ripe, I'd add it. Give everything a good stir and set aside.

TO MAKE THE BISCUIT TOPPING: Whisk together the flour, sugar, baking powder, salt and baking soda in a medium bowl. In a measuring cup or another bowl, whisk together the cream and buttermilk. Pour the liquid ingredients over the dry and, using a table fork, stir until the flour is evenly dampened and you've got a moist batter.

Using a medium (1½-tablespoon capacity) scoop or a tablespoon, dollop the topping over the fruit — leave a little space between each pouf of batter.

Bake the cobbler for 45 to 55 minutes, until the topping is golden brown and, most important, the fruit juices are boiling under, and maybe up, through and over, the biscuits. Transfer to a rack and let cool for at least 20 minutes, or until the cobbler reaches room temperature, before serving, with or without ice cream or whipped cream.

⸻

STORING: The cobbler is best the day it is made. You can keep it covered overnight at room temperature or in the refrigerator, but the biscuit topping will never make you as happy as it does soon after it comes out of the oven.

## BISCUIT SHORTCAKES

The same batter that makes the topping for the cobbler makes lovely shortcakes. Preheat the oven to 425 degrees F and line a baking sheet. Use a large (3-tablespoon capacity) scoop or a tablespoon to portion out the batter, dropping the biscuits on the baking sheet 3 inches apart. Bake for 17 to 19 minutes, until the biscuits are golden and set. You'll get 10 biscuits for sure, and maybe another one or two. Let them rest until they're just warm or at room temperature before serving. These won't be very high, but they will be very tender, so either cut them in half or just smush them and put juicy fruit on top. Choose whatever soft fruit and/or berries you'd like, cut the fruit into bite-sized pieces, if necessary, and toss them with some sugar, so that they create a syrup. Serve the shortcakes with whipped cream.

# APPLE CUSTARD CRISP

Makes 8 servings

This is an unusual crisp. Instead of tossing fruit with some sugar and topping it with an oatmeal mix, I pour a simple custard over the apples and finish the crisp with streusel. Think crustless tart.

The crisp leans toward France, but not in any strict way. The apples that I use most often in the kitchen are Fujis and Galas, but the apple of choice in France is the Golden Delicious, an apple we American bakers shrug off as uninteresting. Here's the surprise: It's lovely in this crisp. Of course you can use any apples you like, or have on hand, but if you're shopping for the crisp, pick up Golden Delicious apples and give them a try.

I've gone easy on the streusel, speckling rather than spackling the top of the crisp so that the apples and custard peek through, but please, feel free to cover the fruit completely — for those of us who love crunch, there can never be too much streusel. Any leftover streusel can be baked in a 350-degree-F oven until golden, cooled and served over ice cream or pudding.

## Playing Around

If you'd like to make a classic crisp, omit the custard and add about ⅓ cup sugar (or more to taste) to the apples. You can also use the oatmeal-flour topping on page 278. Any pie filling or the peaches in the cobbler on page 273 would make a good base for a crisp. And, of course, you can swap pears for the apples.

### For the streusel

¾ cup (102 grams) all-purpose flour

3 tablespoons sugar

1 tablespoon brown sugar

¼ teaspoon ground cinnamon

¼ teaspoon fine sea salt

5½ tablespoons (2¾ ounces; 78 grams) cold unsalted butter, cut into small cubes

½ teaspoon pure vanilla extract

### For the crisp

1½ pounds (680 grams) apples, such as Golden Delicious, Fuji or Gala, peeled, halved, cored and cut into 1- to 2-inch cubes

Finely grated zest and juice of ½ lemon or lime, or more to taste

½ cup (120 ml) heavy cream

¼ cup (50 grams) packed brown sugar

Pinch of ground cinnamon, nutmeg, ginger or cardamom (optional)

1 large egg

1 large egg yolk

1 tablespoon Calvados or dark rum (optional)

2 teaspoons pure vanilla extract

Ice cream or lightly sweetened whipped cream, for serving (optional)

**WORKING AHEAD**
The streusel should be chilled for at least 1 hour, and it can be refrigerated for up to 5 days.

TO MAKE THE STREUSEL: You can make the streusel by hand or in a mixer: Whisk the flour, both sugars, the cinnamon and salt together in a bowl (or the mixer bowl). Drop in the cubes of cold butter and toss everything together with your fingers until the butter is coated.

*If you're making the streusel by hand,* squeeze and rub the ingredients together until you've got moist clumps

and curds. Pinch a bit of the streusel, and it should hold together. Sprinkle over the vanilla and toss to blend. *If you're working with a mixer,* fit it with the paddle attachment and mix on medium-low speed until the ingredients form moist, clumpy crumbs. Reaching this stage takes longer than you think it will — you might have to mix for 5 to 10 minutes. When the grainy crumbs have turned moist and formed clumps and curds, sprinkle over the vanilla and mix until blended.

Refrigerate the streusel in a covered container for at least 1 hour. (*The streusel can be refrigerated for up to 5 days.*)

TO MAKE THE CRISP: Center a rack in the oven and preheat it to 375 degrees F. Place a 9-inch pie plate on a baking sheet lined with parchment or a silicone baking mat.

Toss the apples into the pie plate, spreading them evenly. If they mound in the center, that's fine. Stir in the lemon or lime zest and juice.

In a medium bowl, whisk the cream, brown sugar, spice (if you want a bit), egg and yolk together for a minute to blend thoroughly. Whisk in the Calvados or rum, if you're using it, and the vanilla. Pour the custard over the apples and jiggle the apples and/or the pie plate to encourage the custard to slide into all the spaces.

Scatter over about half of the streusel — that's as much as I usually use, but if you'd like more, scatter over more. Tap the streusel lightly with your fingers so that it "sticks" to the crisp.

Bake for 50 to 60 minutes, until the streusel is golden brown and a tester inserted into the center of the crisp comes out clean. If it looks as if the crisp is browning too quickly or too much, tent it loosely with foil. Transfer the baking sheet to a rack and let the crisp rest before serving it only just warm or at room temperature. Ice cream or whipped cream is optional but nice.

STORING: "Here today, gone tomorrow" is custard's fate, but if you can't bear to bid farewell to any leftovers, don't — refrigerate them and enjoy them straight from the fridge the next day.

## APPLE CRISP WITH OATMEAL TOPPING

To make a more traditional topping for this or any crisp, whisk together 1 cup all-purpose flour, 1 cup rolled oats (not instant), ¼ cup packed brown sugar, 2 tablespoons sugar, ¾ teaspoon fine sea salt and, if you'd like, ½ teaspoon cardamom (or ginger, cinnamon or nutmeg). Cut 1 stick (8 tablespoons) very cold unsalted butter into small pieces and drop the bits into the bowl. Using your hands, mash and rub the ingredients together until they form moist clumps. Stir in 1 teaspoon pure vanilla extract. If you've got time, chill the topping for at least 1 hour before using it.

# ETON MESS

Makes 6 servings

To set the record straight from the start: This is not a traditional Eton Mess. The dish, served on June Fourth at the British school Eton, is, by custom, composed of meringue, whipped cream and strawberries, usually saucy, like a compote. My reading of the classic has these elements and then some. I've fiddled with the meringue, adding even more crunch to it — I fold in chunkily crushed store-bought Biscoff (speculoos/spice) cookies or toasted nuts. And I've added a new element: a rhubarb compote mixed with fresh strawberries and spiked with lime juice and an optional splash of crème de cassis. Of course there's whipped cream. It's a dessert with many good textures and flavors and, because of the variety, so many surprises: Every spoonful offers delights, but no spoonful is the same as any other. (The Eton Mess in the photograph on page 280 is the one made with lemon curd and cranberry jam.)

If you're not expert at making meringue, this is the dessert for you: You just spread it out on the baking sheet — no piping or fussing — and then, when you're ready to use it, you crumble it, so that you get what is essential in meringue — sweetness and crunch.

## WORKING AHEAD

If your kitchen is cool and dry, you can make the meringue a couple of days ahead and keep it on the counter. The compote can be made up to 5 days ahead and refrigerated. You can even sugar the berries a few hours ahead and whip the cream—put in a cheesecloth-lined strainer over a bowl in the refrigerator, it will be fine for a few hours. Once the dessert is assembled—minus the meringue—you can chill it in the glasses for an hour.

### For the meringue

½ cup (100 grams) plus 2 teaspoons sugar

1½ teaspoons cornstarch

2 large egg whites, at room temperature

¼ teaspoon cream of tartar or ½ teaspoon distilled white vinegar

Pinch of fine sea salt

½ teaspoon pure vanilla extract

3 tablespoons Biscoff crumbs (see headnote) or chopped toasted nuts

### For the fruit compote

½ pound (226 grams) rhubarb, trimmed and cut into ½-inch-thick slices

⅓ cup (67 grams) sugar

5 to 8 strawberries, hulled and halved, or quartered if very large

1 teaspoon crème de cassis (optional)

½ lime

### For assembly

1 quart (680 grams) strawberries, hulled and halved

2 tablespoons sugar

1½ cups (360 ml) heavy cream, lightly whipped

TO MAKE THE MERINGUE: Center a rack in the oven and preheat it to 250 degrees F. Line a baking sheet with parchment paper or a silicone baking mat.

Push the 2 teaspoons sugar and the cornstarch through a fine-mesh sieve and set aside.

Working in a stand mixer fitted with the whisk attachment, or in a large bowl with a hand mixer (no matter what you use, make sure your tools are impeccably clean and free of even a trace of fat, grease or yolk — egg whites' enemies), beat the whites, cream of tartar or vinegar and salt on medium-high speed until the whites form soft peaks, about 3 minutes. Add the remaining ½ cup sugar, 1 tablespoon at a time. It will take about 5 minutes to get all the sugar into the whites, but it will

be worth your patience. After all the sugar is incorporated, add the vanilla and beat for another 2 minutes or so. You'll have stiff, glossy, beautifully white peaks. Switch to a flexible spatula and fold in the reserved sugar-and-cornstarch mix, followed by the cookie crumbs or nuts.

Use the spatula to scoop the meringue out onto the baking sheet and spread it about 1/2 inch thick. Size and shape don't matter here.

Bake the meringue, undisturbed, for 1 hour and 15 minutes. It will puff and it may crack, but it shouldn't color much (it might be pale beige here and there, and that's fine). Turn off the heat and prop the oven door open just a crack, to let the hot air out (use the handle of a wooden spoon if necessary), and leave the meringue to finish drying for another 2 hours, or for as long as overnight. It's ready when you can easily peel away the paper or mat. Set aside until needed. (*The meringue can be made up to 2 days ahead and kept loosely covered in a dry place at room temperature.*)

TO MAKE THE COMPOTE: Stir the rhubarb and sugar together in a medium heavy-bottomed saucepan. Place the pan over medium heat and cook the fruit, stirring regularly, until it softens — it might fray around the edges or lose its shape, but that's fine; the mixture should thicken like applesauce. Toss in the strawberries and cook for another 2 minutes. Off the heat, stir in the crème de cassis, if you're using it, and a squirt or two of lime juice. Hold on to the lime — you might want to add more juice later. Scrape the compote into a jar or bowl, cover by pressing a piece of plastic wrap against the surface and cool to room temperature. (*Once cooled, the compote can be left out for a couple of hours or refrigerated for up to 5 days.*)

TO ASSEMBLE THE DESSERT: A few minutes before you're ready to put the dessert together, mix the strawberries and sugar together in a bowl and let them stand until there's a little juice in the bowl. (*You can sugar the berries a few hours ahead.*)

I make the Mess in dessert coupes, but any bowl, jar or parfait glass will do. For each serving, start with a couple of spoonfuls of the compote. Add a few spoonfuls of whipped cream and top with some berries and a little more cream. (*You can make the Mess up to this point, cover it and refrigerate for up to 1 hour.*) Crumble meringue generously over the dessert. You will probably have compote and meringue left over, and that's a good thing. Serve immediately, while the meringue still has all its crunch.

───────

STORING: The dessert is really best served as soon as it's constructed.

CHOICES: This dessert can go high or low: You can layer it prettily in dessert coupes or parfait glasses and serve it at your fanciest dinner or you can pile it up in a bowl and serve it with a big spoon. The ingredients are inherently beautiful, so the Mess will look great no matter how you combine them.

# CRANBERRY-LEMON ETON MESS

Replace the rhubarb compote with the cranberry filling on page 266 and Lemon Curd (page 324), using some of each for every portion. Instead of topping with strawberries, use raspberries — there's no need to sugar them. I like to finish this version with a sprinkling of chopped toasted pistachios.

# BOOZY JUMBLED-FRUIT CROUSTADE

Makes 6 to 8 servings

I've given up trying to define a croustade precisely, shape-shifter that it is. These days, I go with "pie" — double-crusted or open-faced. It can be made with many different types of dough, but because the first croustade I ever had was made with phyllo, it's become my standard. In this version, layers of phyllo are brushed with butter and sprinkled with cinnamon sugar. Halfway through the eight double layers is a mix of dried fruit and fresh apple moistened with bourbon. And, if you're feeling playful, you can finish the croustade with a fillip of crushed phyllo that crisps and ruffles in the oven.

Even if you've never baked before, you can build a beautiful croustade — the operative word here is "build": It's a construction project.

½ cup (120 ml) water

¼ cup (60 ml) bourbon

20 pitted prunes, cut into small pieces

6 pitted dates, cut into small pieces

4 dried pears or 6 dried apple rings, cut into small pieces

2 teaspoons chopped crystallized ginger

1 medium to large apple, preferably Fuji, peeled, cored and cut into small pieces

1 mandarin or clementine or ½ tangerine, peeled and finely chopped, seeds removed (optional)

2 tablespoons sugar, plus more for dusting the top

¼ teaspoon ground cinnamon

7 tablespoons (3½ ounces; 99 grams) unsalted butter, melted

16 sheets phyllo (9 by 14 inches), thoroughly defrosted if frozen

**WORKING AHEAD**
The fruit should be steeped in the bourbon for at least 1 hour, and it can sit for up to a day. You can make the croustade a couple of hours ahead.

Bring the water and bourbon to a boil in a small saucepan. Stir in the prunes, dates, dried pears or dried apples and ginger, cover and set aside to steep for at least 1 hour. (*You can steep the fruit for up to 1 day.*)

Stir the fresh apple and the mandarin (or clementine or tangerine), if you're using it, into the dried fruit mixture.

When you're ready to assemble and bake the croustade, center a rack in the oven and preheat it to 400 degrees F. Line a baking sheet with a double layer of parchment paper or use a silicone baking mat or foil.

Mix the sugar and cinnamon together in a small bowl. Have the butter and a pastry brush nearby (I prefer a silicone basting brush here).

Lay a piece of plastic wrap, a sheet of parchment or a clean kitchen towel on the counter and put the phyllo sheets on it. Using a ruler and scissors, cut the stack of sheets, a few at a time, into 9-inch squares. Keep the squares and the trimmings covered with a lightly moistened kitchen towel. (Phyllo dries almost instantly, so always keep it covered.)

Place 2 squares of phyllo in the center of the lined baking sheet, brush with melted butter and sprinkle with some cinnamon sugar, then repeat until you've got 4 sets of double sheets. As you're working, the phyllo may tear and you might have some gaps and some shaggy pieces — it's annoying, but not fatal: You can use the phyllo trimmings as patches. There are so many layers that cracks, tears, creases and folds won't amount to much in the end.

Spoon the fruit onto the phyllo — if there's any liquid in the saucepan, you can include a tablespoon or so of it. Spread the fruit out, leaving about an inch of dough bare as a border all around.

Cover the fruit with another set of 4 double-phyllo sheets, again buttering and sugaring each set and not worrying about how even or smooth the sets are. When you've got this batch in place, work around the edges of the croustade, folding them up and in with your hands to form a border. The border will be rippled and ragged, but it will be fine. Brush a little butter along the turned-up edges, then butter and sugar the top of the croustade. If you'd like to give the croustade a fancy finish, scrunch up some pieces of leftover phyllo and place them on top. Dab or sprinkle melted butter over the scrunchies and then dust them with some plain sugar.

Bake for 15 minutes, then cover the croustade loosely with a foil tent and bake for 15 to 20 minutes more. There's really no test for doneness with the croustade — when it's golden brown, call it finished (look for good color; pale phyllo is not tasty). Transfer the baking sheet to a rack and allow the croustade to cool until it is only just warm or reaches room temperature before serving.

———

STORING: This is not a storable sweet: The croustade is best the day it's made and awfully nice slightly warm. If you'd like, you can pop the croustade into a 350-degree-F oven for a few minutes to rewarm it before serving.

## Playing Around

I think of this recipe as a blueprint—follow its outline and fill in the details as you'd like. While I'm fond of prunes here, raisins, cherries, cranberries, papaya and/or figs can happily stand in for the prunes, dates and pears. Keep the ginger, but if you don't have crystallized ginger, use fresh ginger or ginger in syrup. And don't worry too much about the proportions—work to taste. As for the bourbon, it can be swapped for cognac, Armagnac, kirsch, Grand Marnier or even straight orange juice (if you use the latter, use ¾ cup and skip the water).

# MIXED BERRY PIE

Makes 8 servings

As soon as there are berries in the market, there's pie in our house. This pie has blueberries, raspberries and blackberries and leans heavily on blueberries' natural tendency to thicken over heat. So that the filling will be juicy, but not so juicy that you'd have to serve the pie in bowls with spoons, I quickly cook some of the blueberries with sugar, add a few spoonfuls of flour and use this luscious jam to hold the fresh-berry filling together. It has only enough flour to thicken it — the slices of pie hold together, but there's still runaway juice, which, for me, is a hallmark of a good homemade pie. The filling doesn't call for much sugar — I don't want to hide the berries' natural sweetness or their acidity — and it includes lemon zest and juice, both of which boost the flavor of sweet fruits.

### WORKING AHEAD
You can wrap the rolled-out dough and refrigerate it overnight or freeze it for up to 2 months.

1 recipe All-Butter Pie Dough (page 326), divided in two and shaped into disks, each disk rolled into an 11-inch circle

1½ pounds (2 pints; 680 grams) blueberries

½ cup (100 grams) sugar

2 tablespoons water

2 to 4 tablespoons all-purpose flour

Finely grated zest and juice of ½ lemon

12 ounces (1 pint; 340 grams) blackberries

6 ounces (½ pint; 170 grams) raspberries

Butter a 9-inch pie plate. Fit one piece of the dough into the plate — don't trim the edges — and place the other piece on a baking sheet lined with parchment, foil or a silicone baking mat. Cover both and put in the refrigerator while you make the filling. (*The rolled-out dough can be well wrapped and refrigerated overnight or frozen for up to 2 months.*)

Put half of the blueberries, ¼ cup of the sugar and the water in a medium saucepan and bring to a boil over medium heat, then lower the heat and simmer, stirring with a heatproof spatula, until the jam thickens a little and your spatula leaves tracks as you stir, about 5 minutes. Off the heat, stir in the flour (I use 2 to 3 tablespoons of flour and get a pie that leaves lots of juice in the pan; if you'd like a less juicy pie, add 4), zest and juice and the remaining ¼ cup sugar.

Pour the jam into a large bowl and add the remaining blueberries, as well as the blackberries and raspberries. Stir gently to blend the berries into the jam as evenly as you can. Don't be overly concerned about crushing the berries — they'll pop and flatten in the oven anyway. Let the filling cool while you preheat the oven.

Center a rack in the oven and preheat it to 425 degrees F.

Remove the top crust from the baking sheet (leave the parchment in place) and put the pie plate on the lined sheet. Spoon the filling into the bottom crust — it's fine if it mounds above the edges.

(*Recipe continues*)

Test the crust — if it's supple enough to bend without cracking, carry on; if not, wait a couple of minutes.

Moisten your fingers with a little cold water and run them along the rim of the bottom crust, then center the top crust over the filling and press down along the edges to seal the top and bottom crusts together. Using a sharp knife, either trim both crusts flush with the plate and press the rim down with the back of a fork, or cut the crusts to leave some overhang, fold the overhang under on itself and flute the edges. Cut at least 3 slits in the top crust and cut out a small circle of dough from the center.

Bake the pie for 30 minutes. Lower the oven temperature to 375 degrees F and bake for another 30 to 40 minutes or — this is the real test — until the filling is bubbling up through the slits. (Trust the bubbling more than the timer.) A juice-stained pie is a beautiful pie and a fully baked one, so don't be tempted to pull it out of the oven too early. However, if you think that the crust is browning too quickly or too much, cover the pie loosely with a foil tent or make a foil cover for the edges of the pie (the part that browns first and most).

Transfer the pie, still on the baking sheet, to a rack and let cool until it is barely warm or reaches room temperature.

STORING: I always say that pie is best the day it is made, but not everyone agrees with me — there are plenty of people who like cold pie. You can have it both ways, of course; just cover whatever is left over and keep it refrigerated. It'll hold for 2 days.

## BLUEBERRY PIE

You can make an all-blueberry pie using this same method by replacing the blackberries and raspberries with equal amounts of blueberries. If you'd like, swap lime juice and zest for the lemon — it's a small but surprising change.

# MOSTLY RHUBARB TART

Makes 8 servings

Almost as soon as you say "rhubarb," you're tempted to say "strawberries." They grow together, ripen at about the same time and play a lively point-counterpoint of sweet and not-sweet. And yet, when it comes to this tart, I don't want too many strawberries. I want them there for color and sweetness, but not so many that they cut away too much of rhubarb's edge or give in too easily to the oven's heat and go soft and watery.

The rhubarb for the tart filling is macerated in sugar — a nice move, because the sugar and juices become a rhubarb-flavored syrup that you can use in the custard, a classic cream-and-egg custard flavored with vanilla and (if you'd like) a little rose extract. It's everything you want in a spring-into-summer dessert: It's beautiful, aromatic and delicious.

1¼ pounds (567 grams) rhubarb, trimmed

½ cup (100 grams) plus ⅓ cup (67 grams) sugar

½ cup (120 ml) heavy cream

1 large egg

1 large egg yolk

1 teaspoon pure vanilla extract

½ teaspoon pure rose extract, such as Star Kay White (optional)

One 9- to 9-½ inch tart shell made from Sweet Tart Dough (page 327), partially baked and cooled

12 strawberries (fewer if they're very large), hulled and halved lengthwise

Lightly whipped cream or crème fraîche, for serving (optional)

Strawberries, hulled, cut and lightly tossed with a little sugar, for serving (optional)

**WORKING AHEAD**

The rhubarb must be macerated in the sugar for at least 30 minutes, and it can sit for up to 2 hours.

Cut the rhubarb into slices about ½ inch thick. (If you've got fat stalks, halve them the long way first and then slice.) You should end up with about 3 cups rhubarb. Put the pieces in a bowl, stir in the ½ cup sugar and let sit, stirring now and then, for about 30 minutes. You want a syrup to form. (*You can macerate the rhubarb for up to 2 hours.*)

When you're ready to bake, center a rack in the oven and preheat it to 375 degrees F. Line a baking sheet with parchment paper or a silicone baking mat.

Drain the rhubarb, reserving the syrup.

Whisk the heavy cream, the remaining ⅓ cup sugar, the egg and yolk together in a bowl until blended. Stir in the vanilla, the rose extract, if you're using it, and the rhubarb syrup.

Place the tart shell on the baking sheet and spoon in the rhubarb, nudging it so that it covers the bottom. Pour the custard over the rhubarb (it should be just enough

to fill the shell with a little room to spare; if you think you've got too much and that it might bake over the sides of the shell, hold back whatever's necessary). Add the strawberries, arranging them so that they speckle the top evenly.

Bake the tart for 50 to 60 minutes (cover the edges of the crust if it starts to brown too deeply), until the custard has risen slightly but evenly and a tester inserted close to the center of the tart comes out clean. Transfer the baking sheet to a rack and let the tart cool to just slightly warm or room temperature.

Serve the tart plain, with whipped cream or with whipped cream and berries.

STORING: This tart is really best enjoyed soon after it's baked, but you can keep it for several hours at room temperature. Refrigerate any leftovers — they won't be as luxurious as just-baked, but they'll still be satisfying.

# FLOGNARDE WITH PLUMS OR BERRIES OR PEARS

Makes 6 servings

A *flognarde* (flow-*nyard*) is a custardy French dessert of fruit — plums, prunes, pears or berries — baked in a batter that most resembles the mix you'd use to make crepes. No matter what fruit you use, you'll enjoy the way it softens and sweetens as it bakes for about an hour. Tender fruits, like plums and berries, become almost jammy in the oven, the perfect consistency for the cake, which is soft and custardy — almost like a chubby pancake. Because the cake is purposefully plain, it's important that you flavor it with good vanilla extract and, more traditionally, alcohol. If the flognarde tips toward boozy, many will declare it a success. (If you'd rather not use alcohol, up the extract a bit.)

A flognarde is a flognarde is a flognarde . . . unless it has cherries, in which case it's a *clafoutis* (cla-foo-*tee*). That's a specialty of the Limousin region, and according to local custom, the cherries should be baked whole and unpitted, so that they remain juicy — and dangerous to the unsuspecting: Warn everyone at the table. (The clafoutis in the photo on page 292 is made with frozen pitted cherries.)

1 pound (454 grams) small plums (about 4), not too ripe or juicy

½ cup (68 grams) all-purpose flour

½ teaspoon baking powder

¼ teaspoon ground star anise or a pinch of ground allspice

Pinch of fine sea salt

4 tablespoons (2 ounces; 57 grams) unsalted butter

½ cup (100 grams) sugar

3 large eggs

2 tablespoons cognac or other brandy (see headnote)

1½ teaspoons pure vanilla extract

1 cup (240 ml) whole milk

About ¼ cup (25 grams) sliced almonds, for topping (optional)

Confectioners' sugar, for dusting (optional)

### WORKING AHEAD
The flognarde can be kept loosely covered at room temperature for 4 to 6 hours.

Center a rack in the oven and preheat it to 350 degrees F. Choose a 9-inch pie plate, a porcelain quiche pan or another ovenproof pan (preferably not metal) with a capacity of 1 quart. Butter the pan and place it on a baking sheet lined with parchment paper.

Cut the plums in half, remove the pits and cut each half into 8 slices. Toss the slices into the pie plate and jiggle them around so that you get an even layer.

Whisk together the flour, baking powder, spice and salt.

Melt the butter in a medium saucepan. Remove the pan from the heat and whisk in the sugar. When the mixture is homogeneous, beat in the eggs one at a time, followed by the liquor and vanilla. Whisk in the dry ingredients. The mixture will be thick, so get it as well blended as you can without beating it, and then start stirring in the milk, which will thin the batter considerably. You'll

have a pourable batter that might have a few lumps —
ignore them. Pour the batter over the plums and scatter
over the almonds, if using.

Bake for 60 to 70 minutes, until the flognarde is
puffed all the way to the center, feels firm to the touch
and is golden and cracked across the surface; the juice
from the plums might be bubbling — so much the better.
A skewer inserted into the center will come out clean.
Transfer the flognarde, on the baking sheet, to a rack and
let cool to room temperature.

Dust the flognarde with confectioners' sugar, if you'd
like, slice and serve.

STORING: Some people think you must eat the flognarde at room temperature the day it's made. I love it
like that, but I also think it's nice straight from the refrigerator the next day. If you've got leftovers, cover and
chill them, and see what you think.

## BERRY FLOGNARDE

Because strawberries can be watery and tend to become
even more so when baked, it's best to use blueberries,
raspberries and/or blackberries for a berry flognarde.
Figure on about 1 pint berries — you want them to
loosely fill the pie plate. While you can still use brandy
or cognac, berries are lovely with kirsch (a floral cherry
liqueur), Grand Marnier or (in lesser quantities, say
1 tablespoon) a nut liqueur like amaretto or Frangelico.
Skip the star anise and go for a pinch of cinnamon or a
few scrapings of fresh ginger instead.

## PRUNE AND PEAR (OR APPLE) FLOGNARDE

Snip 15 pitted prunes into bite-sized pieces and soak
them in hot (or boiling) water for 3 minutes; drain and
pat dry. Peel and core 1 large or 2 small pears and cut
into chunks about 1½ inches on a side. Put the fruit
in the buttered pie plate. Make the batter and bake as
above. If you'd like, use apples instead of pears and raisins or dried cranberries instead of prunes. Do that, and
I'd opt for Calvados as the booze.

## CHERRY CLAFOUTIS

How you want to treat the cherries — you'll need about
1 pound — is up to you. Your choices are: Do nothing to
them except remove the stems (but warn your guests
about the pits); pit the cherries and leave them whole
(you can do this with a cherry-pitter or a chopstick);
or halve and pit the cherries. You can also use 1 pound
frozen cherries; just be certain to drain and dry them as
thoroughly as possible. For the spice, you can keep the
star anise or choose cinnamon, ginger or even coriander. As for the liqueur, kirsch is a smart choice, since it's
made from cherries, but cognac or another brandy is
good too. If you'd like, use 1 teaspoon vanilla extract plus
½ teaspoon almond extract.

# DARK CHOCOLATE PUDDING

Makes 6 servings

The men in my family are pudding heads. Give them anything slippy and slidey, soft and creamy, and they're happy. Give them chocolate pudding, and they're ecstatic.

While I think of chocolate pudding as being very American, when I served it in Paris, my friends licked their spoons and said I'd made a really good chocolate *crème pâtissière*. Indeed, I always forget that our pudding is their pastry cream, a cooked custard thickened with a little cornstarch and eggs.

If you were to follow my husband's lead, you'd pour some heavy cream over the pudding; if you were to follow my son's, you'd have it plain; if you were to follow tradition, you'd have the pudding with some whipped cream or crème fraîche; and if you were to follow my druthers, you'd finish the dessert with a sprinkle of Chocolate Crunch (page 325).

## a word on mixing

When company's coming, I give the pudding a little extra smoothing by beating it with an immersion blender for a minute or so. It's optional, but it does further silken the texture.

1½ cups (360 ml) whole milk

¾ cup (180 ml) heavy cream

⅓ cup (67 grams) sugar

2 tablespoons cornstarch

2 tablespoons unsweetened cocoa powder

¼ teaspoon fine sea salt

1 large egg

2 large egg yolks

¼ pound (113 grams) semisweet or bittersweet chocolate, melted in a double boiler or on low power in a microwave and still warm

1 teaspoon pure vanilla extract

2 tablespoons unsalted butter, at room temperature

Chocolate Crunch (page 325), for serving (optional)

Whipped cream, for serving (optional)

**WORKING AHEAD**
The pudding needs to be refrigerated for at least 4 hours to set.

Set out six bowls or cups for the pudding.

Scald the milk and cream in a medium saucepan over medium heat. (When you see small bubbles in a circle around the edges of the milk, it's scalded.)

Whisk the sugar, cornstarch, cocoa and salt together in a large heatproof bowl. Whisk in the egg and yolks. (Once the yolks go in, you must start whisking immediately, or the sugar will cause the yolks to develop a film.)

Put the bowl on a kitchen towel to keep it steady and, with the whisk in one hand and the pan of hot milk and cream in the other, start adding the liquid to the bowl in a drizzle, whisking nonstop. When you've incorporated about a quarter of the mixture, you can whisk it in more quickly. Pour everything back into the pan.

Place the pan over medium heat and, once again whisking without stopping, cook the cream until it thickens, about 3 minutes — you'll notice that the whisk will begin to leave tracks, your sign that you're almost there. When the first bubble breaks the surface, whisk

energetically and then continue to whisk for another minute or two.

Set a strainer over a bowl and push the pudding through the strainer. If anything has stuck to the pan, leave it behind. Whisk in the melted chocolate, vanilla and butter, stirring until smooth and fully incorporated. If you'd like, give the pudding a last mix with a hand-held (immersion) blender — just a minute or so is all you need. It's not necessary, but it does smooth and ever so slightly aerate the pudding.

Pour or spoon the pudding into the bowls or cups, cover (press a piece of plastic wrap directly against the surface of each pudding if you want to avoid having a skin form) and refrigerate until cold and set, at least 4 hours.

When you're ready to serve, sprinkle a little of the crunch, if you're using it, over each pudding. Using the crunch doesn't preclude the possibility of adding other toppings, such as whipped cream.

———————

STORING: The pudding is best the day it is made, but it can be kept for up to 3 days in the refrigerator. Make sure to keep it well covered and away from foods with strong odors.

# SALTED-CHOCOLATE HOT FUDGE SUNDAES

Makes 4 to 6 sundaes

If I made a cake as elaborate as the Taj Mahal, I don't think it would surprise — or delight — my friends more than when I serve this ice cream sundae. It has everything needed for perfection: good ice cream, of course; hot fudge sauce (the queen of ice-cream toppers); and crunch — toasted almonds and bits of salted dark chocolate. The chocolate is the most unexpected addition and the most enchanting. With it, you get all the childish joy of sundaes and a touch of grand sophistication.

## a word on portions

You can make this sundae with as few or as many scoops of ice cream as you'd like. I usually go with two or three, depending on what's come before.

### For the salted-chocolate bits

½ pound (227 grams) bittersweet chocolate (not chips), finely chopped

¾ teaspoon fleur de sel or ½ teaspoon sea or kosher salt

### For the hot fudge sauce

6 ounces (170 grams) bittersweet chocolate (not chips), finely chopped

¾ cup (180 ml) heavy cream

3 tablespoons light corn syrup

2 tablespoons sugar

### For the sundaes

About ¾ cup (75 grams) toasted slivered almonds

About 1 pint (480 ml) coffee (or other favorite flavor) ice cream

About 1 pint (480 ml) vanilla (or other favorite flavor) ice cream

Lightly sweetened whipped cream

**WORKING AHEAD**
You can make the chocolate bits up to 2 weeks ahead; wrap them well and keep them frozen. The hot fudge sauce can also be made up to 2 weeks ahead; keep it in a sealed jar in the refrigerator. You can even scoop the ice cream onto a baking sheet a few hours in advance and keep the balls in the freezer. (I line the sheet with parchment paper or a silicone baking mat.)

TO MAKE THE BITS: Line a pie plate with plastic wrap. Melt the chocolate in a double boiler or on low power in a microwave. Add the salt and stir to blend, then, using an offset spatula or a table knife, spread the chocolate in the pie pan, making a layer that's ⅛ inch thick (shape doesn't matter). Press a piece of plastic wrap against the surface and freeze for at least 45 minutes. When the chocolate is solid, chop it into bite-sized bits. Keep frozen until needed. (*You can do this up to 2 weeks in advance.*)

*(Recipe continues)*

TO MAKE THE SAUCE: Put the chocolate, cream, corn syrup and sugar in a medium saucepan over medium-low heat and cook, stirring constantly, until the chocolate melts and the mixture comes to a light simmer, about 5 minutes. Still stirring, let it burble for a minute or two more, then scrape it into a heatproof container. Use now or cover and refrigerate until needed. (*The sauce will keep for up to 2 weeks in the refrigerator.*)

TO MAKE THE SUNDAES: If necessary, warm the fudge sauce in a double boiler or microwave on low. For each sundae, sprinkle some salted-chocolate bits and almonds into the bottom of a bowl, snifter or sundae glass. Top with a scoop or two of coffee ice cream and some hot fudge sauce, almonds and bits. Finish with a scoop or two of vanilla ice cream and more fudge sauce, whipped cream, almonds and chocolate bits. Serve immediately.

# WHITE WINE-POACHED PEARS

Makes 6 servings

Poached fruit is an elegant end to a meal. It's light, simple and lovely, full of flavor, but not filling or fussy. It's just what you want after hearty dishes, like meat or pasta, and it's perfect in fall and winter, when fruit isn't very lush but we're all craving it.

Most recipes for poached pears call for red wine — and you could use red wine in this recipe — but I think you might appreciate the softness of white wine (no tannins) and the slight acidity that perks up pears' natural sweetness.

Choose the variety of pear you enjoy most, but pick fruit that's still firm. Since it's often difficult to find ripe, juicy pears, this is a great recipe for making fruit that falls short of perfection delicious.

These take really well to sauce — caramel, chocolate or berry — and/or cream.

6 firm pears (see headnote)

1 lemon, halved

2 cups (480 ml) white wine

¼ cup (50 grams) sugar

2 tablespoons honey

4 quarter-sized slices peeled fresh ginger

1 or 2 vanilla beans, split and scraped (use the pulp, reserve or discard the pods) or 1 tablespoon pure vanilla extract

1 or 2 cinnamon sticks

1 whole star anise, broken into points

Pinch of Urfa pepper (see page 335), cayenne pepper or crushed red pepper flakes (optional)

Caramel, chocolate or berry sauce, store-bought or homemade, for serving (optional)

Lightly sweetened whipped cream or crème fraîche, for serving (optional)

**WORKING AHEAD**
Packed in a tightly covered container, the pears can be refrigerated for up to 3 days.

To poach the pears, you'll need a lidded pot large enough to hold them upright snugly in a single layer; I use a soup pot and one of the pears is always a little squished and slightly higher than the others, but it works out. You'll also need a piece of parchment (or wax) paper cut to fit inside the pot. (Covering the pears with parchment will slow the reduction of the syrup and keep the fruit from bobbing about.)

One at a time, peel the pears, leaving a circle of skin at the top of each, if you'd like, as well as the stem, if the pear has one. Immediately rub the pear with a lemon half to keep it from browning. Using a long vegetable peeler, an apple corer or a knife, working from the bottom, remove the pear's core, being careful not to cut through the top. Squirt a bit of juice inside the pear.

Cut a couple of slices from the other lemon half and

toss them into the pot, along with the remaining ingredients *except* the pears. Place the pot over medium heat and bring the liquid to a boil, stirring to dissolve the honey and sugar. Lower the heat and carefully fit the pears into the pot — extra points if they're all standing up. The pears will not be covered by the liquid, and that's fine. Put the parchment circle over the pears, pressing down lightly so that the paper touches the fruit, and cover the pot with the lid.

Simmer gently for 15 to 20 minutes, or until the fruit is still firm (you want it to hold its shape) but easily pierced with a small sharp knife. Carefully transfer the pears to a bowl or container. Turn the heat up and boil the syrup for about 5 minutes to further concentrate the flavors. Pour the syrup over the pears and allow them to cool to just warm or room temperature, then catch and discard the points of star anise, or do it before serving.

You can serve the pears warm or chilled. I usually serve them cold and plain — one pear in a nice bowl or a stemless glass with syrup poured around it is perfect.

# BASICS & TRANSFORMERS

# DEMI-GODDESS DRESSING

Makes about 2 cups

This is not a real green goddess dressing — the reason for the "demi" in the name — but it is one that's very green, very delicious, very versatile and naturally very low in fat. Because it's made with buttermilk and yogurt instead of mayonnaise, there's tang and brightness, making it perfect as a dressing over anything from beans, vegetables (it's wonderful with boiled or steamed potatoes) and greens to fish (try it with grilled or fried fish, hot, warm or at room temperature), chicken, omelets, burgers and wraps. Or use it as a dip for crisp raw vegetables or as the base for a refreshing soup that can also be a sipper or a shot (page 84).

½ cup (120 ml) buttermilk (well shaken before measuring)

½ cup (120 ml) plain Greek yogurt

¼ cup (60 ml) white balsamic vinegar

1 tablespoon freshly squeezed lime or lemon juice

½ teaspoon fine sea salt, or more to taste

1 ripe avocado, halved, pitted and cut into chunks

1 small or mini (Persian) cucumber, scrubbed and cut into chunks

1 garlic clove, germ removed (see page 320) and finely chopped

¾ cup loosely packed (30 grams) coarsely chopped mixed fresh herbs, such as chives, basil, cilantro, mint and/or parsley

3 fat scallions, white and light green parts only, cut into inch-long pieces

Freshly ground pepper (optional)

## WORKING AHEAD
You can refrigerate the dressing in a tightly covered container for up to 3 days—shake before using.

Put the buttermilk, yogurt, vinegar, juice and salt into a blender or a food processor and whir until smooth. Drop in the avocado, cucumber, garlic, herbs and scallions and blend until the dressing is once again smooth. Taste for salt and, if you'd like, add white pepper.

You can use the dressing now, but if you have time, chill it for at least 1 hour — it's best served cold.

# HOUSE DRESSING

Makes about ¼ cup

This is the vinaigrette I use pretty much every day. It's my all-purpose dressing for greens both hearty and delicate. I also use it on bean salads and fish salads. I make a small amount, but you can multiply the dressing as many times as you'd like, so that you have enough in your refrigerator for a week.

**WORKING AHEAD**
You can refrigerate the dressing in a tightly covered container for at least 1 week—shake before using.

3 tablespoons extra-virgin olive oil

1 tablespoon white wine vinegar

1 tablespoon white balsamic vinegar

1 teaspoon Dijon mustard (preferably French)

Fine sea salt and freshly ground pepper, to taste

*Optional add-ins*

1 small garlic clove, germ removed (see page 320) and minced

1 small shallot, minced, rinsed and patted dry

Minced mixed fresh herbs, such as tarragon, thyme, rosemary and/or chives

*Optional swaps*

Grainy mustard (preferably French) for Dijon

Traditional balsamic for white balsamic

Red wine vinegar for white wine vinegar

1½ teaspoons walnut oil for 1½ teaspoons of the olive oil (best with white balsamic and white wine vinegar)

Put all the ingredients in a jar with a tight-fitting lid and shake well to blend. Taste for salt and pepper and use immediately or refrigerate. If it's cold, let the dressing sit at room temperature for 10 minutes and then shake vigorously before using.

# MAKE-IT-EASY COLESLAW DRESSING

Makes about 1 cup (enough for 6 cups vegetables
or two 12-ounce bags)

I buy ready-shredded vegetables for coleslaw. Sometimes I'll buy cabbage slaw, sometimes broccoli. Often
I'll add a few extras, like apple, onion or poppy seeds, and
I always make my own dressing. The leftover dressing is
delicious drizzled over salads, burgers or pulled pork.

The dressing makes enough for 6 cups of vegetables
or two 12-ounce bags.

## a word on making slaw

Coleslaw is best when it's had time to sit, so the vegetables can take in the dressing and soften just a little. If
you can swing it, mix the slaw and dressing together at
least 30 minutes ahead. (*You can make the slaw as much
as 2 days ahead and keep it in the fridge.*) Stir it a few
times during this period. Alternatively, put the slaw in
a zipper-lock plastic bag and turn the bag from time to
time to distribute the dressing.

½ cup (120 ml) mayonnaise

¼ cup (60 ml) cider vinegar

3 tablespoons plain Greek yogurt

3 tablespoons sugar

2 tablespoons honey

½ teaspoon fine sea salt, or more to taste

½ teaspoon Old Bay seasoning or celery salt, or more
to taste

¼ teaspoon freshly ground pepper, or more to taste

Hot sauce, to taste (optional)

### WORKING AHEAD
You can refrigerate the dressing for up to 5 days in a
tightly covered container—shake before using.

Whisk all the ingredients *except* the hot sauce together
in a bowl. Taste and adjust the salt, Old Bay (or celery
salt) and pepper, if you'd like to, then add as much hot
sauce as you want (or skip it).

Use the dressing now or, better yet, refrigerate until
cold.

# LEMON "GOOP" VINAIGRETTE

Makes about ⅓ cup

The flavor of this vinaigrette, which uses both Lemon "Goop" and Syrup (page 308), is hard to pin down — it spans the taste spectrum, having elements that are sweet, sour, bitter and salty. But listing those qualities goes only a short way to describing this very particular vinaigrette. Use it on bitter greens like endive; on dark vegetables like broccoli rabe, chard and spinach; and on salads with strong ingredients like grains, beets, beans or smoked fish.

1 tablespoon Lemon Syrup (page 308)

1 teaspoon Lemon "Goop" (page 308)

1 tablespoon sherry vinegar

1 tablespoon cider vinegar

3 tablespoons extra-virgin olive oil

¼ teaspoon honey, or more to taste

Fine sea salt and freshly ground pepper

**WORKING AHEAD**
You can refrigerate the dressing in a tightly covered container for at least 1 week—shake before using.

Put all the ingredients in a jar with a tight-fitting lid and shake well to blend. Taste for salt and pepper and use immediately or refrigerate. If it's cold, let the dressing sit at room temperature for 10 minutes, then shake vigorously before using.

# LEMON "GOOP" AND SYRUP

Makes about ⅔ cup goop and ¾ cup syrup

6 large lemons

2 cups (480 ml) water

1½ cups (300 grams) sugar

2 teaspoons fine sea salt

**WORKING AHEAD**
Refrigerate the goop and syrup separately until needed. In a tightly covered container, the syrup will keep forever, and the goop's lifespan is only slightly shorter.

I had something like this years and years ago at a restaurant near Le Dôme in Paris. It was served with tuna; perhaps tuna cooked in olive oil, I don't remember. What I do remember is that I loved it, went home, tried to re-create it and came up short. The second time I had it was at a Paris bistro called Les Enfants Rouges, where the chef, Daï Shinozuka, served a dab of it with fish. Daï gave me a recipe — and this is based on it — but his started with preserved lemons. The recipe I finally came up with uses ordinary lemons and finishes up as a glossy jam that tastes a little like preserved lemons but is sweeter and more complex.

You'll have more syrup than you need to make the jam — aka "goop" — but the syrup is as good as the jam. I've added it to vinaigrettes (page 307), roasted beets, sautéed green beans, tuna salad, chicken salad and more. It's a terrific "tool" to have in the fridge.

I serve the goop with fish and shellfish, pork and chicken. To start you on the road to playing around with this, try it on Twice-Flavored Scallops (page 193).

Using a vegetable peeler or small paring knife, remove the zest from 3 of the lemons, taking care not to include any of the white pith; set aside.

One by one, cut a slice from the top and bottom of each lemon, cutting deeply enough to reveal the fruit. Stand the lemon upright on a cutting board and, cutting from top to bottom, slice away the rind and pith, again cutting until the fruit is revealed. Slice between the membranes of each lemon to release the segments.

Bring the water, sugar and salt to a boil in a medium saucepan. Drop in the segments and reserved zest and bring back to a boil, then lower the heat so that the syrup simmers gently. Cook for about 1 hour, at which point the syrup will have thickened and the lemons will have pretty much fallen apart. It might look as though the lemons have dissolved, but there'll still be fruit in the pan. Remove from the heat.

The fruit needs to be pureed, a job you can do with a blender (regular or immersion) or a food processor; if you have a mini-blender or mini-processor, use it.

Strain the syrup into a bowl and put the fruit in the blender or processor. (Save the syrup in the bowl!) Add a spoonful of the syrup to the lemons and whir until you have a smooth, glistening puree. Add more syrup as needed to keep the fruit moving and to get the consistency you want. I like the goop when it's thick enough to form a ribbon when dropped from a spoon. Thicker is better than thinner, because you can always adjust the consistency with more of the reserved syrup.

## citrus, inside and out

There aren't many ingredients that I consider absolute musts in my kitchen, but I count citrus, particularly lemon, among them and close to the tippy-tippy top. All citrus, whether it's the zest, the juice or the fruit, adds freshness and pizzazz to dishes both sweet and savory. Just like acidity in a wine, which is so important in balancing the fruit, a little zest or a squirt of juice makes rich dishes a little lighter, heavy dishes a little brighter and sweet dishes a little more nuanced. Citrus is magic.

The skins of many citrus fruits are treated, sometimes with wax, to preserve them, so make sure to wash and dry the fruit before you use it.

Zest is the thinnest, brightest outer part of the fruit; it's the colored part of the rind without the pith, the white, cottony underside. You can remove the zest with a vegetable peeler—it's what I use when I want to slice the zest into strips and/or chop it. Or you can grate it. I use rasp-type Microplane graters, most often the one with the very fine blade made specifically for zesting.

When you need segments of any citrus, here's the easiest way to get them: Cut off a slice from the top and bottom of the fruit—cut far enough down to reveal the fruit. Stand the fruit up on a cutting board and, working from top to bottom, cut along the contours of the fruit, slicing away the rind and pith, until you get to the fruit. In fact, you'll find it easiest to cut segments if, when you're removing the rind and pith, you also remove a thin layer of the fruit. Working over a bowl and holding the fruit in one hand, use a paring knife to cut (again from top to bottom) between the segments and the membranes, cutting as close to the membranes as you can, and letting the segments fall into the bowl. You'll be left with a handful of membranes; squeeze the membranes if you want to capture every last bit of juice.

# STORE-BOUGHT MAYO MIX-INS

As good as store-bought mayonnaise is straight out of the jar, it's often even better mixed with other flavorful ingredients, some of which might also be out of a jar or tube. Using mayo as a base for other sauces gives you smoothness, richness and spreadability or sometimes pourability, and you get it with no work — it's all built into the mayo.

I was brought up on Hellmann's mayonnaise, but depending on where you live, you may have a hometown favorite — use it.

These mayo sauces are more play-around ideas than true recipes. I've given you measurements, but you may want more or less of the hot stuff or spice than I've prescribed — so just fiddle and come up with your own special blend. All are great sauces to have in your repertoire or, better yet, in your fridge — they can transform a dish immediately. For another mayonnaise sauce, take a look at chipotle cream (page 196).

# KOREAN-STYLE MAYO

Makes about ½ cup

Rusty red gochujang, as popular in Korea as ketchup is here, is billed as a sweet-and-spicy sauce. When I first tasted it, I was convinced that the manufacturers had made an error — the sauce was sweet and a little spicy, but mostly sweet. By the time I finished reading the label to check its veracity, the heat had come through. The sauce is certainly sweet, but it's certainly hot too . . . in the end. It's also a little smoky. And if you like it, the chances are you'll like it a lot. It has a way of growing on you.

Both the gochujang and soy sauce in this mayonnaise are salty, so wait until everything is blended before adding salt, or deciding not to. Lemon juice often reduces the need for salt, so play with the juice and then the salt. When I've got a Meyer lemon, I pick it for this mayonnaise — its soft orange flavor is nice with the gochujang. Also nice is regular lemon juice with a squeeze of tangerine or clementine juice.

½ cup (120 ml) store-bought mayonnaise
4 teaspoons gochujang (see page 334)
1 tablespoon soy sauce
½ teaspoon Asian sesame oil
Juice from ½ lemon, or more to taste (see headnote)
Fine sea salt, if needed

**WORKING AHEAD**
You can refrigerate the sauce in a covered container for up to 1 week.

Mix all the ingredients *except* the salt together in a bowl. Taste for salt. If you'd like, add a squirt or two more lemon juice.

# PONZU MAYONNAISE SAUCE

Makes about ⅓ cup

Ponzu is a store-bought blend of soy sauce and citrus-spiked vinegar. If you can find yuzu ponzu, grab it — the flavor of yuzu, which is somewhat like a Meyer lemon, is wonderful with soy. This mayonnaise is thin, more sauce than spread, and good over roasted vegetables, fresh tomatoes and cucumbers and roast chicken or fish, especially salmon.

⅓ cup (80 ml) store-bought mayonnaise

1 lime

1½ tablespoons ponzu sauce (see headnote)

1½ teaspoons harissa paste or slightly less harissa powder (see page 334)

Fine sea salt, if needed

**WORKING AHEAD**
You can refrigerate the sauce in a covered container for up to 1 week.

Put the mayonnaise in a bowl and stir with a flexible spatula just to get it moving. Grate over the zest of the lime and squeeze in the juice from half of the lime. Add the ponzu and harissa, stir well, taste and add more lime juice, if you'd like (I usually think the sauce needs the juice from the whole lime). If you think the sauce needs salt, add it.

# GARLIC-SCAPE PESTO

Makes about 1 cup

Scapes are the beautiful, often looping and curlicued stalks that grow out of a garlic plant. Their flower, more like a topknot, looks like a baby garlic head. The scapes are meant to be cut in June, so that the garlic root — the part we're accustomed to using — can thicken, which is why you might see scapes at farmers' markets early in the season and then not again. While scapes smell and taste like garlic, their gorgeous green color and lanky stalks make them useful in ways that garlic often isn't. You can slice scapes and add them to salads; cook them as you would — and along with — other aromatics as a base for soups or braises; stir-fry them for a side-dish vegetable or topping for rice; or puree them to make this pesto, which is stronger-flavored than traditional basil pesto but can be used in all the same ways.

## a word on buying and keeping scapes

Buy scapes as soon as you see them in the market — their season is short and sometimes unpredictable. (If you find slender scapes, grab those first.) If you're not going to use them within days, lay them out on a baking sheet lined with parchment or a silicone baking mat, freeze them and then wrap them airtight — they'll keep for months.

10 garlic scapes, flowers removed, finely chopped
About ¾ cup (180 ml) olive oil
¼ cup (25 grams) finely grated Parmesan
¼ cup (25 grams) sliced or slivered almonds
Fine sea salt

**WORKING AHEAD**
You can pack the pesto airtight and refrigerate it for about 4 days or freeze it for up to 2 months.

If you want to preserve the color of the scapes, bring a pot of salted water to a boil, drop them in and boil for 60 seconds, then drain and immediately plunge them into a bowl of cold water and ice. When cool, drain and pat dry, then coarsely chop.

Put the scapes and ½ cup of the oil in a blender or food processor. Whir until the scapes are reduced to bits. Add the cheese, almonds and 1 teaspoon salt and blend well. Drizzle in as much more oil as needed to get the consistency you want. Taste for salt.

Use now or store tightly covered in the refrigerator.

# SPICED YOGURT: TWO VERSIONS

Each makes about 1 cup

Plain yogurt, particularly thick Greek yogurt, is an all-around teammate, an ingredient that can step in when you're looking for something to cool down a dish, blend into a soup, lighten a dressing or add zip to vegetables that have been roasted, grilled or simply steamed. Chefs figured this out years ago, which explains why so many dishes come to the table on a bed of artfully swirled yogurt. Unadorned yogurt — or perhaps yogurt with a gloss of good olive oil — is lovely, but there are times when you want a little more excitement; those are the times you'll turn to these two blends. One is seasoned with smoked paprika (sometimes called pimentón) and the other gets its lingering flavor and fragrance from a blend of spices most associated with the Middle East and North Africa: cumin, sumac, za'atar and harissa. Both are terrific with beets, carrots, cucumbers, eggs, greens and even grains.

### Harissa Yogurt

1 cup (240 ml) plain yogurt, preferably Greek

½ to 1 teaspoon ground cumin (to taste)

½ teaspoon harissa powder or ¼ to ½ teaspoon harissa paste (see page 334)

½ teaspoon ground sumac (see page 335) or grated zest of ½ lemon

½ teaspoon za'atar (see page 336) or dried oregano

Fine sea salt

1 tablespoon extra-virgin olive oil, or more to taste

### Smoked Paprika Yogurt

1 cup (240 ml) plain yogurt, preferably Greek

1 tablespoon honey

½ teaspoon smoked paprika (sweet or hot), or more to taste

¼ teaspoon piment d'Espelette (see page 334) or cayenne pepper

Fine sea salt

1 tablespoon extra-virgin olive oil, or more to taste

### WORKING AHEAD

You can refrigerate the yogurt in a tightly sealed container for 2 to 3 days; stir before using.

For either yogurt, mix all the ingredients *except* the salt and olive oil together. Season with salt, taste and see if you'd like more of any spice. Depending on how you want to serve the yogurt, you can stir in the oil now or drizzle it over at serving time.

# bean basics

My pantry is always stocked with cans of beans—chick-peas, black beans, cannellini, pinto—and I also store bags of best-quality dried beans and cook them when I've got time. Nothing beats homemade beans for flavor and texture. And when you prepare beans at home, you get a bonus: bean broth, so good as a base for soups.

I cook beans in a pasta pot (the kind with a perforated insert)—it makes draining them and reserving the broth easy. It also means that whatever aromatics I use won't have to be picked out of the beans once they're cooked; they stay in the bottom of the pot. You can use any large pot. If you want to cook the beans in a pressure cooker, Instant Pot or slow cooker, follow the directions that come with it.

I learned the following method from Rancho Gordo, the company that makes the beans I prefer. I buy a dozen bags at a time and have them shipped from San Francisco; they're also available in specialty stores.

You can soak the beans overnight in the refrigerator—it shortens the cooking time—but I rarely do this. If you've soaked them, keep the soaking liquid and use it for the beans.

If you're cooking in a pasta pot, remove the insert. No matter the pot you're using, heat 2 tablespoons of oil over medium heat and add 1 thickly sliced onion, rinsed and patted dry; 1 carrot, scrubbed, trimmed and thickly sliced; 1 celery stalk, thickly sliced; 2 garlic cloves, smashed and peeled; a bay leaf; and sprigs of thyme and/or rosemary, if you've got and like them. Stir to coat with the oil and cook, stirring now and then, for about 10 minutes, or until the vegetables are softened (they can color or not).

Meanwhile, rinse the beans well and discard any debris.

Fit the pot with the pasta insert (if you're using that kind of pot). Add the beans and cover with the soaking liquid or cold water, to a depth of 2 inches. Turn the heat up to high and bring to a boil. Keep the heat high and the bubbles strong for 10 to 15 minutes. Reduce the heat to the lowest setting you can, cover the pot and relax—depending on the type, quality and age of your beans, this can be hours. It's impossible for me to give you a time, so cook beans when you know you're going to be around.

Check on the beans every once in a while to see that the simmer is low, and lift the lid occasionally to let out steam. If it's easier to keep a simmer with the lid partially open, do that—just be sure that the beans are always amply covered with water. It's best to add boiling water when you need to top off the pot.

When the beans are al dente or a little softer—I'm sorry; I can't be precise here—remove the lid and start adding salt, a little at a time. The beans won't take in the salt immediately, so start with about ½ teaspoon and keep adding it at 5-minute intervals. Cook until the beans are just the texture you like.

Drain, reserving the cooking broth and discarding the aromatics. Use the beans now or store them, covered in broth, in a tightly sealed container in the refrigerator. They'll keep for up to 5 days. They can also be frozen airtight and kept for up to 1 month.

# SLOW-ROASTED TOMATOES FOR EVERYTHING

Makes 4 cups, or about 8 servings

¾ cup (180 ml) olive oil, or more as needed

3 garlic cloves, smashed but not peeled

8 to 10 sprigs fresh herbs, such as rosemary, thyme, parsley, basil and/or oregano

Fine sea salt and freshly ground pepper

2 pounds (907 grams) large plum or Roma tomatoes (about 8)

In late spring, when field-ripened tomatoes are an almost-here promise, and again in winter, when their warm sun-filled flavor is least attainable, I yearn for real tomatoes. It's during those long stretches that this recipe is most welcome — it takes not-so-good tomatoes, the kind you wouldn't want to slice into a salad or onto a sandwich, and transforms them into something luscious and satisfying. Not a substitute for great ripe tomatoes, but wonderful in its own way.

Although they are good just as they are, I also like to make these tomatoes the foundation for a chunky sauce that's lovely warm or at room temperature, over pasta, fish, chicken or a hefty steak; see page 316.

This recipe can be easily doubled, tripled or quadrupled — the only constraint is oven space.

## a word on the tomatoes

If you use your ripest, juiciest, most flavorful tomatoes to make these, you'll be defeating the purpose of the recipe. It is meant to make middling tomatoes better — you don't want to mess with great tomatoes.

**WORKING AHEAD**
You can refrigerate the tomatoes, packed in a tightly sealed container, for about 2 weeks. Or freeze them for months. Whether refrigerated or frozen, the tomatoes should be covered with oil. If you don't have enough of the roasting oil to do the job, pour in additional olive oil.

Center a rack in the oven and preheat it to 250 degrees F. I usually roast these in a 9-by-13-inch Pyrex pan, but you can do them in an ovenproof skillet or a glass pie plate or two, or on a baking sheet lined with parchment paper.

Pour about ¼ cup of the oil into the pan and tilt the pan so that the oil coats the bottom. Toss the garlic into the pan, along with half of the herbs. Season this little "landscape" with salt and pepper.

Using a paring knife, remove the little core in the top of each tomato (just chisel out a small cone), then cut the tomatoes crosswise in half. Cut a very small slice to serve as a base for any tomato halves that are too wobbly to stand up. Put the tomatoes cut side up in the pan, pour over the remaining ½ cup olive oil, strew with the remaining herbs and sprinkle with salt and pepper.

Roast the tomatoes for 3 to 4 hours, until they are very soft. Gently squeeze them, and they should give easily. If you happen to walk by the oven while the tomatoes are roasting, you can baste them, but it's not necessary.

You can use the tomatoes now, when they're warm, or when they've reached room temperature. Or you can pack them for keeping. They're best covered with oil.

# MAKE-EVERYTHING-BETTER TOMATO SAUCE

Makes 4 servings

This sauce starts with Slow-Roasted Tomatoes for Everything (page 315), and its name is not an exaggeration: It really does make everything better. The additions to the slow-roasted tomatoes are simple — capers, basil, chives, garlic and lemon — but their effect is outsized. I've used the sauce over rice, mixed it into pasta and topped chicken (try it over chicken Milanese, page 109), seafood, fish and even a hunk of beef with it. Don't miss having it over roasted or grilled eggplant. Most of the time I use the sauce at room temperature, but it can be heated. And while I usually make a batch when I need it, you can certainly make it ahead — the flavors will only get better.

8 pieces Slow-Roasted Tomatoes for Everything (page 315)

¼ cup (60 ml) oil from Slow-Roasted Tomatoes for Everything or extra-virgin olive oil

3 tablespoons capers, rinsed, patted dry and chopped if large

1 piece smashed garlic from Slow-Roasted Tomatoes for Everything, peeled, or 1 fresh garlic clove, germ removed (see page 320) and chopped

3 to 4 tablespoons snipped fresh chives

2 to 3 tablespoons finely sliced fresh basil leaves

1 lemon

Crushed red pepper flakes, piment d'Espelette (see page 334) or cayenne pepper

Fine sea salt and freshly ground pepper

### WORKING AHEAD

You can refrigerate the sauce in a covered container overnight (it will keep a day longer if you don't add the lemon juice). If you want to heat the sauce, warm it in a saucepan over low heat or in the microwave; don't overdo it.

Using kitchen scissors (my preference) or a small knife, cut each piece of tomato into quarters. Or cut into smaller pieces, if you'd like. Put the tomatoes in a bowl and mix in the oil, capers, garlic, chives and basil. Finely grate the zest of the lemon into the bowl, stir and then squeeze in the juice from one half. Season with red pepper, salt and black pepper, taste and decide if you'd like more lemon juice and more salt and/or pepper. Even though the capers are salty, I find that this sauce usually wants a generous amount of salt.

The sauce is ready to use now or it can be refrigerated until needed.

# BLACK (OR GREEN) OLIVE TAPENADE

Makes a generous ½ cup

Anyone who loves olives knows their capacity for transforming a simple dish into something surprising. With tapenade, a blend of olives, garlic and herbs (with citrus and anchovies as boosters), all the goodness of olives is concentrated and enhanced. Add a dab — or a spoonful — to charred peppers (page 39), a tian (page 234) or frittata (page 27), any chicken dish, any egg dish and almost every kind of fish or seafood dish. When I'm freestyling seafood en papillote, I usually grab a little tapenade and some Slow-Roasted Tomatoes for Everything (page 315). And, yes, if you'd like to switch it up, you can use green olives.

## a word on the olives

If you buy medium-sized olives with pits, you'll need about 5 ounces; however, the measurement needn't be precise.

About ¾ cup (113 grams) packed pitted oil-cured black (or regular green) olives, coarsely chopped

1 oil-packed anchovy, drained and coarsely chopped

¼ garlic clove, germ removed (see page 320) and coarsely chopped, or to taste

Grated zest and juice of ½ lemon

½ teaspoon herbes de Provence or ¼ teaspoon dried thyme, or more to taste

Pinch of cayenne pepper, or more to taste

About 3 tablespoons olive oil

### WORKING AHEAD

You can refrigerate the tapenade in a well-sealed jar for at least 1 week. Stir before using.

You can make the tapenade in a food processor (a mini works best) or a blender (a handheld works better than a full-sized blender). Put all the ingredients in the bowl and process, scraping down the bowl frequently, until the olives and garlic are pureed; you can make the tapenade chunky or smooth — the choice is yours. If you'd like a thinner tapenade, add more oil little by little. Taste and add more lemon juice, herbs and/or cayenne, if you'd like.

# TOMATO CHUTNEY

Makes about 1½ cups

This chutney will never replace ketchup, but you can use it like ketchup — it's great on burgers (beef or salmon) and over, under or alongside grilled meats and fish. The mix of tomatoes with vinegar and brown sugar — chutney stalwarts — and the addition of ginger make it welcome year-round. And, because it doesn't depend on lovely ripe tomatoes, you can make this in every season.

You can double this recipe, if you'd like.

1½ pounds (680 grams) tomatoes, peeled and cored

1 medium red or Texas spring onion, cut into 8 wedges, thinly sliced crosswise, rinsed and patted dry

6 quarter-sized slices peeled fresh ginger, finely chopped

½ cup (100 grams) packed brown sugar

½ cup (120 ml) cider vinegar

½ cup (120 ml) water

Pinch of fine sea salt, or more to taste

Pinch of cayenne pepper or crushed red pepper flakes (optional)

**WORKING AHEAD**
You can refrigerate the chutney tightly covered for about 2 weeks.

Cut the tomatoes into chunks, about 1 to 2 inches. Toss all the ingredients *except* the hot pepper into a saucepan and bring to a boil over medium heat. Stir, adjust the heat so that the mixture boils healthily (but not rollickingly) and cook, stirring now and then, for 20 to 25 minutes (keep a close eye on it after about 15 minutes), until most of the liquid has boiled away and the chutney has thickened to your liking.

Taste the chutney to see if you'd like a bit more salt and some cayenne or pepper flakes, then scrape into a jar or other container and cover. When it's cool, refrigerate it.

# QUICK-AS-A-WINK PICKLED STRAWBERRIES

Makes 2 cups

1 pint (340 grams) strawberries, hulled and quartered

½ cup (120 ml) balsamic vinegar (*not* your best stuff)

½ cup (120 ml) water

5 tablespoons sugar

½ teaspoon fine sea salt

5 thin slices peeled fresh ginger

1 kaffir lime leaf, fresh or freeze-dried (see headnote)

A strip of lime or lemon zest

3 tablespoons unseasoned rice vinegar (see page 335)

Strawberries are so wonderful fresh from the basket that, with the exception of jams and compotes, I'm usually hesitant to do anything with them that involves heat. But one day when I got back from the market and saw that my berries hadn't fared well on the return journey — they were pretty banged up — I thought to pickle them. My idea was to serve them with sliced mozzarella, and balsamic seemed like the best vinegar for the job.

Because strawberries are soft, fleshy and porous, they'll pickle quickly. Unfortunately, these same qualities mean they'll go mushy quickly. Pickle the berries the day you want to use them, or no more than 2 days ahead. Since it takes under 10 minutes to make these, same-day pickling isn't a hardship.

The pickling syrup is as good with blueberries, blackberries and raspberries as it is with strawberries, but use any of these berries whole. Once you've gone through the pickled berries, you can gently reheat the syrup and make another batch with it, or just save it to use on its own. I like it as the vinegar in a vinaigrette. It's also good drizzled over everything from green salads, cheese and vegetables to chicken, fish and seafood. Oddly and wonderfully, it's also good stirred into a cup of hot water to make a comforting sipper.

## a word on kaffir lime leaves

Kaffir lime leaves are powerfully fragrant and, once you've tasted them, memorable. It's not easy to find fresh leaves, so I use freeze-dried. If you can't find them, add another slice of ginger and another strip of zest.

**WORKING AHEAD**

You can refrigerate the strawberries in a tightly sealed jar, submerged in the pickling syrup, for up to 2 days; the syrup is good for up to 3 weeks.

No more than 2 days before you want to use them, pack the berries into a clean heatproof 1-pint jar with a tight-fitting lid. A canning jar is perfect.

Stir all the remaining ingredients *except* the rice vinegar together in a small saucepan. Place the pan over medium heat and, keeping your head away from the pan — hot vinegar stings your eyes and burns your nose — bring the mixture to a boil. Lower the heat and simmer gently for 5 minutes. Remove the pan from the heat and stir in the rice vinegar.

Pour the hot liquid over the strawberries, cover the jar and leave it on the counter until it's cool. Chill for at least 2 hours before using.

Serve the berries straight from the refrigerator.

CHOICES: Spoon some berries over sliced mozzarella or beets or both — if you want to add tomatoes, go for it! — drizzle with olive oil and speckle with pickling syrup. Use the berries and syrup in a salad of bitter greens, such as arugula or kale; make a vinaigrette with the syrup; or, for something different and fun, serve the berries and their syrup over vanilla ice cream.

# QUICK PICKLED ONIONS OR CUCUMBERS

Makes about ¾ cup brine (enough for 1 medium onion or 1 large cucumber)

This is a quick no-cook brine that you can use to make pickled cucumbers or onions, just what you want when you're thinking sandwiches, salads or a picnic. The brine recipe is for a small amount — it's enough to pickle one onion or English cucumber. You can multiply it as needed.

## onions, shallots and garlic

To help get all the good flavor from onions and shallots, I take a quick extra step at prep time. After I've sliced or chopped them, I rinse them under cold water and then pat them dry. The short rinse washes away the bitter liquid that's drawn out when you cut them. If I'm using the onion (or shallot) raw in a salad, I sometimes rinse it and then let the slices sit in a bowl of cold water—the chill gives them added crunch.

Unless I'm using whole garlic cloves, smashed or otherwise, I always cut each peeled clove in half the long way so that I can chisel out the green germ that runs the length of it. I learned this trick years ago when I was working with the chef Daniel Boulud, who had learned it years before when he was an apprentice in France. Removing the germ tones down garlic's brashest flavors, and it may make the garlic more easily digestible—the jury's still out on that.

### For the brine
½ cup (120 ml) cider vinegar

5 tablespoons water

1 tablespoon sugar

½ teaspoon fine sea salt

### For pickling
1 medium onion (a red onion is nice here) or 1 English (seedless) cucumber

### WORKING AHEAD
You can refrigerate the onions tightly covered for about 1 week. The cucumbers will keep for no more than 3 days, since after that, they will soften in the brine.

TO MAKE THE BRINE: Combine all the ingredients in a bowl or jar and stir until the sugar and salt dissolve.

TO PICKLE THE VEGETABLES: If using an onion, cut it in half from top to bottom and then cut each half into thin half-moon slices. Rinse under cold water and pat dry. If using a cucumber, peel it or just scrub it, trim the ends, cut it lengthwise into quarters and cut each quarter into 1- to 2-inch-long chunks. Or cut the cucumber into rounds to make pickle chips.

Add the onion or cucumber to the brine, stirring the pieces around so that the liquid covers them. Let the slices or chunks pickle for at least 30 minutes before serving. If you're not going to use the pickles now, pack them into a jar (if you haven't already), cover and refrigerate.

# hard-boiled eggs

Hard-boiled eggs, so simple, so nutritious and so versatile, can also be so frustrating. Sometimes they don't peel easily. Sometimes they peel perfectly and then you cut them in half and the yolks have a dark line around them, indicating that they're overcooked. These two ways of boiling eggs are the best I've found and turn out the most consistently good results. If it makes you feel any better, sometimes it's the egg, not you.

THE BOIL-AND-WAIT METHOD: Put the eggs in a saucepan and cover with cold water by at least 2 inches; salt the water. (Salt tends to keep the eggs from cracking and the whites from popping out.) Bring the water to a full rolling boil over high heat, then turn off the heat, cover the pan and let the setup sit on the warm burner for 12 minutes. When your timer dings, drain the eggs and place them in a bowl with ice cubes and cold water to stop the cooking. After a couple of minutes, the eggs are yours to do with as you wish.

If you have an induction range, you might want to opt for the steam method, below. Or you can turn the heat to the lowest setting for the rest period.

THE STEAM METHOD: Bring an inch or so of water to a boil in a pot over medium heat. Fit the pot with a steamer rack. Lay your eggs in the steamer, cover and steam the eggs for 12 minutes. When time's up, transfer the eggs to a bowl with ice cubes and cold water and let them cool for a few minutes before using them.

The unshelled eggs can be refrigerated for up to 1 week.

# SPICED GRANOLA

Makes about 6 cups

For me, granola is an ingredient, not a breakfast cereal. I serve sweet granola with fruit and ice cream and use it in the topping for a crisp, and I love using savory granola to finish a vegetable gratin (page 230). What makes this granola stand out and also makes it so comfortable switch-hitting are the three types of ginger in the mix: ground, fresh and crystallized. The sweet version is not really very sweet, but if you want to go more savory, see the variation on the opposite page.

## a word on the crystallized ginger

In order to get all the flavor of the ginger and have it be pleasant to chew, it must be very moist. If the ginger is hard, soak it for a few minutes in hot water, then drain, dry and cut it into very small pieces. Alternatively, you can steam it.

¼ cup (50 grams) packed brown sugar

¼ cup (60 ml) honey

3 tablespoons olive oil

2 cups (160 grams) rolled oats (not instant)

1 cup (120 grams) chopped mixed nuts, such as almonds, pecans, walnuts, pistachios and/or hazelnuts

½ cup (80 grams) pumpkin seeds

½ cup (62 grams) sunflower seeds

2 tablespoons wheat germ or additional oats

2 tablespoons millet (optional but nice for crunch)

2 teaspoons ground cardamom

2 teaspoons ground ginger

1 teaspoon fine sea salt

3 quarter-sized slices peeled fresh ginger, minced

Finely grated zest of 1 lemon or lime

½ cup (40 grams) unsweetened coconut flakes (such as Bob's Red Mill) or shredded coconut

2 tablespoons finely chopped or diced crystallized ginger (see headnote)

1½ teaspoons pure vanilla extract

**WORKING AHEAD**
You can pack the granola in tightly sealed containers—humidity is its foe—where it will keep for at least 1 month at room temperature.

Center a rack in the oven and preheat it to 325 degrees F. Have two 9-by-13-inch Pyrex pans at hand, or use baking sheets lined with parchment paper or silicone baking mats.

Put the brown sugar, honey and oil in a small saucepan and bring to a boil, then lower the heat and cook, stirring, just until the sugar dissolves.

In a large bowl, mix together all the remaining ingredients *except* the coconut, crystallized ginger and vanilla. Pour over the warm oil mixture, add the vanilla and stir, preferably with a silicone spatula, until everything is evenly moistened. Divide the mixture between the two pans and spread the granola out as evenly as you can without pressing down on it too much.

Bake for 20 minutes, then stir the granola, making sure to get any bits that have stuck to the pan. Rotate the pans and bake for 15 minutes more. Once again, stir the granola, then stir in the coconut. Bake for 5 minutes more, or until the coconut is very lightly toasted.

Remove the pans from the oven, scrape the granola into a big bowl and stir in the crystallized ginger. When the granola has come to room temperature, use your hands to break up any clumps.

## NOT-SO-SWEET GRANOLA

Reduce the brown sugar to 1 tablespoon and omit the cardamom, ground and fresh ginger and vanilla. Increase the salt to 1½ teaspoons and add ½ teaspoon freshly ground pepper. Depending on how you'll be using this version, you might want to add a little cumin, coriander or chile powder. You may or may not want to include the crystallized ginger. When I use this for the granola-topped vegetable gratin (page 230), I skip it.

# LEMON CURD

Makes a generous 2 cups

While I use this curd for the cranberry version of my Eton Mess (page 279), I like having a jar in the fridge to serve with other fruit desserts and ice cream. Curd is most traditionally made with lemon juice, but you can make it with lime, grapefruit and/or orange juice — a mixed-citrus curd is nice. If you use orange, include some lemon juice too — it will give the sweet orange juice some needed edge.

1¼ cups (250 grams) sugar

4 large eggs

1 tablespoon light corn syrup

About ¾ cup (180 ml) freshly squeezed lemon juice (from 4 to 6 lemons)

1 stick (8 tablespoons; 4 ounces; 113 grams) unsalted butter, cut into chunks

### WORKING AHEAD
You can refrigerate the curd in an airtight container for at least 3 weeks.

Whisk the sugar, eggs, corn syrup and lemon juice together in a medium heavy-bottomed saucepan. Drop in the pieces of butter.

Put the saucepan over medium heat and start whisking. You want to get into the corners of the pan, so if your whisk is too big for the job, switch to a wooden or silicone spatula. Cook, continuing to whisk — don't stop — for 6 to 8 minutes, until the curd starts to thicken. When it is noticeably thickened and, most important, you see a bubble or two come to the surface, then stop; the curd is ready.

Immediately scrape the curd into a heatproof bowl or a canning jar or two. Press a piece of plastic wrap against the surface to create an airtight seal and let the curd cool to room temperature, then refrigerate.

# CHOCOLATE CRUNCH

Makes about 2 cups

Here's a dark cocoa crunch that's made to sprinkle over ice cream sundaes, puddings (it's exactly what you want over Dark Chocolate Pudding, page 294) and tarts. The crunch is really a baked streusel.

If you want to scatter it over a crisp or any other dessert destined for the oven, use it raw.

1 cup (136 grams) all-purpose flour

⅓ cup (67 grams) packed brown sugar

¼ cup (21 grams) unsweetened cocoa powder

2 tablespoons sugar

½ teaspoon fine sea salt

5½ tablespoons (2¾ ounces; 78 grams) cold unsalted butter, cut into small cubes

### WORKING AHEAD
You can put the baked crumbs in a sealed container, where they'll keep at room temperature for up to 1 week. Or, refrigerate for about 2 weeks, or freeze airtight for up to 2 months. Run the crumbs through your fingers to de-clump before using.

Put all the ingredients *except* the butter in a large bowl and, using your fingers, mix them together, making sure that the brown sugar and cocoa powder don't have any hard lumps. Drop in the butter bits and squeeze, rub or otherwise mash everything together until you have clumps and curds. Cover the bowl and refrigerate for at least 2 hours, or for up to 3 days.

When you're ready to bake, center a rack in the oven and preheat it to 300 degrees F. Line a baking sheet with parchment paper or a silicone baking mat.

Scatter the chilled mix over the baking sheet and use your fingers to loosen the clumps.

Bake for 15 to 18 minutes, until you've got crumbs and small clusters. They'll look sandy and you'll have some pebble-sized clumps here and there. Transfer the baking sheet to a rack and let cool to room temperature.

# ALL-BUTTER PIE DOUGH

Makes two 9-inch crusts

3 cups (408 grams) all-purpose flour

¼ cup (50 grams) sugar

1½ teaspoons fine sea salt

2 sticks (16 tablespoons; ½ pound; 226 grams) unsalted butter, frozen or very cold and cut into small pieces

Up to ½ cup (120 ml) ice water

The right recipe for all pies, from fruit to cream and custard. Because it's made with only butter, it's flavorful as well as sturdy. And because it's got a sufficient amount of both sugar and salt, it's got character. I like it when a crust makes as strong a statement as the filling.

This recipe makes enough dough for a double-crusted pie. You can cut the recipe in half, but I wouldn't — roll the extra dough out and freeze it (either between sheets of parchment or fitted into a pie pan) so you'll be one step ahead the next time pie is on the menu.

## WORKING AHEAD

You can refrigerate the crusts, wrapped well, for up to 3 days or freeze them for up to 2 months. If the crust is in the pan, freeze it uncovered and then, when it's solid, wrap it in foil, pressing the foil against the crust to get a tight seal; you can bake it without defrosting. If it is rolled out, freeze it between pieces of parchment paper and then, when it's solid, wrap it well. Leave frozen rolled-out dough at room temperature until it's pliable enough for you to use without cracking.

Put the flour, sugar and salt in a food processor and pulse to blend. Scatter the pieces of butter over the mix and run the machine in long spurts until the mixture looks grainy. This could take a dozen or more blitzes, and there'll still be some nuggets of butter here and there. Add the ice water a little at time, processing after each addition. Stop when you have moist clumps and curds (you may not need all of the water) — don't process until the dough forms a ball; if you pinch some of the dough, it should hold together easily. Turn the dough out, divide it in half and shape each half into a disk.

If the dough is still very cold (as it probably will be), you can roll it immediately; if not, wrap the disks and refrigerate them for 30 minutes.

If you're making a pie now, have a buttered 9-inch pie pan at hand and a baking sheet. (*If you're not baking a pie, just roll out all the dough. Place the dough, which will be between sheets of parchment, on a baking sheet and freeze. When the rounds are solid, wrap them airtight.*)

Flour a sheet of parchment paper, center a disk on it, flour the dough and cover with a second sheet. Roll the dough into a circle that's between 11 and 12 inches in diameter. Fit the dough into the buttered pan; leave whatever dough hangs over the edge. Roll out the second piece of dough between paper and slide it onto the baking sheet. (Or roll out both pieces and put on two baking sheets.) Freeze (first choice) or refrigerate the lined pie plate and the rolled-out dough while you preheat the oven and make the filling.

# SWEET TART DOUGH

Makes one 9- to 9½-inch crust, for a 9- to 9½-inch fluted tart pan with a removable bottom or a 9-inch pie pan

This dough is like shortbread — in fact, if you have leftover dough, you can bake it into cookies. It's crisp, flavorful and rich, which is everything a tart crust should be. To get the full measure of flavor, I prebake crusts even when they'll get a long bake after they're filled. In addition, a partial prebake helps keep the bottom crust from going soggy.

If you'd like, you can press this dough into the pan rather than rolling it out and fitting it into the pan. If you press, you might have some dough left over.

1½ cups (204 grams) all-purpose flour

½ cup (60 grams) confectioners' sugar

¼ teaspoon fine sea salt

1 stick plus 1 tablespoon (9 tablespoons; 4½ ounces; 127 grams) very cold unsalted butter, cut into small pieces

1 large egg yolk

**WORKING AHEAD**
Well wrapped, the dough can be refrigerated for up to 3 days or frozen for up to 2 months. You can freeze the fully baked crust wrapped airtight, but I prefer to freeze it unbaked in the pan, wrapped tightly in aluminum foil, with the foil pressed against the crust to create as tight a seal as possible. Bake it directly from the freezer—it will have a fresher flavor. Just add about 5 minutes to the baking time.

Put the flour, confectioners' sugar and salt in a food processor and pulse a couple of times to blend. Scatter the pieces of butter over the dry ingredients and pulse until the butter is cut in coarsely — you'll have some pieces the size of oatmeal flakes and some the size of peas. Stir the yolk just to break it up and add it a little at a time, pulsing after each addition. When the egg is in, process in long pulses — about 10 seconds each — until the dough, which will look granular soon after the egg is added, forms clumps and curds. Reach in and squeeze a bit of dough — it should hold together. Turn the dough out onto a work surface and knead it gently to bring it together.

Shape the dough into a disk, pat it down to flatten it and put it between sheets of parchment paper. Roll the dough out evenly, turning the dough over frequently and lifting the paper often so that it doesn't roll into the dough and form creases. If you're making a pie now, have a buttered 9-inch pan and a baking sheet at hand. Roll the dough into a circle that's about 11 inches in diameter. If the dough is still cool, you can fit it into the tart (or pie) pan now; if it's not, slide it, still between the sheets of paper, onto a baking sheet and refrigerate it for 2 hours, or up to 3 days; or freeze it for 1 hour, or up to 2 months. If you're chilling or freezing for more than a few hours, wrap the dough airtight.

If the dough has been chilled, let it rest on the counter until it's just pliable enough to bend without breaking. Remove both sheets of paper, fit the dough into the buttered pan and trim the excess dough even with the edge of the pan. (If you'd like, you can fold the excess over and make a thicker wall around the sides of the tart.) Prick the crust all over with the tines of a fork. Freeze for at least 30 minutes, but an hour or two is better. (*The crust can be frozen for up to 2 months before baking.*)

TO PARTIALLY BAKE THE CRUST: Center a rack in the oven and preheat it to 400 degrees F. Butter the shiny side of a piece of aluminum foil and fit it snugly against the crust. Fill it with dried beans or rice (which you can reuse for crusts, but not for eating).

Bake the crust for 25 minutes, then carefully remove the foil and weights. If the crust has puffed, press it down gently with the back of a spoon. Transfer the crust to a rack (leave it in its pan).

TO FULLY BAKE THE CRUST: Center a rack in the oven and preheat it to 400 degrees F. Butter the shiny side of a piece of aluminum foil and fit it snugly against the crust. Fill it with dried beans or rice (which you can reuse for crusts, but not for eating).

Bake the crust for 25 minutes, then carefully remove the foil and weights. If the crust has puffed, press it down gently with the back of a spoon. Bake the crust for another 7 to 10 minutes, until it is firm and golden brown. Transfer the crust to a rack (leave it in its pan).

# PÂTE BRISÉE

Makes one 9- to 9½-inch crust, for a 9- to 9½-inch fluted tart pan with a removable bottom or a 9-inch pie pan

This is the dough for savory tarts, like the Tomato Tart with Mustard and Ricotta (page 48), and the one you should roll out when you're making your favorite quiche. But you can use it for sweet tarts, too, if you'd like.

1¼ cups (170 grams) all-purpose flour

1 teaspoon sugar

½ teaspoon fine sea salt

6 tablespoons (3 ounces; 85 grams) very cold unsalted butter, cut into bits

1 large egg

1 teaspoon ice water

## WORKING AHEAD

You can refrigerate the dough for up to 3 days or freeze it for up to 2 months. While you can freeze the fully baked crust, wrapped airtight, for up to 2 months, I prefer to freeze it unbaked in the pan, wrapped tightly in aluminum foil, with the foil pressed against the crust to create as tight a seal as possible. Bake it directly from the freezer—it will have a fresher flavor. Just add about 5 minutes to the baking time.

Put the flour, sugar and salt in a food processor and pulse to blend. Scatter the pieces of butter over the dry ingredients and pulse until the butter is cut in coarsely — you'll have some pieces the size of oatmeal flakes and some the size of peas. Beat the egg and water together and add to the machine in three additions, pulsing after each bit goes in. Then whir until the dough forms moist clumps and curds — you're aiming for a moist dough that holds together when pinched.

Shape the dough into a disk, pat it down to flatten it and put it between sheets of parchment paper. Roll the dough out evenly, turning it over frequently and lifting the paper often so that it doesn't roll into the dough and form creases. Roll the dough into a circle that's about 11 inches in diameter. If you're making a pie now, have a buttered 9-inch pan and a baking sheet at hand. If the dough is still cool, you can fit it into the tart (or pie) pan now; if it's not, slide it, still between the paper, onto a baking sheet and refrigerate it for 2 hours, or up to 3 days; or freeze it for 1 hour, or (well wrapped) for up to 2 months. If you're chilling or freezing for more than a few hours, wrap the dough airtight.

*(Recipe continues)*

If the dough has been chilled, let it rest on the counter until it's just pliable enough to bend without breaking. Remove the paper, fit the dough into the buttered tart pan and trim the excess dough even with the edge of the pan. (If you'd like, you can fold the excess over and make a thicker wall around the sides of the tart.) Prick the crust all over with the tines of a fork and freeze for at least 30 minutes — an hour or two is better — or up to 2 months before baking.

TO PARTIALLY BAKE THE CRUST: Center a rack in the oven and preheat it to 400 degrees F. Butter the shiny side of a piece of aluminum foil and fit it snugly against the crust. Fill it with dried beans or rice (which you can reuse for crusts, but not for eating).

Bake the crust for 25 minutes, then carefully remove the foil and weights. If the crust has puffed, press it down gently with the back of a spoon. Transfer the crust to a rack (leave it in its pan).

TO FULLY BAKE THE CRUST: Center a rack in the oven and preheat it to 400 degrees F. Butter the shiny side of a piece of aluminum foil and fit it snugly against the crust. Fill it with dried beans or rice (which you can reuse for crusts, but not for eating).

Bake the crust for 25 minutes, then carefully remove the foil and weights. If the crust has puffed, press it down gently with the back of a spoon. Bake the crust for another 7 to 10 minutes, until it is firm and golden brown. Transfer the crust to a rack (leave it in its pan).

# GALETTE DOUGH

Makes 1 galette

This dough is one of my favorites. It's flaky, the way pie dough is, and flavorful, the way tart dough is. It's a cinch to work with, and even first-timers can make a perfect galette with it. Of course, "perfect galette" is an oxymoron — a galette is a rustic, freestanding, open-faced tart that's only perfect when it's higgledy-piggledy.

**WORKING AHEAD**
You can refrigerate the dough, wrapped airtight, for up to 3 days or freeze it for up to 2 months. (I like to roll the dough and then freeze it.) If you've frozen the dough, leave it on the counter to come to a workable temperature.

1½ cups (204 grams) all-purpose flour

2 tablespoons sugar

½ teaspoon fine sea salt

1 stick (8 tablespoons; 4 ounces; 113 grams) cold unsalted butter, cut into 16 pieces (frozen butter is good here)

¼ cup (60 ml) ice water

Put the flour, sugar and salt in a food processor and pulse a couple of times to blend. Scatter the pieces of butter over the dry ingredients and pulse until the butter is cut into the flour. At first you'll have a mixture that looks like coarse meal and then, as you pulse more, you'll get small flake-sized pieces with some larger pea-sized pieces. Add a little of the ice water and pulse, add some more and pulse and continue until all the water is in. Now work in longer pulses, stopping to scrape the sides and bottom of the bowl if needed, until you have a dough that forms nice, bumpy curds that hold together when you pinch them.

Turn the dough out onto a work surface and knead it gently to bring it together. Gather the dough into a ball, flatten it into a disk and put it between two large pieces of parchment paper. Roll the dough, while it's still cool, into a circle about 12 inches in diameter. Don't worry about getting the exact size or about having the edges of the round be perfect — ragged is pretty here. The dough will be thicker than you might think it should be, and that's fine — it's what you need for a free-form pastry. Slide the rolled-out dough, still between the sheets of paper, onto a baking sheet or cutting board and refrigerate for at least 2 hours, or (well wrapped) for up to 3 days.

When you're ready to use the dough, leave it on the counter for a few minutes just so that it's pliable enough to lift and fold without cracking.

# A PANTRY ALPHABET

## A Glossary of Specialized Ingredients and Some Substitutions

The majority of the ingredients I use regularly are available in supermarkets. A very few are a bit more exotic, but they can be ordered online. If you can't find an ingredient locally, here are some good sources:

**AMAZON,** amazon.com
**KALUSTYAN'S,** kalustyans.com, foodsofnations.com
**PENZEYS SPICES,** penzeys.com
**THE SPICE HOUSE,** thespicehouse.com

---

**ALEPPO PEPPER:** Red pepper flakes that are moderately hot and a tad fruity. I have seen the pepper — a native of Syria and Turkey — sold ground, but I prefer the flakes, which are sometimes a bit chewy. Kalustyan's, Penzey's and Spice House are good sources for this. Cayenne or crushed red pepper flakes are substitutes.

**ASIAN SESAME OIL:** This roasted — or toasted — oil is found in the Asian section of most markets. Its flavor is full and forthright — use it sparingly. While it can be heated, it shines when it's added to a dish at the last minute — that's when you get the best of the oil's fragrance.

**BOUILLON BASE:** A paste that can be diluted in hot water to make a broth, bouillon base is particularly convenient when you need only a small amount of broth or want to quickly flavor a soup or stew. Bases, which come in chicken, beef, vegetable, fish and seafood, are concentrated — a teaspoon will make a cup of broth — and serve the same purpose as bouillon cubes. The most popular brand is Better Than Bouillon, but there are others — taste and decide which you like most.

**BULGOGI SAUCE:** This Korean barbecue sauce (there's also a Korean dish with the same name) is a little sweet but mostly tangy and spicy. Its predominant ingredients are soy sauce, sesame, ginger and a fruit puree (either apple or pear). Bulgogi sauce can be used in marinades, and I like a little of it on a bun for a burger.

**CHIPOTLES IN ADOBO SAUCE:** Chipotles are smoked dried jalapeño peppers. Sold in cans in the Latin American/Mexican food section of supermarkets, the peppers are packed in a thick rust-colored sauce called *adobo*. You can use both the peppers and sauce, separately or together, but always sparingly — they're hot!

**FURIKAKE:** A Japanese seasoning mix, often sprinkled over rice, furikake can flavor soups, vegetables and fish. There are many different kinds, but the most popular have sesame seeds, dried seaweed and spices, often including chiles. Furikake is sold in jars with shaker tops.

**GARAM MASALA:** An Indian spice blend, garam masala does not have a precise recipe. It can vary from region to region, household to household and merchant to merchant. The blend is fragrant and tilts toward the sweet side, with cinnamon an important ingredient. It usually also includes cardamom and nutmeg, as well as more savory spices like cumin, coriander and bay. In addition to online sources, both Simply Organic and McCormick market garam masala.

**GOCHUJANG:** Sometimes called Korean ketchup or Korean miso, gochujang is a fermented sauce and therefore its flavor is complex. It can be just the least bit sweet, but you'll know it by its heat. Made of fermented soybeans, red chiles and glutinous rice, it's a terrific ingredient to add to marinades, beef stews and even mayonnaise. The most popular and most widely available brand is Annie Chun's — you can find it in some large supermarkets or online. As with many blended condiments and spices, brands differ, so if you find you like gochujang, you might want to taste a few different ones. There really isn't a substitute for it, but if you don't have it, try making a paste of crushed red pepper flakes, soy sauce and a small amount of sugar.

**HARISSA:** A ferociously hot North African spice blend, harissa can be bought as a ground spice mix or as a paste in tubes, cans and jars. Chiles, primarily red ones, are the most important and abundant ingredient, but they're blended with garlic and other spices (like cumin and coriander) and, in the case of the pastes, oil. If you buy harissa powder, you can mix it with oil or water to make a paste. Harissa powders and pastes vary from brand to brand. I find the most variation in the pastes — some are stronger, some are sweeter. If harissa interests you, search for your favorite. Instead of harissa powder, you can use chile powder. For the paste, substitute your favorite hot sauce, Thai red chili paste or sambal oelek.

**KAFFIR LIME LEAF:** These leaves — thick, tough, shiny on one side and dull on the other — are most often found in Southeast Asian cooking, particularly in Thai dishes, and are used in much the same way that bay leaves are used in European cuisines. The leaves are usually sold dried. The aroma is so particular that there is no substitute.

**KECAP MANIS:** Although it's sometimes referred to as Indonesian ketchup — it's the most popular condiment in that country — the sauce bears no resemblance to what we know as ketchup. Its color is dark, almost black; its consistency is thick and syrupy; and its flavor is sweet. A mixture of soy sauce and palm sugar, it can be cooked into dishes or used as a condiment.

**LEMON/LIME OIL:** Pure lemon or lime oil is intense and should be used sparingly, the way you would a citrus extract, which makes a fine substitute. The most popular brand (and the one I use) is Boyajian.

**MISO, LIGHT (WHITE OR YELLOW) AND RED:** Made from fermented soybeans, miso is sold as a paste in tubs and jars. Stored in the refrigerator, it seems to keep forever. Its flavor is salty and savory, and it's one of the foods that defines the "fifth flavor," umami.

**PIMENT D'ESPELETTE:** Espelette is a village in the Basque region of France famous for its red chile peppers — after harvest, almost every house in the area hangs peppers out to dry in the sun. Once dried, the peppers are finely ground. Cayenne is a good substitute.

**POMEGRANATE MOLASSES:** Although pomegranate molasses is made by boiling pomegranate juice and sugar down to a syrup, it is more sour than sweet. Popular in Middle Eastern dishes, it is good in glazes and sauces for vegetables and poultry. You can find it in most supermarkets.

**PONZU SAUCE (SOMETIMES LABELED PONZU SOY SAUCE OR YUZU SOY SAUCE):** This Japanese sauce has a sharp tang that comes from a mixture of vinegar and citrus. Traditional ponzu includes yuzu, a Japanese citrus fruit that resembles lemons; today many sauces use other citrus. The soy blends are so full of flavor they can be used on their own as marinades, salad dressings or dipping sauces. Popular brands include Kikkoman, Eden, Marukan and Mitsukan. Ponzu is available in many supermarkets.

**RAS EL HANOUT:** This North African spice blend is most closely associated with Morocco. The name means "head of the shop," implying that the spices come from the vendor's best selection. There is no fixed recipe for ras el hanout — each merchant blends his own — but you can usually count on there being cardamom, cumin, cloves, cinnamon, ginger, turmeric and nutmeg, and often many other ingredients, including rosebuds. The blend is always warm and just a little sweet. If you can't find ras el hanout, opt for garam masala (not the same, but similar in spirit). Ras el hanout is available from spice purveyors and can even be found in some supermarkets under the McCormick label.

**RICE VINEGAR:** Milder than most vinegars, rice vinegar is used to flavor Asian food and also to quick-pickle ingredients like onions and cucumbers. You'll find it plain and seasoned — the seasoned vinegar is sweetened and, with a splash of oil (olive or sesame), makes a nice dressing for simple salads or steamed vegetables.

**SAMBAL OELEK:** A spoonable red chile paste popular in Thai and Malaysian cooking, sambal oelek is thicker than Sriracha, and can be hotter, but it's made with many of the same ingredients. In a pinch, substitute Sriracha. I sometimes use Chinese chile-garlic paste instead as well.

**SRIRACHA:** Slightly sweet, slightly garlicky and certainly spicy, this bright-red chile-spiked sauce is now almost as ubiquitous as ketchup and almost as easy to find. The most popular Sriracha is made by Huy Fong Foods, but other brands provide just as much punch. Sriracha can be used straight, the way you would any other hot sauce, or it can be mixed with other ingredients to season meat and fish.

**SUMAC:** A tangy spice, ground sumac has a flavor reminiscent of lemon. You can find it readily in shops specializing in foods from the Middle East. If you don't have sumac, substitute freshly grated lemon zest.

**THAI CURRY PASTE, RED OR GREEN:** Both red and green Thai curry pastes are made with ginger, galangal, kaffir lime, lemongrass and spices, but the red paste is made with dried chiles and the green with fresh. Both pastes should be used sparingly. Thai Kitchen and Maesri are brands that are widely available.

**THAI SWEET CHILI SAUCE:** The name tells you almost everything you need to know about this popular condiment. Sweeter than it is hot, the orange sauce is thick, pourable and as easy to add to dishes as ketchup. It's found in supermarkets under popular labels like Thai Kitchen, A Taste of Thai, Kikkoman and even proprietary brands like Trader Joe's. I use Mae Ploy, found in many specialty markets.

**TOGARASHI:** Shichimi togarashi — that's usually how you'll see it labeled — is a Japanese blend of seven spices. The primary flavor is peppery, but, depending on the brand and blend, you'll also taste ginger, orange, sesame and perhaps seaweed. I use S&B brand. It comes in a small shaker tube and may look familiar to you if you eat at ramen or home-style Japanese restaurants — it's often on the table alongside the soy sauce. Cayenne can be used as a substitute.

**URFA PEPPER:** This Turkish chile pepper is always found dried and crushed into flakes. Even dried, the pepper retains some moisture. Its heat is mild, and it may have the aroma and slightly sweet tang of dried fruit. This chile is optional in many of my recipes; where it's not, substitutions, such as smoked paprika or crushed red pepper flakes, are suggested.

**YUZU KOSHO:** A paste made from yuzu, the Japanese lemon-like citrus, and chiles, this comes in both red and green versions (the difference is the type of chiles). Sold in small jars, it is used in very small quantities — it packs a punch. Yuzu kosho is sold in Asian and specialty markets and online. If you can't find it, substitute Thai curry paste, which is more easily found in supermarkets.

**ZA'ATAR:** A blend of dried thyme, oregano and marjoram, sometimes mixed with sumac and roasted sesame seeds, za'atar is a popular Middle Eastern seasoning. If you don't have za'atar, you can substitute ground thyme, oregano or marjoram, or a mix of these herbs, and add sesame seeds or not.

# INDEX

Note: Page references in *italics* indicate photographs.

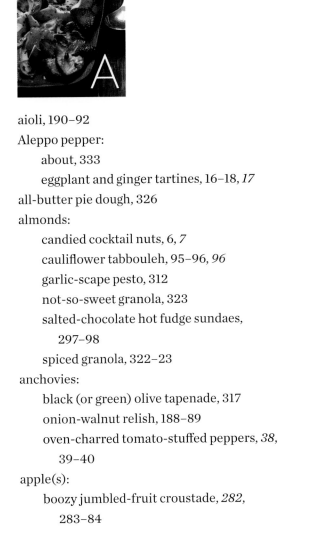

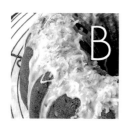

B

carrot(s) *(cont.)*

    ginger fried rice, 239–40, *241*

    roasted butternut squash soup, 58–59

    subtly spicy, softly hot, slightly sweet beef stew, *148,* 149–50

    sweet and smoky roasted, 214, *215*

    and sweet potatoes, slow-cooker brisket with, 151–52, *153*

    tempura'd vegetables, seafood or even fruit, 30–32, *31*

cauliflower tabbouleh, 95–96, *96*

celery root:

    beef carbonnade chockful of vegetables, 147

    granola-topped squash and root vegetable gratin, 230–31

    tempura'd vegetables, seafood or even fruit, 30–32, *31*

chai-tea bars, chocolate-covered, 248–50, *249*

chard:

    Rosa Jackson's bourride, 190–92, *191*

    tomato tart with mustard and ricotta, 48–50, *49*

cheddar:

    bean and tortilla soup, 60–62, *61*

    my newest gougères, 8–9, *9*

    pimento cheese, 24, *25*

    savory bread pudding, 237–38

    sharp, buying, 24

    three-pepper burgers, 138–39, *139*

cheese:

    bean and tortilla soup, 60–62, *61*

    caramelized onion galette with Parm cream, 54–55

    carrot-and-mustard rillettes, 10–12, *11*

    garlic-scape pesto, 312

    mushroom-bacon galette, 51–53, *52*

    my newest gougères, 8–9, *9*

    pimento, 24, *25*

    ricotta spoonable, 22, *23*

    savory bread pudding, 237–38

    sharp cheddar, buying, 24

    tangerine-topped cheesecake, 270–72, *271*

three-pepper burgers, 138–39, *139*

tomato tart with mustard and ricotta, 48–50, *49*

*see also* cream cheese

cheesecake, tangerine-topped, 270–72, *271*

cherry clafoutis, 293

chewy chocolate chip cookies, 246–47

chicken:

    balsamic, with baby potatoes and mushrooms, *120,* 121

    breasts, oven-roasted, 108

    -chili sandwiches, Luang Prabang, 106, *107*

    -chili tamale pie, 125–27, *126*

    ginger fried rice, 239–40, *241*

    herb-butter, 122–24, *123*

    lemon-fennel, in a pot, 133–34, *135*

    Mediterranean shepherd's pie, *160,* 161–62

    ponzu, 112–13

    roast, with pan-sauce vinaigrette, 128–29

    and salad Milanese style, 109–10, *111*

    spatchcocked, *130,* 131–32

    tarragon spatchcocked, 132

    thighs, sweet chili, 114–16, *115*

    and winter squash tagine, 117–19, *118*

chickpea(s):

    cauliflower tabbouleh, 95–96, *96*

    and noodle soup, Moroccan-spiced, 66–68, *67*

    -tahini salad, 93–94

chiles:

    bean and tortilla soup, 60–62, *61*

    chicken-chili tamale pie, 125–27, *126*

    chipotle cream, 196–98, *197*

    chipotles in adobo sauce, about, 333

    cowboy caviar salad or side, 90–92, *91*

    poke to play around with, 44–45, *45*

    three-pepper burgers, 138–39, *139*

    Urfa, about, 335

chili, chicken-, tamale pie, 125–27, *126*

chipotle(s):

    in adobo sauce, about, 333

    –black bean dip, 19

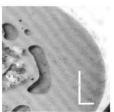

oats:

    apple crisp with oatmeal topping, 278

    chewy chocolate chip cookies, 246–47

    not-so-sweet granola, 323

    spiced granola, 322–23

oil, Asian sesame. *See* Asian sesame oil

oil, lemon or lime, about, 334

olive(s):

    black (or green), tapenade, 317

    lamb or veal osso buco, 164

    and tomatoes, braised lamb shanks with, 163–64, *164*

onions, spring. *See* spring onions

onion(s):

    beef and beer stew, 146–47

    beef carbonnade chockful of vegetables, 147

    bourbon-roasted pork loin, 170, *171*

    caramelized, galette with Parm cream, 54–55

    and kale frittata, 28

    quick pickled, 320

    savory bread pudding, 237–38

    sliced, rinsing, 320

    summer vegetable tian, 234–36, *235*

    tempura'd vegetables, seafood or even fruit, 30–32, *31*

    tomato chutney, 318

    -walnut relish, 188–89

orange(s):

    chocolate-covered chai-tea bars, 248–50, *249*

    citrus-marinated halibut with mango salsa, 180–82, *181*

    gremolata, *148*, 149–50

    working with, 309

osso buco, lamb or veal, 164

oven-charred tomato-stuffed peppers, *38*, 39–40

oven-roasted chicken breasts, 108

panzanella, tomato and peach, 99–101, *100*

paper-thin roasted potatoes, 224

Parmesan:

    caramelized onion galette with Parm cream, 54–55

    garlic-scape pesto, 312

    mushroom-bacon galette, 51–53, *52*

    savory bread pudding, 237–38

parsley:

    cauliflower tabbouleh, 95–96, *96*

    demi-goddess dressing, 304

parsnip(s):

    beef carbonnade chockful of vegetables, 147

    and cranberry cake, triple-layer, 266–69, *267*, *269*

pasta:

    with cabbage, winter squash and walnuts, 232–33, *233*

    meatballs and spaghetti, 157–59, *158*

    Moroccan-spiced chickpea and noodle soup, 66–68, *67*

    with sardines, fennel and pine nuts, 202–3

    seafood, 207–9, *208*

    with shrimp, squash, lemon and lots of herbs, 204–6, *205*

pastry dough:

    all-butter pie dough, 326

    galette dough, 331

    pâte brisée, 329–30

    sweet tart dough, 327–28

pâte brisée, 329–30